THE LETTERS OF GEORGE LONG BROWN

Contested Boundaries

UNIVERSITY PRESS OF FLORIDA

Florida A&M University, Tallahassee
Florida Atlantic University, Boca Raton
Florida Gulf Coast University, Ft. Myers
Florida International University, Miami
Florida State University, Tallahassee
New College of Florida, Sarasota
University of Central Florida, Orlando
University of Florida, Gainesville
University of North Florida, Jacksonville
University of South Florida, Tampa
University of West Florida, Pensacola

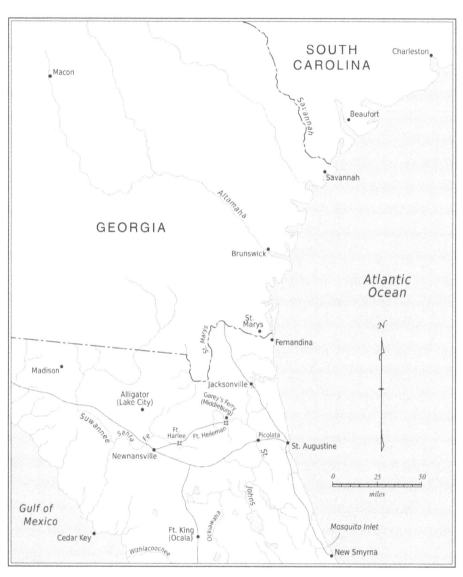

George Long Brown's commercial world. Map by Peter Krafft.

THE LETTERS OF

George Long Brown

A Yankee Merchant on Florida's Antebellum Frontier

EDITED BY

James M. Denham and Keith L. Huneycutt

University Press of Florida

Gainesville · Tallahassee · Tampa · Boca Raton

Pensacola · Orlando · Miami · Jacksonville · Ft. Myers · Sarasota

First cloth printing, 2019
First paperback printing, 2024

29 28 27 26 25 24   6 5 4 3 2 1

Library of Congress Cataloging-in-Publication Data
Names: Denham, James M., editor. | Huneycutt, Keith L., 1956– editor.
Title: The letters of George Long Brown : a Yankee merchant on Florida's
antebellum frontier / edited by James M. Denham and Keith L. Huneycutt.
Other titles: Contested boundaries.
Description: Gainesville : University Press of Florida, 2019. | Series:
Contested boundaries | Includes bibliographical references and index.
Identifiers: LCCN 2018047757 | ISBN 9780813056388 (cloth) | ISBN 9780813080635 (pbk.)
Subjects: LCSH: Brown, George Long—Correspondence. | Newnansville
(Fla.)—History. | Alachua County (Fla.)—History.
Classification: LCC F319.N56 L48 2019 | DDC 975.9/79—dc23
LC record available at https://lccn.loc.gov/2018047757

The University Press of Florida is the scholarly publishing agency for the State University System
of Florida, comprising Florida A&M University, Florida Atlantic University, Florida Gulf Coast
University, Florida International University, Florida State University, New College of Florida,
University of Central Florida, University of Florida, University of North Florida, University of
South Florida, and University of West Florida.

University Press of Florida
2046 NE Waldo Road
Suite 2100
Gainesville, FL 32609
http://upress.ufl.edu

CONTENTS

FIGURES

ACKNOWLEDGMENTS

We wish to acknowledge the invaluable assistance of descendants of George Long Brown. Principal among these is the late Miss Mannevillette Sullivan, the great-granddaughter of George's sister Ellen Brown Anderson. Our relationship with Miss Sullivan began in 1993, when James M. Denham came across the Brown family correspondence while visiting the U.S. Military Academy at West Point on a military history fellowship. At the time, Alan Aimone, director of special collections, encouraged Denham to contact Miss Sullivan, who, only a year or so before, had sent the collection to the academy library with the intention of bequeathing it. Since then, Miss Sullivan and other family members have been instrumental in the publication of this book as well as of a previous book, *Echoes from a Distant Frontier* (Columbia, 2004), and other articles, which focused on the lives of George's sisters Ellen and Corinna Brown. Miss Sullivan's cousin Jane Gill, her husband, Raymond Gill, and another family member, Elizabeth Traynor, provided us with permission to publish all their family's correspondence. Over the past two and a half decades, Jane, Raymond, and Elizabeth have offered advice and shared family genealogy, photographs, additional letters, diaries, and artwork. Without this constant support, advice, and cooperative spirit, which extends back to 1994, this book could never have been written.

Another person associated with this project that deserves special recognition is Norm La Coe, of Naples, Florida. Mr. La Coe shared with us a great deal of useful information about the provenance of the letters and his own research concerning the Browns in Florida over a long period of time.

We also wish to acknowledge the support of Gene Smith, professor of history at Texas Christian University in Fort Worth, Texas, and editor of the Contested Boundaries series at the University Press of Florida. We are proud to include George Long Brown of Newnansville, Florida, among the titles in his series.

We also wish to thank numerous librarians, archivists, and other professionals who have assisted us since the publication of the above book. They are, in alphabetical order:

Paul Backhouse, Ah-Tah-Thi-Ki Museum; Tara Backhouse, Ah-Tah-Thi-Ki Museum; Alan Bliss, Jacksonville Historical Society; Christophe Boucher, College of Charleston; Jim Cusick, P. K. Yonge Library, University of Florida; Nora Galbraith, Florida Southern College; Tom Hambright, Monroe County Library; Andy Huse, University of South Florida; Joe Knetsch, former head of Florida Bureau of Land Archives; Peter Krafft, former director of the cartography lab at Florida State University; Emily Lisska, Jacksonville Historical Society; Peggy MacDonald, Matheson History Museum; Randall MacDonald, Florida Southern College; Boyd Murphree, P. K. Yonge Library, University of Florida; Jim Powell Jr., Alachua County Clerks Office; Mary Beth Rosebrough, Ah-Tah-Thi-Ki Museum; Peter Schreffler, Florida Southern College; Samuel Sfirri, Addlestone Library, College of Charleston; Charles Tingley, St. Augustine Historical Society; and Jim Vearil, Jacksonville. We also wish to thank those of our colleagues who read all or portions of this book: John M. Belohlavek, Canter Brown, Jim Cusick, Andrew Frank, and Larry Rivers.

We also wish to thank Florida Southern College, which provided financial support to us both for travel and other expenses in pursuance of this project. Especially helpful was a sabbatical leave for Keith L. Huneycutt during the spring semester of 2013 and for James M. Denham in the spring semester of 2016. We also want to acknowledge the support of the Florida Southern College administration, which has enthusiastically supported this as well as other projects over the years, especially Brad Hollingshead, dean of the School of Arts and Sciences, a colleague in every sense of the word.

BROWN FAMILY CHART

Elihu Dearing Brown (1777–1819) and Elizabeth Dearing (1785–1832)
married in Portsmouth, N.H., 1806

CHILDREN

Henry Alexander Brown (1807–1825)

Adelaide Mary Brown (1808–1833)

Mannevillette Elihu Dearing Brown (1810–1896)

Corinna Elizabeth Brown (1812–1854)
married Edward Aldrich (1811–1870) in 1837

Ellen Maria Brown (1814–1862)
married James Willoughby Anderson (1812–1847) in 1840

Charles Burroughs Brown (1816–1840)

George Long Brown (1817–1857)
married Matilda Stewart (1827–1914) in 1852

Introduction

ON JULY 18, 1846, twenty-nine-year-old merchant George Long Brown wrote from Newnansville, Florida, to his artist brother, Mannevillette Elihu Dearing Brown, in Paris, France, "I am still in business at this village, and have slowly, but I hope surely, prospered. My trade is large, though of a <u>small kind</u>. My customers are a curious sort of people, very different from the close-calculating folk of New England. My receipts are mostly in raccoon hides, and 'sea Island' cotton." Brown had shipped about two hundred bales over the past year, and as he explained to his brother, "I purchase it in the seed from the plantations, and grow it on my own. . . . Although I have much to be glad for, and much to complain of, still being of a contented sort of a disposition, I live on without a murmur, and manage to enjoy myself. I keep an old Bachelor's establishment, no woman as yet having touched my tender spot. I . . . am much addicted to pets—a tame raccoon, and tame parakeet being part of my household— most gladly would I welcome your face within my house."[1]

When George Brown came to Newnansville in 1840, he established a business partnership with his sister's husband, Dr. Edward Aldrich. Brown's seventeen years in Florida brought him wealth and a happy marriage to Matilda Stewart, who bore him three children. Brown's letters to his brother, sisters Corinna Aldrich and Ellen Anderson, and other family members and associates shed light on southern business practices and social mores of the time and place. Even so, as a native of Portsmouth, New Hampshire, Brown would have been very much the "Yankee Merchant" to his neighbors, even as he adjusted to his new surroundings. The letters narrate George's daily activities in the isolated Alachua County seat. At the same time, they provide a vivid picture of life on Florida's antebellum frontier through the eyes of a transplanted New Englander in a southern community. Before this work, we have published articles and a monograph using George Brown's sisters' letters.[2] The purpose here is to use George's letters to tell his story.

George was born to Captain Elihu and Elizabeth Dearing Brown on November 1, 1817, in Portsmouth, New Hampshire, the youngest of seven children. Only two years old when his father, a ship designer and captain of the privateering vessel *Fox* and other ships, died in a prison in Cádiz, Spain, George grew up in a large comfortable house in Portsmouth with his mother, three aunts (Delia, Mary, and Ann), and six siblings.[3] George's life changed dramatically in 1832 when his mother died and the family decided to leave Portsmouth. The next year, sixteen-year-old George joined brothers Mannevillette and Charles in Philadelphia as the family began to settle the Portsmouth estate.

Details about George's early education are unavailable, but according to Michael Hugo-Brunt, Portsmouth set "an example to other New England towns in the development of its cultural activities . . . [including] constant attempts to develop the educational facilities of the city."[4] The Brown family placed strong emphasis on education: reading, writing, and education were regular topics in family correspondence written during George's teens when the family was still mostly together in Portsmouth. In 1831, George's mother wrote a letter to her son Charles, who was with his brother Mannevillette in Philadelphia, thanking Charles for writing to her recently but chastising him for poor spelling and urging him to use a dictionary.[5] In a letter two months later, she praises Charles's wording in his letters but again criticizes his spelling and adds that she would mail him a dictionary. In the same letter, she comments that George, age fifteen, was doing well in school.[6] Although Charles was enrolled in writing school by February 1833, George's formal education apparently had ended by the time of his mother's death late in October 1832.

Of the four Brown siblings who survived into adulthood in the 1840s and 1850s, the other three—Mannevillette, Ellen, and Corinna—were literary and artistic, but their talents should not overshadow those of George, whose energy was channeled into business; their abilities suggest that all the children shared a cultured upbringing. Hundreds of letters by Mannevillette, Corinna, and Ellen survive, and they often run to four detailed pages, whereas most of George's seventy or so letters are shorter.[7]

Figure 0.1. Elizabeth Dearing Brown of Portsmouth,
New Hampshire, circa 1820s, painting from memory
by Mannevillette Elihu Dearing (M.E.D.) Brown.
Courtesy of Jane and Raymond Gill.

Still, George's letters reveal the mind of an educated man with considerable composition and narrative skills, and he represents the typical letter
writer of his day, the man of business.[8]

George's training as a clerk during his late teens and early twentics in
Boston, Pittsburgh, Philadelphia, and Charleston would have reinforced
his earlier education and further strengthened his writing. In addition to
leaving a detailed account of the economic, community, and social affairs
of mid-nineteenth-century Newnansville, George occasionally took time
out from his business affairs and correspondence, showing a more con-
templative character in his reflections on his own situation and interests.
When discussing business in his letters—notably those with his partner,
Edward Aldrich—George employs a direct, clear, and straightforward

Figure 0.2. Mannevillette Elihu Dearing Brown, self-portrait,
as a young man during his years in Europe.
Courtesy of Jane and Raymond Gill.

style quite different from the more relaxed and descriptive style he uses
in personal correspondence with his siblings.[9]

George's Aunt Delia Dearing had migrated to the Florida Territory in
the fall of 1833. Not long after establishing a millinery shop in St. Augustine, she married Dr. James Hall, an elderly, well-to-do planter from Mandarin on the St. Johns River.[10] The seventy-four-year-old Hall (also a New
Hampshire native) was one of the most substantial planters in the area,
having come to the region during the Spanish period. Delia Hall soon
welcomed other family members to her new home. The first to join the
Halls was George's sister Adelaide, but she died only months after arriving
in the territory on October 10, 1833.[11] Undaunted, other family members
migrated to Florida. By November 1835, George's brother Charles (nineteen), sisters Corinna (twenty-three) and Ellen (twenty), and Aunts Ann
and Mary had homesteaded acreage adjacent to the Halls.

Figure 0.3. Aunt Delia Dearing Hall (a), Ellen Brown (b), and Corinna Brown (c), portraits by M.E.D. Brown. Courtesy of Jane and Raymond Gill.

George Brown's letters touch upon several interesting themes appropriate to the study of relationships among siblings. George's letters to his sisters and his male correspondents were decidedly different, and they reflect gender roles and expectations of the time. George's letters to his brother Mannevillette and to his business partner, brother-in-law Edward Aldrich, contain business details and political speculations. They also contain racy, even graphic, sexual content. His missives to his sisters, while often jocular and humorous, discuss matrimony, domestic concerns, and speculations as to differences between the sexes. Ellen and Corinna were always solicitous of their brother's matrimonial plans. For instance, about the time George began courting Matilda Stewart, Corinna wrote to Mannevillette that George "says when he intends to take a sleeping partner he will let us know." She hoped he would find the "right kind of lady so as Aunt Mary used to say that we might have somewhere to go & take tea—now and then."[12]

George's letters also display attitudes about manhood that were prevalent in mid-nineteenth-century America. Anthony Rotundo argues, "There were . . . three ideals of manhood held up to middle-class men in the nineteenth-century North . . . the Masculine Achiever, the Christian Gentleman, and the Masculine Primitive. The first two held sway throughout the nineteenth century." Although George certainly displayed characteristics of the Christian Gentleman, he more closely followed the ideals of the Masculine Achiever as Rotundo describes the type: "What made the ideal of the Masculine Achiever so distinctive to its own era was the way it focused on self-advancement as the primary goal for a man's active nature. . . . Man had to work hard and with unfailing persistence."[13] George's rejection of a safe occupation as an employee in a northern city demonstrates this drive for self-advancement and independence. George ambitiously headed into an uncertain venture on the Florida frontier in pursuit of achievement in business. As David Pugh points out, "In brief, the acquisition of wealth became a test among men for those who, knowing that life was short and time was money, were willing to chase the main chance with leaps and bounds, often risking all in the hope of gaining everything. Some rushed to the west for gold and furs; others challenged a different kind of economic frontier in the East, one every bit as brutal and forbidding, by gambling in industry and commerce."[14] Although his brother Charles and especially his brother-in-law Edward Aldrich gave

Figure 0.4. George Long Brown as a young man about
the time he came to Florida, painting by M.E.D. Brown.
Courtesy of Raymond and Jane Gill.

George his start, there can be no doubt that his own drive and ability were
the main factors in his success.

George's letters include his observations on fundamentalist religion as
practiced on the Florida frontier. George's religious roots in New England
were not Calvinist, as might be expected, but Episcopal. George could
have occasionally attended the St. John's Episcopal Church in Jacksonville, where his brother Mannevillette's friend David Brown was pastor.[15]
The Methodist church had established inroads into the Alachua region as
early as the 1820s. Circuit riders visited Newnansville and environs into
the 1840s. In 1845, the Florida Conference of the Methodist Church created the Newnansville district.[16] Local pioneer-preacher Maxey Dell, one
of George's customers, operated a sawmill and furnished the lumber for

the community's first Methodist church. In 1846 and 1847, George might have witnessed two Methodist revivals in the area.[17] George's letters occasionally refer to more rustic services he attended mainly for a chance to socialize, to meet friends, or even to gain amusement. He sometimes regaled his brother Mannevillette with what he considered the ludicrous scenes of fundamentalist religious worship in the area.

George's letters make frequent reference to roughly fifty settlers in the Newnansville and Alachua County area with whom he socialized and had business relations. As with the community itself, these persons are in large part lost to history, but their names can be verified in numerous sources.[18] George also interacted with military and political figures and with lawyers and judges who came and went, such as David Levy, Isaac Bronson, Thomas Douglas, and William Forward. Two young lawyers, James A. Peden and George's business partner's brother Louis Aldrich, boarded with him for a time. George attended the superior (later circuit) court in Newnansville frequently as a litigant, juror, or spectator. His letters also discuss numerous state and national political issues of the day, such as the presidential elections of 1844, 1848, and 1852, the Mexican War, and foreign relations, especially as they related to commerce. From his letters it is easy to ascertain that George was decidedly a Whig, as was typical of merchants.[19] His positive references to Henry Clay, Zachary Taylor, and Winfield Scott and his disparaging comments on Martin Van Buren and James K. Polk prove the point. Though he never dabbled in politics himself, George was a keen observer of territorial, state, and national political affairs and regularly associated with men who were directly involved in politics. His brother-in-law and business partner, Edward S. Aldrich, ran unsuccessfully for a seat in the state legislature. Later, Edward's brother Louis was elected to the Florida House of Representatives and eventually also served in the state senate as a Democrat.

As George's family members moved to various Florida and Georgia locations during the next few years, George pursued a career in commerce, finding employment in merchant houses in Philadelphia and Charleston, South Carolina. During this time, George remained in touch with Mannevillette and with other family members in Florida, especially after the fall of 1837, when George's sister Corinna married Dr. Aldrich, who was attached to the army. A native of St. Marys, Georgia, and a graduate of the South Carolina Medical College in Columbia in 1833, Aldrich was especially helpful to George because of his many contacts.[20] Edward's

Figure 0.5. Likeness thought to be Edward Aldrich.
Courtesy of Elizabeth Traynor.

father, Dr. Whipple Aldrich, was a prosperous merchant in St. Marys; Edward also had relatives in Charleston with commercial contacts. His uncle Robert "Bob" Aldrich might have assisted George while he was in Charleston.[21] George's sister Corinna was especially grateful to her husband for his assistance to George in Charleston. On October 14, 1838, Corinna wrote from Macon, Georgia, where Edward was attempting to establish a medical practice, thanking Mannevillette for his efforts to assist George in his journey south and adding that Edward had "done his best to get him a situation [in Macon] at a salary of fifteen hundred dollars per year. They will await G's arrival. E. will befriend him to the last. He is very anxious to meet him."[22] By that time the Aldriches had moved from Macon, Georgia, to Mineral Springs in Columbia County, but they would soon relocate to Newnansville, the Alachua County seat.[23]

The Aldriches, Corinna's sister Ellen, and her brother Charles moved to Newnansville in August 1839. Aunt Ann soon joined them. As Corinna explained to Mannevillette, the town offered brighter prospects than their previous location: "Our quarters [are] more comfortable, and present business much more active." Corinna expected Newnansville to prosper, writing, "[Once] efficient means are taken to close the war this Winter & then this County of Alachua (with its rich hammock lands) must flourish." Corinna already saw signs of prosperity and explained, "Money always has been and will be plenty here—the farmers live in their log house—though they keep their carriages and spend money wholesale—and they get rich—the lands are so prolific."[24]

Formerly known as Dell's Post Office, Newnansville was established in 1828 but exists today only as a cemetery and historical marker bearing silent witness to a once vibrant community that included numerous stores, churches, hotels, rooming houses, a newspaper, a federal land office, and the entire region's only superior court.[25] Newnansville was strategically located just south of the Santa Fe River and about fifty miles south of the Georgia-Florida Line. The town was approximately sixty miles (a three-day journey) west from St. Augustine. Travelers heading from St. Augustine to Newnansville would cover the eighteen miles west to Picolata, cross the St. Johns River, and then continue on the Bellamy Road to the Alachua County seat.

George arrived in Newnansville two years before the end of the Second Seminole War (1835–1842). Regular army and militia leaders frequented the town, as did political leaders and officials of various sorts, and George associated with many of them. There were numerous forts within a ten-mile radius of Newnansville: Fort Gilliland was in the town itself; Fort Harlee was about ten miles to the east; Fort Clarke was ten miles south of the town on the edge of San Felasco Hammock; and Forts Tarver and Walker rested roughly eight miles south of Newnansville between San Felasco Hammock and Paynes Prairie. Also only a few miles east of Newnansville on the Bellamy Road was Post #12 commanded by Lt. James W. Anderson, who would soon marry George's sister Ellen. Roughly fifty miles northeast of Newnansville was Fort Heilman (Garey's Ferry) on

LINE OF STAGES,
BETWEEN ST. AUGUSTINE & PICOLATA.

The Travelling Public, is informed that Stages run regularly between the above places, as follows:

Leaves Picolata on Monday night, immediately after the arrival of the Mail steamer from Savannah.

Leaves St. Augustine at 5 o'clock Tuesday morning, to meet the Mail Boat on her way to Savannah.

Leaves on Friday at 5 o'clock, A. M., to meet the Wm. Gaston on her way from Savannah to Picolata.

Leaves Picolata on Friday morning, after the arrival of the steamer Wm. Gaston, from Savannah.

For passage apply to GEORGE W. COLE, Florida House, St. Augustine. No seat can be secured unless paid for.   May 31

NOTICE.

ALL persons having claims against the estate

Figure 0.6. "Line of stages between St. Augustine and Picolata." Regularized travel in antebellum Florida, while difficult and arduous, was well established by the 1840s. George Brown often traveled by stage and steamboat to and from such places as Picolata, St. Augustine, Garey's Ferry, and Jacksonville. *Jacksonville Florida News*, January 30, 1846.

Black Creek, an army supply depot with access to the St. Johns River, eighteen miles away.[26] Henry Whipple, who visited the village in 1844, thought Black Creek came "the closest to total depravity of any village" he "had ever seen. The demoralizing effects of the war are exhibited in glaring colours by the dissipation, profanity, & drunkenness of the place."[27] South Carolina Planter Whitfield Brooks, who traveled through there one

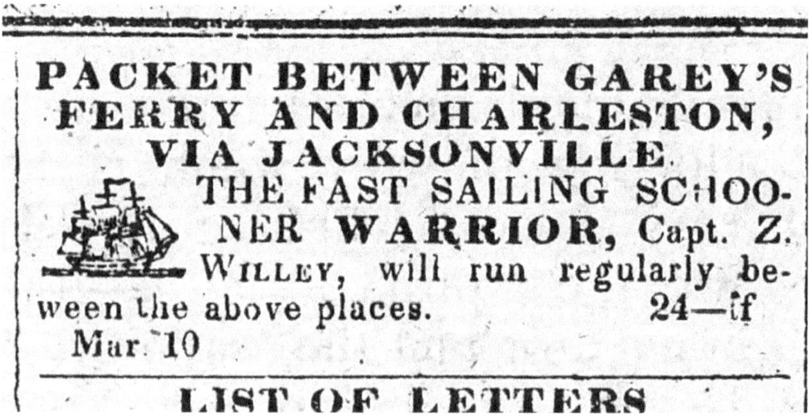

PACKET BETWEEN GAREY'S
FERRY AND CHARLESTON,
VIA JACKSONVILLE.
THE FAST SAILING SCHOO-
NER **WARRIOR**, Capt. Z.
WILLEY, will run regularly be-
ween the above places.   24—tf
Mar. 10

LIST OF LETTERS

Figure 0.7. "Packet between Garey's Ferry and Charleston via Jacksonville." George Brown could reach Savannah, Charleston, and points north via Garey's Ferry on Black Creek. *Jacksonville East Florida Advocate*, April 21, 1840.

year later, agreed. He described Black Creek as a "small and dirty little place, consisting of a few houses. It is a landing place, where a post office has been established and from which a line of stages are running to Newnansville."[28]

George visited the location for the first time in 1839, but in later years he often traveled to Garey's Ferry (later known as Middleburg) on his way to Jacksonville, Savannah, and Charleston. Middleburg was twenty-five miles from Jacksonville by land, but most travelers took the forty-mile route via Black Creek and the St. Johns. By 1855, the location was shipping between 1,500 and 2,000 bales of cotton per year.[29] Most visitors to this village were uncomplimentary of the makeshift settlement that served as a vital connecting point to the interior. The famous travel writer Charles Lanman spent a miserable night there in 1855. He noted that the town consisted of a few buildings on a "desolate hill, with a pine barren on one side" and a cypress swamp on the other. He found one merchant "selling goods and shipping cotton; a grocery store, where were assembled about twenty planters and teamsters, several of them intoxicated; a miserable tavern, where I occupied the same room and bed in which several individuals had recently died of consumption. . . . The tavern accommodations were very poor, and the doleful aspect of the place was a good deal heightened by the circumstance that our ears were all night saluted with the croaking of innumerable frogs in the neighboring swamp." Large quantities of cotton, cow hides, and deer skins were shipped from this spot. But the place, Lanman asserted, was probably more famous for its numerous alligators. "So abundant are these revolting creatures," he explained, "that in the summer evenings their bellowing, which resembles thunder, is quite annoying even to the inhabitants, and it is a common occurrence for the more ambitious of these amphibious monsters to ascend and sun themselves in the road upon which the cabins of the embryo city are planted."[30]

In 1840, when George Brown arrived in Newnansville, the region was only beginning to recover from the devastation of the Second Seminole War. In the five years before George's arrival, Newnansville became ground zero for the war against the Seminoles after the conflict's outbreak on December 28, 1835. The war tore apart East Florida as settlers fled from their isolated farms to the village in the months following the destruction of Maj. Francis Langhorne Dade's force. News of the panic and devastation spread quickly. The attack came on just as the Superior Court of Alachua, Columbia, and Hillsborough Counties was meeting in Newnansville. Judge Robert Raymond Reid hurriedly ended the proceedings so that everyone could return to their homes.[31] One report noted, "The white families have for the most part, abandoned their homes, in grate [*sic*] alarm and assembled at the different places where the inhabitants have erected, or are erecting forts for protection. At Newnansville, the Courthouse is turned into a fort, and the jail into a block-house."[32] A militia officer described the suffering of the 300 or so refugees in Newnansville as "beyond the power of human endurance."[33] Another report noted that Newnansville and Picolata were essentially under siege. "The Indians are pressing closer and closer upon us," one frightened settler wrote a local newspaper; "They riot and revel upon the ripening crops and on the cattle reluctantly but necessarily left to them by our people."[34] Those settlers who refused to abandon their farms often paid with their lives.[35]

While the terror that many isolated settlers experienced was real enough, George's sisters could not help but see the humor in the ludicrous scenes that often confronted them. In May 1836, Corinna wrote her brother Mannevillette only months after they first arrived in Mandarin, "If the Indians make us run I will take [the silk worm cocoons] with me, confound the scamps, how much trouble they make, but I don't blame them. It must be rare fun for them. You would die laughing to see the crackers (as they call the natives) they are so frightened. Dr. [Hall] went to Mandarin yesterday—he says he never saw such a set of crazy, foolish devils in his life."[36]

While the influx of regular army and militia forces managed to stabilize the situation to a certain degree, by the end of the year, many of George's future neighbors in Alachua County had become vulnerable to attacks and many had lost their lives. For example, in 1837 James Pendarvis, who eventually became a close friend to George, nearly lost his life when Indians fired on him only three miles from town.[37] Deadly attacks on neighboring homesteads and plantations continued for the next several years. But more than that, Newnansville was turned into a kind of armed camp, with the continual comings and goings of refugees and army personnel making for a chaotic and disorderly situation.

Jacob Motte, a surgeon in a regular army unit, arrived in Newnansville in May 1837. In his diary, he noted that before the war the town had only one block house, a courthouse, and a tavern, all "built in the same primitive style of architecture." But by the time Motte visited Newnansville, it consisted of "two rival hotels, a fort, shops in abundance, and dwellings, alias shanties, so numerous that for several days after my arrival I could scarcely find my way through the labyrinth of streets and lanes, laid out with a pleasing disregard to all rules of uniformity." This Harvard-educated scion of a South Carolina Huguenot family had a very low opinion of the town's inhabitants, mostly small farmers who had emigrated from Georgia to Alachua County to "plant corn, hoe potatoes, and beget ugly little white-headed responsibilities." Motte was convinced that the settlers (commonly referred to as Crackers) had brought the war on themselves to gain financial support from "Uncle Sam." At the first sign of alarm, he explained, they "immediately congregated in spots, built pickets of stockades—which they called forts—drew rations—and they designated themselves 'suffering inhabitants.' . . . Finding this a very agreeable way of living, they occasionally united together, and riding though the country in strong parties managed to kill a stray Indian or two. This so exasperated the rest of the tribe that they would break out anew and swear they wouldn't cease hostilities so long as a white-skin of them were left."[38]

George's sister Ellen shared Lt. Motte's dim view of Newnansville and its inhabitants. In 1839 she wrote their brother Mannevillette that the "inland city" contained about 1,500 inhabitants who lived in "cracker [houses] built of logs and surrounded by the dull monotonous uninteresting pine barren. . . . After I have written log-house, pine tree and cracker the only addition I can summon to memory is pig and dog. You mix up these ingredients in any and every possible way, add a little of some proportion of alcohol and the result will always be Newnansville."[39]

In 1840, when George arrived in Newnansville, Alachua County included portions of what would later become Gilchrist, Putnam, Levy, Marion, Citrus, and Hernando Counties. The county contained roughly 2,300 inhabitants, including just over 500 slaves. As might be expected in frontier regions, white men outnumbered white women by about three to one. By 1850, the county had increased by only 200 inhabitants, but the demographics had changed: men only slightly outnumbered women, but the number of slaves had nearly doubled.[40] One close study of the county has found that 111 households out of 274 (or roughly 40 percent) listed in the 1850 census owned slaves.[41]

The 1840 census of Alachua County noted that the county contained only eleven persons involved in commerce, so the county must have offered an open field for Edward and George's commercial enterprise. The precise number of mercantile establishments that existed in the county at that time is unclear.[42] Even so, the 1845 state census noted that the county's merchants had $16,900 stock in trade.[43] The 1850 census was more precise, listing George L. Brown and five other merchants in the county: Jehu Livingston, thirty-eight, a native of New York; John Zawadski, thirty-nine, from Poland; John P. Weeks, twenty-three, from North Carolina; William Dell, twenty-five, a Florida native; and John Parsons, forty, a native of Connecticut.[44] William Dell, with a net worth of two thousand dollars, and Jehu Livingston, with a net worth of one thousand dollars, were the most prosperous merchants after George, whose net worth was listed at two thousand dollars.[45]

By way of comparison with Alachua County, Duval County had thirty-eight merchants listed in the 1850 census out of a population of nearly 5,000. Roughly five were employed chiefly in the burgeoning lumber trade. Fourteen of the merchants hailed from north of the Mason-Dixon Line, and four were foreign born, coming from Germany, Holland, and Ireland (two).[46] One of the pioneer merchants of Jacksonville was Connecticut-born S. L. Burritt, who, as early as 1835, opened a wholesale trade with Cuba. His company shipped lumber, fish, and other commodities to Cuba and brought back rum, cigars, coffee, sugar, and fruits to

Jacksonville. George's sisters Ellen and Corinna had enjoyed his hospitality at his lavish residence, the largest in Jacksonville.[47] With a population of just over 1,000 in 1850, Jacksonville, on the St. Johns River, with an outlet to the Atlantic Ocean, was poised to command the commerce of East Florida. By the mid-1840s, steamboats had connected the town with Palatka, Black Creek, Picolata, and Enterprise to the south and with St. Marys, Savannah, Beaufort District, Charleston, and other points to the north. In 1855, a visitor reported that Jacksonville had two steam sawmills, two iron foundries, two first-class hotels, two newspapers, numerous boardinghouses, and Baptist, Methodist, Episcopal, Presbyterian, and Catholic churches.[48] Steamboat travel along the river and along the lower Atlantic coast grew rapidly. Northerners appreciated Jacksonville's potential as a commercial center, and the town eventually came to dominate economic affairs in the years leading up to the Civil War.[49]

St. Johns County had the second-largest number of merchants in East Florida, with 14 of roughly 2,500 inhabitants. Of that number, five were from the North: George Burt was from Vermont, B. E. Carr and Nancy and Sally Pinkham were from New York, and George Center was from Massachusetts. Thirty-year-old Thomas Nelson was from Ireland.[50] Nearly all the commercial activity of St. Johns County emanated out of the ancient city of St. Augustine. Dominated by the Castillo San Marcos (Fort Marion), St. Augustine was home to a mixed population of white, black, and creole residents and soldiers housed at St. Francis Barracks on the seawall on the southern edge of town. Whitfield Brooks, who visited the town in 1845, thought St. Augustine was a "doomed city" that must in a few years languish from an irredeemable atrophy. He found many of the buildings "literally in ruin" and "scarcely habitable" and wrote that "a few years will see many more tumbling to the earth."[51] Even if Brooks's appraisal of the Ancient City was too harsh, his comments reflected the inevitable eclipsing of St. Augustine by Jacksonville.

Columbia, Levy, Madison, St. Johns, Marion, and Putnam Counties bordered Alachua County in 1850. Of the six, Columbia had the most merchants after St. Johns, with eight. Only one of the merchants, Thomas Dexter of Rhode Island, was born outside the South. The county had nearly double the population of Alachua with almost 5,000 inhabitants. The county seat and largest town was Alligator (eventually known as Lake City), midway between Jacksonville and the Middle Florida settlements.

The county's second-largest village was Mineral Springs on the Suwannee River.[52] Of the remaining counties bordering Alachua in 1850, Putnam had five merchants, Levy had two, Madison had five, and Marion had three.[53]

Historian Lewis Atherton has noted that country stores in new communities served a vital purpose as an "agent of credit extension, as a supplier of merchandise, and as the first agent in collecting farm crops and starting them on their way to market." As such, merchants "became a force in building up the rural towns in which they lived. Along with the lawyer, preacher, editor, and artisan he provided the leadership in such communities." The purpose of southern country stores was to supply merchandise, receive and market farm crops, and provide farmers with a source of credit and exchange. Country store owners such as George Brown often dealt in commodities instead of cash.[54] Again, Atherton notes of southern storekeepers that they "provided the dry goods, groceries, and tools necessary for the operation of farmers. . . . He served as a middleman between seaboard wholesalers . . . and farmers, thus handling the generous and long-range credit which characterized the system. He bartered merchandise for farm crops, and by marketing the latter offered an outlet for southern farms."[55]

Harold Woodman notes, "Next to factors, country storekeepers . . . were the most important Southern middlemen in the cotton trade. Located in the smallest crossroads villages as well as in the larger market towns, grocers, dry goods merchants, and general storekeepers regularly handled cotton in addition to their other business. . . . Storekeepers provided the same important services in marketing of cotton as did the factors. Like the factor, the storekeeper assisted in the sale of the crop, provided long-term credit, and facilitated the movement of supplies to the cotton grower." According to Woodman, small country stores like the one George operated were in a sense "'appendages' to the factorage system."[56] Woodman explains:

> Country storekeepers who combined cotton transactions with his business of selling merchandise for the most part serviced the farmers and small planters. Owning few or perhaps no slaves and producing a relatively small crop, this group required on a lesser scale many of the same services the large planter did. However small the

amount, cotton produced on the farms had to find its way to market. The factorage system could not always meet the needs of the farmer and small planter. The crop was not large enough and the security was usually inadequate to induce factors to take the trouble and risk involved in dealing with hundreds of tiny cotton growers. The country storekeeper stepped into the breach. He offered equipment, food, and dry goods to the farmer as needed and allowed bills, rendered at the end of the season, to be paid in cotton. By providing this service to as many as three or four hundred farmers within shopping distance of his store, the storekeeper accumulated enough cotton to enable him to deal with a factor. The storekeeper thus became an important customer of the factor, and he could, if necessary, receive advances and credit on cotton shipped or to be shipped (just as a planter could), thus enabling him to pass his credit on to his farmer customers. The smallest producer could market his crop through the storekeeper. [A storekeeper bought and sold] not only cotton but all other merchandise of the community. In this manner he replenished his store of goods, filled orders for buyers, and accumulated goods for sale elsewhere. . . . For the small farmer the store might be his only market. Indeed, the storekeeper was in fact—if not in name—the farmer's factor, providing the same necessary services for the small grower that the factor furnished the planter.[57]

George's store in Newnansville, Florida, like other stores throughout the rural south, operated not only as a place to buy, sell, and trade but also as an important social center, especially during courthouse days or when the town's Federal Land Office was auctioning off land. As historian Frank Byrne has noted, stores in rural communities served as hubs where men and women, both white and black, could socialize: "People living relatively close to their neighborhood store often dropped by not to make a purchase but to exchange gossip, whittle sticks, and discuss horse racing or cockfighting. Not surprisingly, this led many people to view their local storekeeper as a neighbor and friend. . . . Personal and business relationships overlapped in southern stores. Friendships developed and pleasantries passed between salesman and customer."[58]

As a merchant in East Florida with experience in larger cities in the North, George would have appreciated the large degree to which his own operations were tied to the health of the national and global economies.

To a large extent, the cotton trade drove the economy of the western world, and by the 1830s New York City had already begun to dominate American markets. According to one source, the "'Cotton Triangle' in which New York brokered the exchange of southern cotton—for British manufacturers, New York ships ran cotton from Charleston or Mobile or Savannah to European ports (primarily Liverpool), returned to New York with manufactured goods (and immigrants) then worked down the coast again to exchange their goods for cotton—ringing up, at every turn, substantial profits, freight charges, and commissions."[59]

The majority of Alachua County settlers made their living in agriculture. Corn was the main staple. The 1850 census recorded that the county produced almost 65,000 bushels of corn, 451 bushels of oats, almost 18,000 pounds of rice, 28,000 bushels of sweet potatoes, just over 2,500 bushels of peas and beans, and fifty-two bushels of Irish potatoes. By 1850, with readier access to slave labor, cotton was offering larger profits than were foodstuffs. The 1850 census recorded that Alachua County farmers produced 561 bales of ginned cotton. If George's claim to his brother that he shipped two hundred bales of cotton was correct, then he would have handled almost half of Alachua County's crop. Alachua County ranked third among East Florida counties behind Columbia County (802 bales) and Marion County (701 bales) in cotton production. Alachua County farmers also turned to sugar as a cash crop. The 1850 census recorded sixty-eight hogsheads produced.[60]

By far the most profitable crop that East Florida settlers produced and George Brown handled was Sea Island cotton (or long staple cotton). As distinguished from upland cotton, which had short, coarse fibers and green seeds that adhered to the fiber, Sea Island cotton had long silky fibers and smooth black seeds that could be more easily removed. Thus, Sea Island cotton required a ginning process that differed from the variations on the Whitney-style gins generally used in most areas of the South. Sea Island cotton was planted in the latter part of March; upland cotton planting ranged from early March through May. Picking went from August through the end of the year, and ginning occurred soon after that. Most East Florida planters used the McCarthy gin, which was designed specifically for the crop by Putnam County inventor Fones McCarthy. Sea Island cotton was grown primarily in the coastal areas of Georgia, South Carolina, and Florida. But more and more farmers found the crop perfectly suited to Florida. According to historians William W. Rogers and Jerrell

Shofner, "because the peninsula was affected by the Gulf breezes from the west and the Atlantic Ocean from the east, it was found that Sea Island cotton thrived as much as sixty miles inland. A fine quality cotton of the long staple variety was grown in Alachua County almost in the center of the state." Sea Island cotton commanded much higher prices than upland cotton. The commodity never fell below thirty cents per pound during the 1850s. By the late 1850s, with high returns on investment attracting more and more planters from South Carolina, Florida surpassed Georgia and South Carolina in the production of Sea Island cotton.[61]

By 1850, more than forty-five settlers in Alachua County had amassed estates valued at least at one thousand dollars, and the wealthiest of these derived their income from farming.[62] Even the largest landholders called themselves "farmers." The designation "planter" is not listed in the Alachua County census. Even so, fifty-six-year-old farmer Bennett Dell had a net worth of twenty thousand dollars (including sixty-five slaves), making him the richest man in the county, and he certainly would have merited the designation of "planter."[63] If owning twenty or more slaves earned a holder the title of "planter," then Zelphia Standley (fifty-six), John B. Standley (twenty-eight), Thomas Prevatt (forty-six), Philip Dell (twenty-nine), M. S. Perry (twenty-seven), Asa Clark (twenty-six), James G. Cameron (twenty-six), Sarah Colson (twenty-four), Samuel Piles (thirty-three), John C. Richard (twenty-six), and Samuel Geiger (twenty-one) also earned the distinction. Eleven other Alachua Countians owned between ten and twenty slaves. Eighty-three others, including George Brown, who owned six slaves, owned fewer than ten slaves.[64]

In the 1850s, Alachua County's population and prosperity burgeoned. At approximately 8,200 by 1860, its population had nearly quadrupled from the 1850 total, and so did the number of slaves. Much of the growth and prosperity was due to the introduction of slave-based agriculture, and in 1860, (three years after George's death) the county produced the state's seventh-largest cotton crop.[65] George Brown witnessed and took part in the East Florida frontier's transformation into an economy based increasingly on slave labor. This transformation moved along slowly during George's residency in Newnansville. Scholars such as Larry Rivers have recognized marked differences between the slave regimes in Middle Florida and East Florida. East Florida's antecedents as a Spanish province resulted in a greater reliance on the task system than on the gang system. This circumstance, notes Rivers, "generally afforded the typical slave fewer restraints and somewhat greater control over daily living conditions than those of Middle Florida. Still, the temperament and whims of owners could result in agonizing pain or relative ease. Because a larger percentage of area owners were small slaveholders and worked directly with slaves, the owners' personal attitudes toward bond servants loomed larger than in Middle Florida. Owners always could display meanness of spirit regarding slave control or evidence of downright cruelty in the wink of an eye."[66] Even as East Florida adjusted to a market economy based in large part on slave labor, settlers in Alachua County also made a living by herding cattle and pigs. East Florida contained the best open range lands east of the Mississippi. These vast tracts were extremely conducive to cattle herding, and this pursuit was endemic to the region going all the way back to the First Spanish Period. Thousands of head ranged freely in the peninsula and attracted pioneers eager to merge them with their own herds. The 1850 census noted that settlers in East Florida counties owned nearly 80,000 head of cattle, and thousands more roamed free on the frontier. This total did not include about 40,000 domesticated milk cows. On its own account, Alachua County contained about 12,000 head of cattle and about 5,200 milk cows. Raising and hunting hogs on the vast open range was also a chief pursuit. The 1850 census noted that Alachua County settlers owned almost 12,000 hogs.[67] Many of those who migrated to East Florida hailed from Georgia or South Carolina, where they practiced this herding culture, and they continued these folkways in Florida.[68]

Although the majority of Alachua County settlers were Scots-Irish farmers and herdsman from adjacent southern states, by 1850 the county had attracted settlers from nearly all the states of the eastern seaboard. Like George, several settlers hailed from New England: fellow merchant John Parson, teacher Augustus Prentiss, and innkeeper George Galpin were from Connecticut and minister George Watson was from Maine. Two Europeans found their way to Alachua County: the previously mentioned merchant John Zawadski, from Poland, and tailor Adam Kiel, from Germany.[69]

George Brown's experience as a Yankee merchant on America's southernmost frontier offers numerous opportunities to explore the commercial life of an isolated region before the advent of railroads. In a sense, George and other merchants were introducing capitalism to a precapitalist frontier society. In the process, many questions arise. Where did George get credit? Where did he get his goods? How did he bring them to this relatively isolated frontier village? What were the logistics? And of his neighbors: How did they view him? Were they suspicious of his Yankee background? The easy answer to the first question is that George's brother-in-law Edward Aldrich provided George with the capital and the connections to get his enterprise off the ground. Edward's merchant father, Whipple Aldrich of St. Marys, Georgia, has already been mentioned. Edward Aldrich's uncle Robert Aldrich, also a merchant in Charleston, may have introduced George to sources of credit. Robert's son (Edward's cousin) Alfred Proctor Aldrich was a leading lawyer-politician from Barnwell District, South Carolina. Through Alfred Aldrich, a protégé of powerful planter-politician James Henry Hammond, George could have gained access to a wider circle of leading commercial and business contacts in the Charleston area that might have included William Gilmore Simms.[70] George traveled frequently to Savannah and Charleston, where he met with factors, dealt with creditors, and secured goods to bring back home. As well as can be determined by George's own letters, newspapers, and financial records, George made semiannual visits to Charleston. In doing so, he traveled on at least twelve different steamboats, side-wheelers, and other craft.[71] His journeys from Newnansville to Garey's Ferry and then to points north via steamboat can be traced in his letters, newspapers, and financial records. Like other merchants and businessmen from isolated locales, George enjoyed his sojourns in the South's largest metropolis, Charleston. He made many friends there, among them mayor-intellectual William Porcher Miles.

Historians have written extensively about commercial activity in the frontier South and have addressed the role of Yankee merchants there.[72] Historian Fletcher Green notes that the "Southern Yankee played an important role in . . . bringing on . . . an agricultural and industrial revolution in the South," making the 1850s the "most prosperous decade experienced in the Old South."[73] George's strange New England accent would have indicated that he was not a native of the South, but the most important distinction between northerners and southerners was usually their attitudes on slaveholding. However, on this score, George Brown had no difficulty adjusting to Southern social and labor customs and had no qualms about the institution of slavery; like most southern whites, he thought that enslavement was the natural condition of an inferior race. His letters often refer to his own slaves, who plowed his garden, cooked in his kitchen, ran errands, and hauled goods from place to place. Surviving correspondence also indicates that George regularly bought and sold slaves on behalf of himself, his family, and his customers. In his first couple of years in New-nansville, he shared the labor of one slave with Edward Aldrich. When George died in 1857, he owned seven slaves, and from the beginning of his time in Florida, his statements about slavery in his letters were indistinguishable from what a southern-born person would have written.

George thought the differences between northern and southern merchants were overstated: "Say what they will of Yankees of their love of money—their bargain downing propensity, etc. the Southern merchants are exactly the same—Cheating, gouging, meanness and amor pecunia[74] flourishes as well south of the Mason Dixon's line as it does elsewhere."[75] George's comments beg the question, How were Yankee merchants viewed by the greater community? Were they despised? Were they accepted? It is probably the case that most farmers were ambivalent toward all shopkeepers (with Northern-born ones held in only slightly more contempt.) Whatever the case, they certainly were numerous. When Episcopal clergyman Henry Whipple visited Savannah in 1844, he found many northerners who had been "successfully engaged in business for many years." "Indeed everywhere in the south," he noted, "you will find enterprising and energetic northerners located & successfully competing with those southerners educated & reared here." There were some successful southern-born men in commerce, but "in point of business talent," Whipple observed, "the preponderance is decidedly in favor of the north."[76]

Daniel Hundley, perhaps the South's most perceptive contemporary social commentator, saw little difference between northern and southern storekeepers. They are, he noted, "pretty much like all other shopmen the world over. They certainly do possess some marked peculiarities, but aside from those which are mainly due to local surroundings, they differ but little from any ordinary shop-keeper in New-England or the North-West. They generally, in all the States, spring from the thrifty middle classes; and their heads are much more constantly occupied with how they may turn an honest penny, than with politics, or science, or religion." Hundley, though, differentiated between the "honest and straightforward tradespeople" of the South and the "less honest class of storekeepers" whom he referred to as "Southern Yankees." For Hundley, these were Southern men who were as "shrewd, sharp, chaffering, oily-tongued, soft-sawdering, inquisitive, money-making, money-saving, and money worshipping individual[s], [as any] who hails from Down East." Even though southern-born, "Southern Yankees" embodied the worst tendencies of northern avarice.[77]

One historian has noted that "successful mercantile newcomers . . . [were often able] to acquire planting kin—and with them land and slaves—through marriage."[78] George Brown's experience fits this pattern. He married into the richest family in Columbia County when he wed Matilda Stewart in 1850.

If George had to adapt himself to Southern cultural, economic, and social mores, one of the other differences he encountered in his new home was the South's penchant toward violence. Historians have determined that antebellum Florida was one of the most violent places east of the Mississippi.[79] The violence associated with slavery and the Second Seminole War was real enough, but George also witnessed shocking scenes of violence among white settlers in his community. Two of his wife's brothers died violent deaths: one died from wounds sustained in a duel, and another was shot dead in an angry confrontation with a man in George's own store. Some of the violence resulted from clashes between settlers and soldiers.[80] For example, in 1838, Asa Smith murdered a soldier named Dunnegan in Newnansville and fled.[81] Most of the violence involved personal slights or economic disputes, and alcohol was often involved. In 1841, the grand jury for Alachua, Hillsborough, and Columbia counties deplored as a "great public evil" the out-of-control liquor traffic that was taking place "at and about the United States Posts."[82] Shootings like the one that took the life of Alfred Tanner at his tavern at Fort Harlee in 1840 were common. After shots were fired in the crowded tavern, everyone fled, leaving Tanner's lifeless body behind. To discover what had happened, U.S. Attorney Thomas Douglas called in George's brother-in-law to perform a postmortem examination. The murder was left unresolved as Douglas was forced to conclude that the circumstances connected with Tanner's death were shrouded in "obscurity and mystery."[83] In 1848, the Alachua County sheriff himself was gunned down during a dispute in a poker game.[84] The mere fact of living in such an isolated region brought with it untold hazards. For example, in 1849, in broad daylight, two men approached an isolated Alachua County plantation, shot its owner, a man named Rains, robbed the house of four thousand dollars while his wife and family were present, and fled.[85] In the seventeen years that George lived in Newnansville, the superior and circuit court prosecuted fifty-five violent assaults and sixteen murders.[86] George also witnessed numerous instances of corporal punishment and public hangings.

By the spring of 1840, George had joined his family in Florida. By that time, Edward Aldrich had established his medical practice in Newnansville, moving Corinna and Ellen with him to a house in town. The family anticipated that Charles Brown and Edward would go into business together there. As Corinna explained in a letter to Mannevillette, Charles and Edward "are about to try the mercantile business. E. is to give his name and capital, and Charles to attend to business. I suspect they will do well. The opening is fine for a small business and they can increase by and by. The headquarters of the army are to be here this winter and it will of course bring much into town. It is said there will be an army of twenty thousand there by the last of next month."[87] Unfortunately, just as they were implementing the plan, Charles died unexpectedly in Savannah. Eventually, George would fill this void, and soon he and Edward formed a close friendship and business partnership.

Edward Aldrich's decision to move to Newnansville was based in large part on his reenlistment in the army as a surgeon. In the summer of 1839, settlers in the area were outraged at the truce or "false peace" that Gen. Alexander Macomb had made with the Seminoles according to which they would be allowed to remain in the extreme south of the territory. On August 3, citizens from Alachua and Columbia Counties met in Newnansville to denounce the pact. "We must distinctly declare," the body stated, "we have no confidence in the arrangement entered into between General Macomb with the Seminole Indians as effecting peace, or restoring quiet and order to the country."[88] Events soon proved that the fighting was far from over. Sporadic attacks on isolated homesteads continued unabated for the next several years. Newnansville remained the center of the army's war against the Seminoles, and as late as 1840 settlers were still exposed to attacks in the area. Although most of the Seminole hiding places were south of Alachua County, Seminole warriors were able to continue their raiding operations near Newnansville. For example, on March 19, 1840, a Methodist minister named McKay was shot and scalped near Newnansville.[89] In April and May 1840, three people were killed near the town. Also in May, only a few miles east of town, Seminoles burned down John B. Standley's plantation, killed his livestock, and destroyed eight hundred bushels of corn, which accounted for his whole year's crop.[90] In the fall three soldiers were killed while on their way from Fort Tarver to Micanopy. The same report also noted that a young man of eighteen was shot by a party of Seminoles seven miles from Black Creek on the Newnansville road.[91] On January 19, 1841, in a brazen attack on Newnansville, Seminoles killed a man named Lindsey, burned down territorial legislator Edmund Bird's house, and tried to break into another residence on the other side of the village.[92]

Even so, time was running out for the Seminoles. A series of retaliatory raids against the isolated Seminole villages effectively removed the Seminole threat from the immediate area. In June 1841, Colonel William Jenkins Worth took charge of operations against the Seminoles and devised tactics to bring the war to a close. A few Newnansville area settlers lost their lives early the next year, but Worth's relentless assaults pushed them deeper and deeper into the peninsula.[93] Campaigning right through the summer months, Worth kept the pressure on until so many Seminoles had agreed to emigrate west that he declared the war over in August 1842. Remaining tribesmen were pushed to the lower Peace River and the Everglades.[94] Congress simultaneously passed the Armed Occupation Act, which was calculated to garrison the frontier with settlers on what had been Seminole lands south of the Alachua County line. Introduced by Senator Thomas Hart Benton of Missouri, the act provided that heads of households or single males could claim 160-acre tracts, build a cabin, occupy it, cultivate at least five acres, and after five years secure title to the land. Claims had to be at least two miles from military posts. This measure gave momentum to Edward Aldrich and numerous other Alachua settlers' appeals to establish a land office in Newnansville. By August 1843, the new land office had issued almost 950 claims.[95] Newnansville boomed as new settlers poured in. Favorable reports of Worth's successes against the Seminoles spurred immigration, and national newspapers trumpeted the opportunities for settlement. In August 1843, for example, a Richmond, Virginia, newspaper reported that owing to Worth's efforts, "no fear is apprehended from the band that now remains with the Territory. Almost every day witnesses the arrival at St. Augustine of emigrants wending their way south in quest of land."[96] However, that was two years after George Brown had arrived in the town.

While his brothers and sisters braved the wilds of the East Florida frontier, Mannevillette Brown was in European cities such as Paris, Rouen, Florence, Venice, and Rome with other American artists who studied, worked, socialized, and visited European art centers and copied the works of the old masters.[97] Beginning in 1838, Mannevillette spent nearly a decade abroad. Thirty years old in 1840, Mannevillette never visited Florida during George's lifetime, but the older sibling served as a life-long confidant to his younger brother. A year before he arrived in Florida, George wrote the aspiring artist from Philadelphia that he must be enjoying "the vine clad hills of France and the glorious sunsets of Italy." George was proud to say that he was "pursuing [his] proper business" and was on the "high road to preferment."[98] Of his brother-in-law and future business partner, George wrote to Mannevillette that Dr. Edward Aldrich "is gaining ground in his profession rapidly–he is surgeon for two military forts . . . besides an extensive practice. Corin has secured an excellent and devoted husband in him. I know you will like the young gentleman if you have the opportunity to know him." Meanwhile Aunt Mary and Aunt Ann lived on their farm near the Halls in Mandarin, but they would soon join the family in Newnansville.[99]

What follows is the story of George Brown's life as a merchant on the Florida frontier as reflected in his letters to his family members. Brown witnessed and discussed the goings on in this isolated frontier outpost from his arrival in 1840 until his death in 1857. In the seventeen years that George lived in Newnansville, he had occasion to interact and carry on business with nearly all the settlers from the area. His letters discuss business, politics (local, state, and national), Seminole affairs, agricultural issues, and, of course, the latest gossip. His letters reveal the challenges and rewards of operating a business in the isolated village of Newnansville, a community that no longer exists and of which we know very little.

Provenance and History of George Brown's Letters

The origin, the intended destination and recipient, and the provenance of the letters are generally clear: George Brown always included in his letters salutations naming his intended correspondent, the location from which he was writing, a complimentary closing, and a signature. The salutation sometimes appears as a term of endearment, such as "my dearest brother," or a shortened name, such as "Dear Mann" (for Mannevillette). George varied his own signature: sometimes he used his full name, George Long Brown, and sometimes he used his initials entirely or partially. To clarify the identifying information for the reader, we include in brackets the names of the intended recipients above George's salutation, along with the intended destination, which usually appears on the outside of the folded letter itself.

The seventy or so letters reproduced in this study generally followed a clear path from George's hand to their current locations, but the journey becomes uncertain at a few points along the way. Like many nineteenth-century Americans, George's family members generally saved letters received from others in the family. However, given the itinerant nature of the family, these mementos were subject to loss or damage. Many of George's letters traveled a long way, especially those to Mannevillette in Europe or upstate New York. Corinna, Ellen, and Mannevillette carefully saved George's letters, and Edward's letters were saved as long as he was with Corinna, which suggests that Corinna saved them for him. When Corinna died in New York City in 1854, Ellen or Mannevillette apparently saved her letters. Ellen passed her collection on to her daughter Villette, who kept them when she moved with her sister Georgia to Washington, D.C., to live with their brother, Edward. When Villette died in 1891, Edward saved her collection and added to them the letters saved by his uncle Mannevillette, who died in 1896. After Edward's death in 1915, the entire collection of more than 850 nineteenth-century family letters stayed in a single-family home in Washington, D.C., for several generations.

In 1975, a family member brought a selection of the letters—those written to and from Brown family members in Florida—to Gainesville, Florida, and offered them for sale to local historians and collectors and to the P. K. Yonge Library at the University of Florida, where they were stored in a vault for several years. Later, the collection was sold to a private individual in Gainesville. In the 1980s, Ms. Mannevillette Sullivan, the great-granddaughter of Ellen Brown Anderson, located and bought the entire collection, including photocopies of originals that had been sold off. In 1994, Ms. Sullivan bequeathed these letters and photocopies to the United States Military Academy at West Point library.

Already familiar with the existence of portions of the Brown-Anderson-Aldrich family correspondence, James M. Denham chanced upon the assembled West Point collection in 1993.

After corresponding with Miss Sullivan, he returned to West Point and carefully arranged the entire collection for microfilming. Since then, Keith Huneycutt has also visited West Point to examine some of the original letters and copies more closely, to take notes on the condition of the collection, and to make digital photographs of a selection of them. We have primarily used these copies and notes to make the transcriptions presented in this book.

While conducting research, transcribing letters, and editing this book, the editors began a correspondence with and eventually met Mr. Norman La Coe, an Alachua County historian and retired Gainesville attorney who was among the first people to view the letters when they arrived in Florida in 1975. Mr. La Coe shared with us a great deal of useful information about the provenance of the letters after 1975 and his own research concerning the Browns in Florida. In addition, he gave us his own excellent photocopies of all of the Florida letters, which were made when they were first brought to Gainesville; we discovered that these copies sometimes reproduced the letters more accurately and completely than the copies at West Point, which in some cases had pages that were missing, out of place, or damaged by handling between 1975 and 1992 when we first examined and copied them. We used Mr. La Coe's copies to improve the transcriptions of a dozen letters. Mr. La Coe also lent us his complete set of transcriptions of the Florida letters, which occasionally proved very helpful.

Another repository for part of the Brown family letter collection recently came to our attention: the Ah-Tah-Thi-Ki museum on the Big Cypress Seminole Reservation in the Florida Everglades. This collection of nearly two hundred Brown family letters, including approximately thirty written by George Brown, consists of original letters, copies of which Ms. Sullivan acquired in the 1990s. These originals found their way to the museum in 1995.

Editorial Procedures and Practices

We have ourselves transcribed George Brown's letters, all of which were handwritten. For each letter, one of us would carefully examine a given letter or photocopy while preparing a transcription of it. Then, the other would also examine the letter independently, read the transcription, and record any disagreement with specific readings. We then collaborated in person concerning any points of disagreement, made alterations where we could now agree, and temporarily noted words or phrases that remained indecipherable. For letters where questions remained, we consulted Mr. La Coe's transcriptions, and when we agreed that his reading of a word was correct, we used it. In the final text, ellipses now indicate the few re-maining indecipherable words or phrases. Likewise, we indicate with an ellipsis places where words are missing owing to tears or smudges in the page. In a few instances, we also use ellipses where we have deliberately left out a passage because it duplicates information appearing in another letter, and we indicate such omissions in a footnote.

We include brackets within transcribed letters to indicate editorial emendations, such as words added to complete the grammar of a sen-tence. Also, we enclose added names or parts of names within brackets to identify persons when George included only a nickname, a first or last name, or initials. For the first appearance of a person, we provide identi-fication in a footnote; additional information about a person appears in appendix A.

We attempted to represent George's spelling, capitalization, punctua-tion, and spacing as accurately as possible. George's spelling is consis-tent with nineteenth-century standard written American English, such as appeared in published newspapers, magazines, and literature of the day, and it is generally clear to a twenty-first-century reader. In cases where George's spelling seems likely to confuse a modern reader, we have let it stand but supplied a footnote to define the word or George's use of it. Where a word requires a precise definition, we have quoted the *Oxford English Dictionary*, which provides historical definitions with examples from English and American authors. We also provide footnotes with translations of foreign words, phrases, or abbreviations. Capitalization practices in the mid-nineteenth century were less standardized than they are today, so the recipients of George's letters would probably not have noticed his inconsistent capitalization; whenever his intent is clear, we have let it stand.

George was usually careful with his grammar and spelling, but he was less stringent and consistent with his punctuation. The majority of his sentences follow standard punctuation practices, with commas, periods, semicolons, and question marks generally used as a modern writer would use them. However, sometimes, especially when he was apparently writ-ing in a rush to beat the departure of the mail, he would be less consistent, and in such cases, he employed dashes freely, often in place of periods and commas and sometimes in the manner that a modern writer would employ an em dash to insert a parenthetical remark or a hurried com-ment. In instances where we could be relatively certain that George was using the dash as a period—as when a short dash appears at the end of a sentence with a long space or paragraph break after it or in a lowered position parallel with the bottom of the last word in a sentence—we supplied a period. In all other cases, we let the dash stand, and in cases where he used longer dashes or a series of consecutive dashes, we did the same.

We did not attempt to reproduce all of George's spacing and positioning of words; for instance, when George wrote a brief business letter, his hand is usually larger with fewer words and more spacing throughout the page than in his more leisurely, personal letters. We did not vary the font size to reproduce the layout and appearance variations that are obvious to a reader viewing the original letters. However, if George left extra space between sentences within a paragraph, we did also, since he seemed to do so to create a longer pause than end-stop punctuation could provide. Also, George sometimes varied the position of his closing and signature, ranging from the center of the page to the far right; we attempted to re-create that placement.

❦ 1 ❦

"I Shall Be My Own Man"

(1840–1842)

GEORGE BROWN ARRIVED IN NEWNANSVILLE on May 21, 1840. Corinna Brown Aldrich wrote to Mannevillette in Paris that George "looks princely and seems in better spirits" than when she had last seen him. She predicted that his business prospects were fair, as he and his brother Charles were "steady, industrious and persevering."[1] One can only imagine what the twenty-three-year-old New Hampshire native would have thought of Newnansville. George must have gaped at his new surroundings. Compared to Portsmouth, Philadelphia, or Charleston, Newnansville and its environs must have seemed like another world. He could not have guessed that during the next seventeen years he would prosper, marry, have three children, and become a leading member of the community.

By the time George arrived in Newnansville, the Aldriches, his sister Ellen, his brother Charles, and Aunt Ann had been in the town almost a year. It certainly would have been a happy reunion. George's immediate living arrangements are unclear, but he most likely would have lived with Charles, and the two would have communicated frequently with Edward about their new commercial venture. On August 2, Corinna wrote to Mannevillette that George "begins to look and act more contented" but suggested that they all might eventually move to Savannah or Charleston. She recognized that the war was far from over and that for the time being they would stay put. She hoped to see Mannevillette but speculated that he would not be contented here "in the wild, wild, woods. No amusements, nothing to interest but solitude. No news but Indian murders and thefts. After you get <u>naturalized</u> you would do better but it takes time for that."[2]

Since arriving in town, Dr. Aldrich had traveled often throughout the region visiting the various posts and treating patients. He bought a town lot and secured a license to sell spirituous liquors.[3] He also began taking an active part in his community. Along with other Alachua County settlers, he signed a petition asking Congress to establish a land office in Newnansville.[4] He was also drawn in to boisterous political debates. For example, on September 19, 1839, Edward's voice was prominent at a meeting at the Newnansville courthouse opposing division of the territory at the Suwanee River to eventually create two different states. Edward helped draft resolutions to that effect.[5] Four months before George arrived, Edward had presided over an official welcoming party for Florida's new governor. President Martin Van Buren had appointed Robert Raymond Reid as superior court judge; the judge, his family, and other dignitaries under military escort arrived in town on their way to Tallahassee. Reid was well-known and beloved in the community, as he had served as judge of the Eastern Judicial District of Florida since 1832. The occasion must have been a joyous one for Corinna and Ellen too since they had frequently visited Mrs. Mary Martha Reid and her stepdaughters, Janet and Rosalie, in St. Augustine. As one report noted, once Reid and his entourage had arrived in town, they were taken to Mrs. Standley's boardinghouse, where the new governor spent the afternoon receiving visitors and congratulations. A salute was fired, and at 3 p.m., the group "sat down to one of the largest and most sumptuous public dinners that had ever occurred in the county and the company continued at the table until a late hour." Edward presided over the festivities that evening, officiating the regular and volunteer toasts.[6] Edward's Whig Party affiliation did not prevent him from supporting Democrats such as Reid and David Levy. A year later, Edward served as president of the day at a Harrison Meeting in Newnansville and offered up a toast in support of Levy in his bid to become Florida's territorial delegate to Congress.[7]

In late July, Charles Brown traveled to Charleston to purchase goods for the new store. Unfortunately, on his return trip, he died in Savannah on August 23.[8] After Charles's death, George stepped in tentatively to move the enterprise forward. A month after Charles's death, Corinna observed that "George seems to be quite busy. He is of an easy disposition, however."[9] In the waning days of 1840, George proceeded to Charleston to secure Charles's affairs and resume purchasing goods for their store in Newnansville. By the first days of 1841, George had arrived on the steamer *Gen. Clinch* in Savannah.[10] From there with his goods George would have continued south by boat to the St. Johns River, then to Black Creek, and then the fifteen miles to the landing at Garey's Ferry, where he oversaw the unloading of goods to a wagon for the eighteen-mile trek to Newnansville. Not long after George returned to Newnansville, Edward himself made a visit to Charleston. Along with his relative the Reverend N. Aldrich, he arrived in the port on the steam packet *Southerner* in late January.[11] George would also make frequent trips to Savannah. He traveled there again in May on the steamboat *Isis* from Palatka.[12]

Figure 1.1. Lt. James Willoughby Anderson,
daguerreotype taken just before the siege of Vera Cruz,
Mexico, 1846. Courtesy of Jane and Raymond Gill
and Elizabeth Traynor.

As George became accustomed to his new surroundings, he witnessed his sister Ellen's courtship with a young army officer, Lt. James W. Anderson, a native of Virginia and graduate of West Point. Coming to Florida in 1838, James was stationed at a nearby fort and probably introduced to Ellen by her brother-in-law. The relationship blossomed, and the two were married on October 26, 1840.[13] Some months later George provided his impressions of his new brother-in-law to Mannevillette: "Our <u>new</u> brother, Lieut. Anderson, is a very fine fellow. . . . He is a very handsome officer too (not in the phiz,[14] but in the frame) and . . . he is important to his regiment [because he has been appointed a staff officer], an appointment [that is] always filled by the smartest lieutenant — he and Ell seem perfectly satisfied with each other, they now reside at Fort King about fifty miles from Newnansville. I am in hopes he will be able to visit Alachua soon, too. He is quite high on the list for promotion and will probably be a captain before you see him."[15]

Even as he settled into his new environs, George was still uneasy about his plans to locate in East Florida permanently. Certainly the area offered fewer refinements than what he was used to in the North, but the financial prospects and the pull of family beckoned. While in St. Marys, Georgia, conducting business and visiting Edward's family, George recounted to his brother the previous year's trials that led him to settle in Newnansville:

> [George L. Brown to Mannevillette E. D. Brown]
> St. Mary's, Georgia [to Venice, Italy]
> June 12, 1841

My Dear Brother,

You might well think me negligent or forgetful of you if brotherly affection and true friendship were to be measured by common forms and compliments. I have not written to you since I left Philadelphia, a year from last March! I own it with mortification. I am sure, however, of your finding a ready excuse for one, when you hear how much has happened to vex me, and unfit my mind for epistolizing. Having been deprived of a very promising situation in Philadelphia, by the unfortunate pressure of 1839–40, I left that city for Florida—the land of flowers, rattlesnakes, and Seminoles, with the intention of passing the mercantile interregnum there, and return with the ensuing fall. I found Brother Charley flourishing in a small store (large for the place) which he had established by obtaining a credit of a merchant of this place. His business promised to be quite lucrative, and I accepted an offer from him to take charge of his books etc. with the option of remaining or leaving when the times got brighter elsewhere. But who can say, I shall live another year, or day, or hour! In a few weeks poor Charley lay in his grave! His sad death you have long since been apprised of. By this sorrowful event, I was compelled to stay another season in Florida, to settle his affairs. He had credited a large amount to the "volunteers," (militia mustered into the U.S. Service to protect the settlements) and had they been paid when mustered out, his assets would have exceeded his debts considerably. But Congress with its usual <u>promptness</u>, made no appropriation for this purpose, and will not for some months to come. The men being all mustered out, without money, I foresaw that all trade must be on the credit system; Having consulted Corinna, I concluded to sell out the few remnants of goods and close the store during the summer. Having done so, I took notes from all the people who owed him for goods, and placed them in a train for collection. I then paid his creditors as far as my limited means permitted, and I made ready to start for Philadelphia, when, (my luck) news came that the Banks had again suspended,— that merchants looked blue,— and all were going to ruin, or the devil. I had been sick with the fevers of Florida <u>only</u> three times during the fall; by then my constitution was so much impaired that Aldrich advised me to go North at any rate, even if I returned again. I left Newnansville with this determination. Having escaped being shot by some devil of an Indian, I was certain nothing could prevent my anticipated journey. Alas! I forgot my <u>luck</u> was still predominant. I had got as far as Charleston and engaged a passage for N. York. The next day I was on my back, prostrated by another fever; and so I remained a fortnight. When I was better my physician advised me <u>not</u> to go north at present—to remain in Charleston was dangerous-; so I concluded to hasten to this place where I arrived ten days since. I am now quite well again–Dr. Aldrich's father resides here, and has invited me to pass the summer with him. St. Marys is a very pleasant and healthy place, so healthy that people don't die at all, but dry up and blow away. So say the "oldest inhabitants"–In the fall I shall either go to Florida and resume business, or return to Philad. You will direct your answer to this (if you think I deserve one) to me here, and if I have left, it will be sent to me. So much for myself. I will now write something about other folks ————

Corinna and Aldrich I left well—he has a fine position but poor pay. The planters are so cramped by the Indians that they dare not plant more than is necessary for their consumption. I doubt if they remain there after this summer. I am certain they will not, if I don't return. Florida will be a fine country when the war is over. When–a long time to wait–it seems no nearer to its end than it was five years since; nor so near, for they have learned to fight since then. . . .

The folks at N— suppose me now near Philad; my retrograde movement has kept me out of letters from them entirely since I left. I presume they have received one from you. I shall direct this, however, as formerly and trust to fortune whether you get it or not. I hope it will come safe to you as I would regret your being any longer ignorant of my assurance that a cessation of letters, the mere mark of the hand, does not interrupt the affectionate pulsations of my heart toward you. Indeed, hardly a day passes by, but I think or talk of you. I look to the future, and fancy I hear your name spoken, with pride by your countrymen. Something whispers to my heart that your works (to be) will one day give you fame. You must write me what you are doing and what pictures you are painting or copying, also the new sights and scenes of the country.

You look with interest, no doubt, to the papers from the United States. You will have seen how General Harrison, the gallant old soldier, was selected by the people to succeed Van Buren. From his election, we had already begun to discover brighter times; But his earthly career ended in one month from his inauguration—like the eagle "he soared to the sun to die"—he reached the uppermost stop of ambition's ladder, and from there sought the skies. Genl. H. was in favor of a U.S. Bank, without which this country cannot prosper. He approved of a higher tariff on luxuries such as silks, . . . etc. to prevent the country from getting into debt—he was in favor of a bankrupt law, that the unfortunate might have a stimulus to exertion and not, as now, live in fear and trembling, lest some scoundrel creditor comes to take the last means whereby he lives. For, the accomplishments of these and many other measures for his country's good, he called an extra session of Congress, just prior to his decease. Congress met on the 30th of May. President Tyler's notions are rather different from his predecessor's, but it is the general opinion that he will carry out the wishes of old Tippecanoe. I am but one of 14,000,000, still, the transacting of this extra session is of great importance. On it will depend my future residence. Whether I am paid in Florida depends on this making an appropriation or not; "nous verrons."[16]

About my decision in the fall, I am somewhat like the often quoted jackass who got between two haystacks & starved—if I return to Fl. I shall be my own man and perhaps in time do well. If I go to Philadelphia, I must be a salesman for two or three years at least, and subject myself to the orders of employers. Good, wholehearted men like Ingraham & Martin I would as soon be ordered by as not, but it is the vulgar, low-bred rich-man that I abhor. It annoys me more to be knocked on the head with a piss-pot than to be struck by a thunderbolt. If peace prevails in Florida, I should certainly steer south; as it is, I turn my hopes northward.

I would tell you something of old Portsmouth, but my advices from that ancient town are not of a very recent date. . . . There is no one there for whom I have a particular attachment, nor is there any one who casts a thought on me. Still, I often let my thoughts wander back to the days past there, and I have even wished to return there, after escaping the many vexations of life, and die at home at last. The thought, though a vain one, has cheered me alike in the bustle of a city café and in the wilds of Florida. Have you not the same thoughts occasionally?

I hope, dear Manne that this letter will reach you in the midst of happiness, and find you content. It is the greatest virtue one can possess to be satisfied with his lot, and be reconciled to any misfortune. The last five years, years that should have been my best, have brought forth nothing but disappointment, yet I manage to keep my good spirits; and can laugh at a joke, let the world wag as it will—if anything crosses you, do likewise. Fare well—I am, and ever shall be, affectionately, thy brother,

George L. B.

One person with whom George struck an immediate friendship was Capt. Samuel Peter Heintzelman, who made frequent visits to the village. Heintzelman was a member of the U.S. Quartermaster Corp. Though he was stationed in Tallahassee, he was paymaster, and one of his chief duties was to gather evidence of militia service for claims. He traveled frequently to the various settlements in East Florida. In June and July, Heintzelman visited Suwanee Springs, Madison, Jasper, and Alligator until finally reaching Newnansville on June 27. On that day, he noted that Newnansville "has an ancient appearance for a Florida town & is of considerable extent." He described "stopp[ing] at the Widow [Zelphia] Standley's[17] at the further end of it" and called her boardinghouse "small, but . . . about as good as usual [and] within is a disposition to oblige."[18] Heintzelman stayed in town thirteen days. On his second-to-last day, July 7, Heintzelman wrote that Mrs. Standley "had been very kind & obliging. I counted this evening on the table seven dishes of meat, hash, butter milk and we had them as often as we wished. She only charged one dollar per day."[19] On July 7, Heintzelman provided military escort to Edward, Corinna, and Aunt Mary to Black Creek. On the way, the party spent the night at Fort Heilman. Heintzelman commented that on the journey, "Mrs. Aldrich was quite talkative & agreeable—her Aunt (Miss Dearing is old & ugly not much to say)."[20] The party boarded a steamer at Garey's Ferry and then traveled on the St. Johns south to Picolata and reached St. Augustine by July 12. Once there, they met Lt. Anderson and his new bride, Ellen. Anderson was on leave and would soon be transferred from Fort King to St. Augustine.[21]

While Heintzelman saw the Andersons and Aldriches frequently that fall in St. Augustine, George remained in Newnansville working to establish his new business. In late October, he traveled to Charleston to buy goods, but he was back in Florida by December, and he met Heintzelman and Edward on his way to Newnansville. Heintzelman had traveled with Edward from St. Augustine, and they were heading to Newnansville when they met George at Fort Harlee. On December 1, George and Heintzelman spent a delightful evening playing chess. Of the five games they played, Heintzelman won the last two. George "plays a good game," he said. The next day they set out for Newnansville but did not get there until an hour after midnight. It was "cold & we slept in a shed room, where the moon shone in, in a dozen places," the captain wrote.[22]

Heintzelman, in town for about a week taking claims, was not as fortunate as before with his accommodations. His office was a room with three doors "& not a latch & no cracker can pass in or out without leaving the door as wide open as possible." He slept in a "shed room, loosely clapboarded," with holes on each side. There were "no fastens to the door or windows." The floor and roof were open, allowing the rain to come

(a)

Notice to Florida Claimants.

THE Subscriber having been ordered to Florida for the purpose of continuing the collection
of Claims connected with the militia service, will
remain in St. Augustine till the 28th inst, and will
then proceed, by the way of Newnansville, Alligator,
Suwanne Springs, &c. to Tallahassee, remaining a
few days in each place.

All persons having such claims, are requested to
present them *immediately*, with any evidence they
may have in their support.

S. P HEINTZELMAN,
Capt. & A. Q. M., U. S. Army.

Nov. 15th, 1841.

(b)

Figure 1.2. S. P. Heintzelman, "Notice to Florida Claimants" (a) and image of Fort Harlee (b). St. Augustine *Florida Herald and Southern Democrat*, December 10, 1841, and Florida State Archives.

through, and he had to move his things to avoid having them soaked. He complained, "Every sound throughout the house can be heard as distinctly as if there was not a partition about. I was very amused at a conversation I heard in the sitting room that was got up between the land lady and several 'crackers' . . . on the subject of Florida Claims." Although Heintzelman did not get much sleep during his one week in Newnansville, he did enjoy pleasant interactions with the Aldriches and George. On December 6, after a long day working with his accounts, Edward paid the West Pointer a visit and they walked together "down town, as far as his brother-in-law's store." "He is just getting his goods," the captain wrote in his diary. Two days earlier, he proudly recorded that George Brown called on him late in the afternoon and that he had beaten George in two games of chess.[23] The amusements that George enjoyed with Heintzelman and his friends were most likely augmented with alcoholic drinks. George intended to make such goods available to his customers and secured a license to sell liquor soon after he went into business.[24]

George's business was in large measure dependent upon credit and establishing commercial contacts in Charleston, which he visited often, developing important business and social relationships. According to historian Walter Edgar, antebellum Charleston was a town of "handsome homes, churches, public buildings, and lush gardens." With a population of roughly forty thousand in 1841, Charleston was still recovering from the aftereffects of the Panic of 1837, but its cotton trade was growing. By 1840, Charleston had received nearly 60,000 bales of cotton, and by 1845, that total would grow to 200,000. Most of the city's commission merchants, brokerage houses, importers, and auctioneers were on Hayne, Broad, and East Bay Streets. King Street contained many fashionable retail shops.[25]

George's extant letters from his early twenties are scarce, but eleven from 1839 through 1842 exist in good condition, all addressed to either Mannevillette or Edward. In his letters to Mannevillette, he wrote about himself, family members living in Florida, and news from Florida and America. In his letters to Edward, he focused on their shared business concerns. Although George arrived in Newnansville in 1840, no letters from that year survive and only two survive from 1841, probably owing to his business responsibilities and the necessities of adjusting to his new way of life. Moreover, living in close proximity to Edward, Ellen, Corinna, and his aunts meant that he would have interacted with them in person.

George's first surviving letter sent from Charleston to Edward details many of the activities on his initial major buying trip:

[George L. Brown to Edward S. Aldrich]
Charleston, S.C. [to Newnansville]
Nov. 21, 1841

Dear Edward,

I arrived here last Thursday and set immediately about getting goods. I have succeeded in getting some 11 or 1200$ worth by paying <u>part cash</u>–I had myself about 250$ and had to borrow 300$ of Mr. Wingate of the House of Townsend, Marshall & Wingate, is an old New Hampshire boy and a good friend of mine for many years past. I have faithfully promised to return the amount to him by the 1st of May 1842, if the troops etc. are paid off–I wrote you from St. Mary's to send me "bills of sale etc." which you see I now shall not need—my goods, in addition to the borrowed money, are purchased on short credit, and I shall find a use for all your spare <u>funds.</u> If you could now raise 2 or 300$ . . . you would afford me considerable assistance—on my punctuality this further will defend my future credit. If we settle at Madison, I shall want to buy on a larger scale–Thus you will see the importance of doing the best you can–I of course consider you a partner with me as formerly. And you will steady your own interest as well as mine–If you can get the few hundred dollars you can remit to S.S. Mills [of S. S. Mills and Beach Commission Merchants][26] Charleston. You [can] leave [it at] St. Augustine, or you can bring it on with you to Newnansville—try my good fellow–I am full of business, and no doubt we will make money if things go smooth—but I am easily depressed, and therefore hope all will or my game is up.

I shall leave here next Wednesday on the <u>Clinch</u> for Black Creek with my goods–I do this because I think the sooner I am out there the better. It will be impossible for you to reach there so soon as I do, but I shall look out for you soon after–If you have written me any letters which will arrive after I leave here, I have given your Uncle Robt. [Aldrich] directions about them–

If it is convenient I should certainly advise Corinna to stay with Ellen in preference to going into the interior, until we get settled.

Give my love to all the folks. Tell them I feel like a steamboat - you may judge of the "go ahead" principle within me, when I tell you that my principle purchases, almost all in fact, were made yesterday between 9 o'clock A.M. and 4 P.M.

Affectionately your brother,
George L. Brown

*   *   *   *   *   *

[George L. Brown to Edward S. Aldrich]
Newnansville [Florida, to Thomasville, Georgia]
April 13, 1842

Dear Edward,

I received your note of the 8th inst[27] quite pleased to hear of your safe arrival <u>so far</u>: and hope this will find you at the village of Thomasville in like health and happiness. Your instructions in relation to the hatchet have been attended to.

Your account on [Woodbridge S.] Olmstead [is] nearly balanced; about $2.50 cts in my favor. I saw Mr. [John B.] Standley yesterday; He gave me his note for his bill of 20$. Mr. S. begged me to write to you and say that his leg (chronic ulceration as per bill) now and then troubles him, although it is in fact well–it occasionally <u>breaks</u> <u>out</u> and makes him lame. He wishes you if possible to send him some of the medicine you gave him to treat it with, yet if this is impossible to send me the prescription and he will get some physician to put it up. Please attend to this; it will facilitate the collection of the note. He was surprised you had left town; would certainly have called on you had he been aware of your intention. Mr. [Lemuel] Willson is somewhat uneasy about his "yard"[28] but has to grin & bear it. Alex[ander] McKay complains of <u>worms</u>; [James] Stephens says he has got the Bolts. No further <u>medical</u> intelligence. I saw Jeptha Knight's Negro man Alfred from Fort Fanning, who says he saw Charles [Aldrich's slave] at Fort F. with Chas. Goodrich en route from Cedar Keys. I have nothing new to write from this place, all is barren. The mail last week did not bring you any letters. All your documents shall be speedily forwarded. I settled P. O. Bill with [Thomas J.] Prevatt. Today is Tuesday; if I have anything to add between now & Thursday night (mail night) you shall hear it. Write me all about Thomasville & the adjacent country. Give love to Corinna and take some yourself. God bless & prosper you both is the prayer of

your brother
Geo. L. Brown

Thursday Eve, 15th, I have nothing new to add, except an entire failure on my part to convince Aunt Ann that "are" is the plural & "is" is the singular—she is beyond the reach of the schoolmaster, and still uses the two words at random.

Yours truly
George L. Brown

*   *   *   *   *   *

[George L. Brown to Edward S. Aldrich]
Newnansville E.F. [to Thomasville, Georgia]
April 24, 1842

Dear Edward:

I received your letter from Thomasville by last night's mail, which has relieved me from some uneasiness I felt about you. As I did not hear from you last mail—I am delighted to hear of your safe progress & that you are pleased with the new country.

Look keenly for your new home, and when you settle, let it be for a long while. I want you to be fixed permanently to your satisfaction, and then I will come with you. I have but one fear, that's that your anxiety to get a good place for me, may induce you to select a lesser one for yourself—I pray, don't do this. I never should consider it a favour. I don't care how selfish you act; my only wish is to see you happily located, and "going ahead." The courts are now in session, [Joseph L.] Smith [and] [John L.] Doggett, are here, and inquire after your health & Corinna's. [U.S. Marshal Joseph S.] Sanchez had no money, but at my hint, borrowed 185 dollars of [W. S.] Olmsted and paid [Judge Isaac] Bronson & [U.S. Attorney Thomas] Douglas—this he told me this morning—tomorrow Monday, I will get the receipts & sign "Uncle John's" Bill. Sanchez says nothing as yet about the deed from the commissioner's office. We have three cases of murder in this court & several for assault and battery—one case [Adam] Keil, the Tailor, vs. Geo. Sanchez will prove exceedingly funny—Judge Smith and Doggett are the opposing lawyers—[George] Mackay made a speech in defense of one of the murderers, and made a damned ass of himself at the same time ~ a lame contemptible affair as I ever heard, and one that did more injury to the poor criminal than good— Mackay puts me in mind of the Lowell boy, who was so remarkably bright, that his mother had to look at him through smoked glass! [Charles] Cushing [of Portsmouth] is here and thinks he will stay for a season, he feels somewhat disappointed at your absence as he depended considerably on your acquaintance. He is stopping with us— Judge Smith is here also—so far he behaves very decently & I trust he will pay his bill. Doctor [Alfred W. H.] Elwes, from Micanopy makes a third at Mrs. [Susan] Watson's. He is a U.S.A. Surgeon, & witness in many of the criminal cases—he brought a letter of introduction to you from Captain [Benjamin L. E.], and gave it to me. I have done the honors of Newnansville for you. Dr. E. is a very clever fellow.

I enclose you a letter for Corinna from Ellen. I sent you one from Mannevillette last week—any letters of importance requiring answers I will forward to you. . . . [Bennett] Maxey Dell was inquiring about you today; he regrets your absence, or says he does, and furthermore, said that he thought you could come back here—I told him I could not say, but I was certain of one thing, that you seemed devilish glad to get away—I will arrange Phil Dell's business as soon as I see him— This letter goes via St. Marys. I will write you next Friday. . . . Dr [John P. Crichton] is still missing—no doctors here.

Love to Corinna—Ann & myself & the rest are all well—I will write Corinna soon—tell her I doubt if the regiment leaves Florida this summer.

Very truly yours
George L B

*　　*　　*　　*　　*　　*

[George L. Brown to Edward S. Aldrich]
Newnansville [Florida, to Thomasville, Georgia]
May 7, 1842

Dear Edward

I am happy to inform you that I have received from Wm. Selden[29] the US Treasurer a check on the S W Rail Bank Charleston for 249 dollars for your services at St. Augustine. With it came a receipt for you to sign, which I have signed as your attorney and sent to Washington. The same mail brought a letter from Dr. [Henry Lee] Heiskell acting Sur[geon] Gen[eral] merely saying your accts had been rec'd and sent to the treasurer to be paid as above. The 249 dollars is safely deposited in my "Black Leather Trunk" where it will remain untouched until I hear from you—I would like extremely well to have the use of it for about six weeks, say until the 1st of July, after which time you could

depend upon having it again. The use I wish to make of it is to pay old Saul Clarke my note for 250$ falling due this month. I have money enough to pay all my own notes and only lack sufficient for this purpose and besides it will save me a trip to Charleston, as I can send your check there with other money to pay my notes & send some Treasury drafts I have to Clarke. I do not want to go to Charleston for fear I shall buy too many goods, but I must show my face there and explain matters, unless you lend me the draft; in which case I shall have no explanation to make, as I can pay every note against me. As I said before you can depend upon having the $249 any time after the 1st of July. I will agree to deposit that much in same Cha'ston Bank for you. This will oblige & help me much. Still if you have any immediate use for the money, or for any part of it, you must with me be open & say so unhesitatingly; and I will take your will for the deed.

I have rec'd your two letters from Macon Ga, much to my surprise, & have duly noticed all you say therein. Your opening at Albany looks well, & I trust will continue so for your sake & mine—but I must caution you against any investments before you are satisfied you will remain there. By next fall you will have a better and safer idea of the country by experience. I wish you to settle in some first rate place, & settle for a long while. Then I will jump to come with you if I have half a chance. It would do to lease or hire some good building for your office, with an eye to the prospect of making a store of it, but I would not buy land unless at a price that you could get again at any time. What I wish you particularly to observe in your new home is, whether the trade is for barter & produce, or for the "ready" "shine." I will have your remaining things here shipped "in good order and condition" as you request.

The Gen'l Clinch broke her shaft lately and nearly stopped

running, but will soon resume her old place. I will advise you in season of the shipment. The goods sent first to S.S. Mills have been forwarded to Port Leon, so says Mr. M. by letter. He did not tell me what house at P. Leon, you will however have no difficulty finding out, as they went <u>to</u> <u>the</u> <u>agents</u> of the regular line. I have written to Mr. M though to inform me who they are. I have heard of <u>Charles</u>[30] once or twice; will attend to your orders about him. I am anxiously waiting to hear from Corinna as she is a writing sort of person and will stir them up at Pilatka. I am anxious to hear from her because I have no letters from Pilatka for a long time. I think you acted wisely not to go to housekeeping right off. You will save considerable expenses this summer, and in the autumn you can tell exactly how to arrange your house, furniture, etc.

Nothing new here except that Halleck Tustenegge has come in after a fight with Col. Worth. His <u>staying</u> in is another affair. Mr. J. Standley found on one of the Indians who came in with Halleck, his rifle which [Samuel] Smart had, who was killed by the Indians in Hope's field some time past. We are expecting <u>some</u> <u>amusements</u> in Newnansville soon. Two men are to be hung; William is to be married; [James] Pendarvis <u>is</u> <u>to</u> <u>have</u> <u>his</u> <u>home</u> <u>finished</u>! And several other new things too trifling to mention. With my sincere good wishes, I am, as ever,

Your brother

George L. Brown

P.S. Look out for <u>George</u> in Baker [County] soon, he won't rest. Baker has been his promised land for more than a year. He will not allow so good a chance to slip past. I forgot to say that the person signing a paper for another as attorney is of daily occurrence and will answer the same purpose. I have written you several letters to Thomasville, Ga.

*   *   *   *   *   *

[George L. Brown to Edward S. Aldrich]

Newnansville E. F. [to Albany, Georgia via St. Marys, Georgia]

May 30, 1842

Dear Edward,

You and Corinna have, at last by your letters, thrown me entirely off of your track. I was certain that you would settle at Albany; when, I am told that you will go to Thomasville; then comes another letter from her that you are settled at <u>Albany</u>. . . . I rec'd two letters from you this mail from the West. One is dated May 14, which stated your plans etc. much to my comfort. The second, however, dated on the road from its <u>uncertainty</u> spoils all until I hear from you again. Your order not to sell the furniture etc. squints a little towards coming back to Newnansville. I hope I misconstrued your letter; I hope, too that you do not think of any such movements. Newnansville grows worse & worse. And this you can be sure of that I shall not stay here longer than this year–My sales during the two weeks past have averaged about <u>twenty</u> <u>dolls</u> <u>per</u> <u>week</u>! Part cash and part credit. Such a business will soon sicken me, and the only thing that buoys me up for any time longer is, that my neighbors do no better. The medical, is no better off than the mercantile interests. Crichten and [James] Kelly are both without patients. You will say that I am not very anxious to see you! I pray you my dear fellow don't think so seriously, for I never was more anxious to see you in my life. Still I would rather not see you for a six-month, if I am only to see you here, unless indeed you come to pay a visit. I don't know that I express myself exactly as I wish in what I have written, but for God's sake, remember that I advise for what I feel is for our good.

Corinna has written once or twice about going North, a journey that I do not approve of without your company. I have never said anything to her for or against it, as I did not know how you liked it. As your letter wherein you say you have written for her to come to Albany is later than her last, I shall write her to day and let her know my views. A journey north would undoubtedly do her great good but at this time I should say it was rather impracticable. Better wait still another year, than to go so far away when we scarcely can determine on a home to return to. I am uneasy about the whole of it, and shall continue so, until I get another letter from you, which I trust will be next Saturday at farthest. Your check for $249 which I wrote you I had used, I shall be ready to refund any time after the first of July. Should Corinna go north, I can if it is necessary remit to her at any time. If you have no use for it, better let it remain deposited with me. It will be safe, and something to depend on bye & bye, and with interest. I owe you besides about $100 on the old score. I will write next

Thursday, via Tallahassee and send you an exact balance of the whole. This goes tomorrow by the Eastern mail, I should say via Tallahassee was the quickest route.

Nothing new here except the Indian murders. You probably know all by this time. 8 were killed and 3 wounded along the Santafee. Yet in the face of this Col. Worth proclaims peace and orders two Regts of infantry out of the Territory. As soon as you tell me to I will commence sending the paper Knickerbocker, Herald, etc. I would now, but I should be sure to send them where you are not. I will venture the Herald today, as a pioneer.

Lem Wilson and Mrs. [Rafaila] Olmstead were put together last Thursday. I saw him through as waiter.[31] Lt. [Nevil] Hopson & Ambury leave their post tomorrow for Ft. Fanning, from thence they go to the Gulf. The Lord rid Florida of all such soldiers as Lt. H. and Capt. Jewell. Aunt Anne has had a slight attack of ague, but I cured her per directions. She is now talking as fast and as sensibly as ever; don't fail to write every week.

Yrs. Very truly,

George

Mr. & Mrs. Wilson are well. I am weller. Chas is still with Capt. Goodrich, he and yr things still wait your orders

*   *   *   *   *   *

[George L. Brown to Edward S. Aldrich]

Newnansville E. F. [to Macon, Georgia]

June 2, 1842

Dear Edward,

Whilst the two criminals sentenced to be hung last court by Judge Bronson are being sent into eternity, I will write you a letter for next Friday's mail, having no curiosity to witness such an exhibition; it takes place today between 10 & 2 o'clock.[32] I wrote you last Sunday, via St. Marys, but this route being rather the quickest it is possible that letter will reach you after this. Your last letter from Pendarvis put me so completely in the dark concerning your future operations, that I wrote to ease my mind, nor am I entirely satisfied yet, particularly as your first (received last mail) from Albany spoke so decisively of your location there. I wrote you in my letter Sunday that I hoped for your own well-being and mine that you did not think of returning to Newnansville. I still repeat it. For I am sure to quit the place as soon as I can and I see no way for me to remain south to my advantage unless you are my pioneer to some new town. 'Tis for this I wish you settled at some place now that you may be enabled to tell in the Fall from your own observation, whether such a place will do for me. To establish a new store is something not to be done hastily, nor till after much deliberation. When I move again I wish it to be at a sure, and permanent home.

I have nothing new to write at all. I have sent as I promised a statement of your affairs in my books, that you may know what you have. The debits & credits I could not well particularize for lack of room, but I can send them to you some other time. They are correct however; I have looked over them to ascertain this fact. Your accts with Phil Dell & [Wilson] Bates are still unsettled. I did not see them again last time & they have not been in town since. There will be no difficulty, however, about getting the two notes. I can arrange them easily—I have paid old Clarke his last note & be d—d to him. I don't know but I shall count upon you for half of the debt I have paid on account of the old store since last Spring[. . . .] You have now a balance in your favor of $324.33—in the $592 charged is included orders, notes, msde, & all.

We have a new company here called the "Alachua Mounted Volunteers" numbering 20 privates & the usual number of officers. They paraded yesterday 10 strong! Alex McKay <u>captaining</u>. Lemuel Wilson & Jeptha Knight, Lieuts. Wilson stands the <u>widow</u> pretty well. "Old" Pendarvis says he intends to go right "point blank" and get married. I don't know who will take pity on his stinking corporation. Write me very often. I promise you a letter by each mail.

Very truly yrs.
George

❧ **2** ❧

"Better to Make Money
as a Cracker Merchant"

(1843–1845)

THE NEW YEAR FOUND George Brown well ensconced in Newnansville. As his circle of friends and customers widened, George found satisfaction in his accomplishments. The rhythm of the cotton growing season pretty much determined his traveling schedule to Savannah and Charleston, but while at home in Newnansville, George worked hard to develop his business. George's living arrangements are unclear. Perhaps he lived for a time in Edward's house when the doctor was away, or he might have lived in a small cabin near his store. George makes frequent references to his friend Thomas Prevatt, who lived with him and minded the store when he was away.

George Brown's ledgers and account books have been lost, but court records and surviving records of local settlers provide some idea of the goods that George supplied settlers in exchange for cotton, corn, or hides or for credit. Cash rarely changed hands. Most annual transactions would have been similar to those of local farmer William Cason in 1846. From May through September 1846 Cason made five separate purchases. Among the items he signed for were shirts, shoes, suspenders, hats, pants, and calico, onasburg, and gambroon cloth. Cason also acquired paper, ink, quills, razors, fiddle strings, tobacco, and linens of various sorts. On

September 26, he signed a note to Brown for his annual purchases for $47.07.[1]

An inventory of the items in George's store at the time of his death in 1857 ran to six pages and included products for the farm such as shovels, buckets, cowbells, brushes, drawing knives, screwdrivers, grindstones, compasses, bridle bits, saddles, plough points, hatchets, axes, hammers, nails, chisels, paints, and bottles of varnish. George's store stocked various consumables, such as candies and bottles of sarsaparilla, cherry, and bitters drinks. There were ointments, pills, and bottles of medicines, including liniment, calomel, and quinine. He also carried a line of men's, women's, and children's clothing, shoes, and boots. The store stocked household items such as boxes of salt, combs, fishhooks, shears, chairs, irons, iron pans, waffle irons, frying pans, scales, brass candlesticks, gridirons, fancy goblets, stationery, and crockery such as stew pans and kettles. The store even stocked beds, bedsteads, mirrors, washstands, tables, chairs, bureaus, and other furniture.[2]

On November 12, 1841, George's sister Ellen gave birth to her first child, Edward Willoughby Anderson, at Palatka, where his father was stationed. Not long thereafter the Second Infantry was transferred to Buffalo, New York. Corinna, Edward, and James Anderson's sister Virginia joined James, Ellen, and the baby for a time. Edward soon returned to Florida, but Corinna remained in Buffalo until late in the year when she traveled to New York City to meet Edward for the journey south.[3] Meanwhile, Edward's Whig friends had nominated him as a candidate for a seat in the Florida Senate. Edward's late entry into the race and his inability to campaign due to the demands of his medical practice resulted in his eighth-place finish. He polled votes only in the larger communities in the district where he was known (St. Augustine, Jacksonville, Newnansville, and Micanopy) and even in those places rarely in the majority.[4] After the election, Edward traveled to New York and picked up Corinna, and on the way home the two spent several days in Washington, where Edward consulted with Captain Heintzelman and territorial delegate Levy over his unpaid accounts. Perhaps a federal appointment might also have been in the offing.[5] Though Edward was dissatisfied with Newnansville, he decided to remain there for a time.

One reason for this decision was the arrival of Edward's brother in the community. Louis Aldrich was admitted to practice law in the superior court of East Florida in November, and on December 1, he announced a

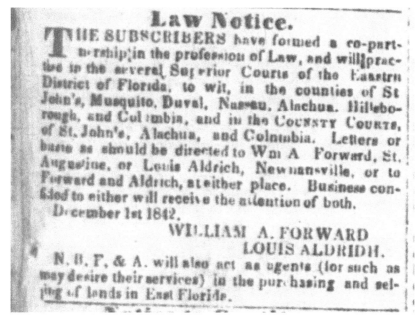

Figure 2.1. "Law Notice," Louis Aldrich and William A. Forward's law partnership, *St. Augustine Florida Herald and Southern Democrat*, January 9, 1843.

law partnership with William A. Forward.[6] George soon formed a close personal friendship with the young lawyer, and Aldrich even boarded with George for a time. Louis thrived in this new environment. His outgoing personality contrasted with his brother's more reserved demeanor. He built up a successful practice, and the Alachua County court records make frequent mention of him; he eventually became a probate judge.[7] Unlike his Whig brother, Louis was a Democrat and was active in political affairs. He eventually served in the Florida legislature.[8]

By the end of the year, Edward had decided to settle his accounts in Newnansville, rent his large house, and relocate to St. Augustine. Corinna was quite pleased with the Aldriches' new location. The next fall she wrote her brother Mannevillette that she expected a visit that winter from "Ellen & and her family. . . and George tells me he will pop in on us." Corinna told her brother that George was still doing business in Newnansville, "but I am in hopes [he] will go to the sea board [in] another year. He is now doing very well—but it is a sorry life, that of being in the woods. I did not realize how miserable it was until I have become settled in a civilized place. We have all the advantages of town & country. It is not a very large

Figure 2.2. Map showing George Brown's East Florida, circa 1850.
Map by Peter Krafft.

place, you know, but the society is refined & and it is innocently gay."[9] The stark contrast between Newnansville and St. Augustine must have been real enough to George.

Only three of George's 1843 letters survive and only seven from 1844, all sent to Mannevillette or Edward. George's first letter of 1843 is a long one and updates Mannevillette on his current situation and on the circumstances of their other family members. The letter immediately following was written on the same day in response to one from Mannevillette:

[George L. Brown to Mannevillette E. D. Brown]
Newnansville, East Florida [to Paris, France]
January 7, 1843

My Dear Brother:

The beginning of another year has caused me to look back on the one just ended, and to reflect on the many duties neglected which I might have performed, among a hundred faults, none seems to me so deserving of censure as this, not writing to you a dozen letters instead of one. My last to you was dated from St. Marys, Georgia, at which time it was my fixed intention to return to Philadelphia; subsequently, however, I concluded to retrace my steps to this place and resume my storekeeping—You will be curious to know what led me to select the barren wilderness again in preference to the more civilized life of a city. I will briefly tell you. After sounding all the depths of my reason and philosophy, I came to this result, that is was better for me to make money as a cracker-merchant, than to waste my time as a dandy salesman—Better to be a slave to L'argent[10] than to a "Tailor and Boot-maker!" After coming to this conclusion, (it was at St Mary's) the next step towards putting in force, was to get a stock of goods. Having but a small capital, I started for Charleston to try what my <u>honest face</u> would do for me. To my astonishment it got me a credit of $2000 in merchandise—which I shipped with myself in a steamboat on the 25th of Nov. and arrived here on the 3rd day of December; since then I have been doing a fair business and am in hopes that the world will henceforth wag more easily for me. I shall visit Charleston again the last of this month for more goods - - so much for myself–Now I will tell you something of the rest of us—Aldrich and Corinna are at St Augustine, & expect to leave there for this place soon—after their return they will visit West Florida, where he has some idea of settling—West Florida is a much better country than the East—The lands and the planters are richer—the climate healthy—The latter quality of the "atmospheric product" is rather against his profession; still there are diseases enough peculiar to any part of the south to occupy his entire time—Anderson & Ellen are at Pilatka on the St Johns River the Head Quarters of the 20th regiment—it is a pleasant place during the <u>cold</u> season; but it is difficult to find <u>any</u> cold weather here. Today—the middle of winter—is as

mild as the first of August in New England—I am writing with my
windows and doors open–while without every tree is green and thousands of birds are enjoying the shade of them—Since I last wrote you,
Ellen has made you and I uncles! She has brought into this scathing
world a boy, which is to pass through life by the high sounding names
of Edward Willoughby; thus giving our respectable handles of Man &
George, to use a parlance of this region—"the go bye," I have however,
secured my immortality by speaking in season for the next time—you
can apply for the third chance—Names remind me of a funny dream
I had once—I dreamt that you had promised Charley & myself once,
that we should go a gunning with you on a certain day—but when the
day came you would not let us start with you, and went off without
us, we, to have some revenge, sat down on "mill–darn–bridge" to
abuse you—we branded you with a variety of names, and this one—
Mannevillette Elihu Dearing shitfinger Brown—which Charley gave
you, at the same time making one of his ugly faces, sat me to laughing
so heartily, that I woke in the midst of my cachinnations—The dream
was so natural that it was some time before I could really believe that
years had passed upon my head since "I went a gunning" and that I
was far away from the scenes of those pleasant days.

To return however to the family relations—Aunt Ann is here keeping house for me. She is the same as ever, excepting perhaps that time
has slightly scored his yearly notches on her—Aunt Dolly is living at
her place La Grange on the St Johns; or was until sometime last week
when an attack of the indians on two or three of her neighbors houses
lately, gave her a scare, and, I hear, she has taken up a temporary
abode at Jacksonville, 15 miles below. The attack of the Indians, one
of the most daring and unexpected ones since the war commenced
in the spot where they committed their depredations was on the St
Augustine road, between Mandarin and St. A. about three miles from
Aunt Doll's—The Indians, 21 in number, laid in wait all day intending
to attack the settlement of Mandarin—Having caught a negro man,
the property of one Mr. [William] Hartley, who told them that M.
was full of soldiers, (it was a lie in season) they altered their plan and
told the negro to lead them to Hartley's House near Aunt Dol's—he
did so, and they on reaching it fired in at the door on a number of
people—at the first fire—Mrs. H, her child and a Mrs. La Costa were
killed—the rest escaped—The Indians then proceeded to burn down

the houses of Hartley & two or three others—and killed two more men—Horrid murders! & these too with a regular force of 3000 men in the country![11] 3000, good for nothing, drunken scapegoats,—the scourings of other countries men. Our army is or ought to be filled with natives. One thousand of them would do more service than the above Brandy drinking sons-of-guns—I am growing in the belief that this Indian war never will end—It is now six years from the commencement and for myself, I see no hope of a termination—When Indians commit their crimes in such exposed places as Mandarin—a town jutting out into the St Johns on a peninsula, as where Indians could be cut off almost to a certainty if people would be cool and determined at such trying moments, - when they do this it argues badly for their cries of peace.

Having told you of friends and foes here, I have written all worth communicating about Florida—At the North hard times, like Roman cement grows harder with age–Mr. Secretary of the Treasury [Walter] Forward has however, presented to Congress a new plan for a new sub-treasury to be called the "Exchequer of the U. S." It is like a bank inasmuch as it receives deposits, issues bills . . . , and draws exchange from one state to another – It is unlike a bank in this respect–it has nothing to do with discounts, or paper accommodations of any kind—it will be a good thing no doubt, and I hope Congress will soon adopt it—really we want some kind of paper money, good over the United States—at present in Florida we get nothing of the kind— gold and silver is the currency—very good money to be sure. But we have to lug it all to Charleston & to carry 1 or 2000$ in silver about us is making <u>pack</u> animals of men.

Your old acquaintance Wm Jones has taken to his bed board & legs Miss Charlotte Brown—They were married about two months ago, I believe—I have no other news from Portsmouth saving the death of old Andrew Bell, who, I will wager my existence, took a bee line from his death bed to the regions of hell–and there may he get <u>his</u> reward.

Some time past Corinna wrote me that you had lost your pictures, or supposed you had. I pray you may find them—it will be too bad to lose them—You must be considerable of a painter and I assure you I am anxious to see you & your <u>copies</u>. You must write me as soon as you get this—let me know how you are & how you flourish & what you intend to do—all everything. Aunt Anne sends love—May you in the ensuing year receive all the happiness that is wished you by yr. affectionate Brother

George–

*   *   *   *   *   *

[George L. Brown to Mannevillette E. D. Brown]
Newnansville, E. F. [to Paris, France]
January 7, 1843

My Dear Brother

I have rec'd a letter from you, dated at Paris, Oct. 21 ult.[12] With the agreeable information that you are to return to the "Land of Freedom" in one of our noble N. Y Packets. Perhaps you are already here and anxiously awaiting this answer. Ellen has no doubt rec'd her letter, but lest she has not I will write her to day. She is still at Buffalo and I believe comfortably settled. Yrs to Corin reached her via Thomasville and remains in my desk, she and her Doctor being still somewhere north. The last I heard from them they were at Washington (Dec. 25) and were to get home as early as possible. If you are now in New York, I don't see how you can help coming together as they will come south by the way of this city; God grant you may meet. It will be so delight-ful to all of you. You can then make one of the party to Newnansville. You will derive but little pleasure in a trip to Florida, save the mutual joy of seeing each other. It is a dreary land to one accustomed to dif-ferent and better residences. You will find Aunt Anne & Aunt Dolly the same old sixpences, only a little older. Dolly, being a "widder" (as Sam Weller says,)[13] is ex officio rather a termagant,[14] "equal to nine women"–she resides at her place "La Grange!" on the St John's River–

Aunt Anne has been my bachelor's hall keeper during Corinna's absence–I wish you had been here. I would show you how to keep house. I am a real "Peter Punctillio"[15]–breakfast at sunrise–dinner at one, and supper at sunset–"exactly"–or, fly goes the cowhide on the darkies' backs. You seem doubtful whether you will recognize me–but I rather guess you are mistaken–A Lieut. [Rose?] of the army, who was once a fellow clerk of mine in Boston, and who had not seen me for six years told me recently that I looked the same counter jumper as I was in 1834. I can only say, I feel the same — — —

The Times, meaning business times, are at present horribly dull—

but not as bad as they are in most parts of the United States—besides we are expecting some 60 or 70,000$ to be paid out in this country very soon by Uncle Sam, which will set matters right. Times, however, be they dull or bright find me just the same,—in good spirits. I have been <u>rubbed</u> <u>bright</u> in my day, and faith I'll keep so.

I was in hopes you would get you a wife in the old country–you must pick one out soon. We must not let the breed of Portsmouth Browns become extinct. Ellen has begun the manufacturing of babies, but they will bear the name of Anderson–a very good name, even better than our <u>rare</u> one, still I like my own best. Seriously, we must try our metal!

You complain of cold weather in yours. You can judge of the difference of climate when I tell you that at present I am suffering with the <u>heat,</u> windows open, & fireplace shut–Our planting season commences about the middle of January!–in New England April is early you know. 3 months difference!—Have you brought many pictures home? I long to see some of your pieces–I am no great connoisseur, but can tell a windmill from a castle.

Our great disturbers, the Indians are rather still just now, but it is difficult to say how long they will keep so–Gen'l Worth grabbed 100 of the rascals on the 22nd of Dec–he invited them to a grand <u>feast,</u> and gave them their <u>deserts</u>. Let me see you or hear from you as soon as you can—and believe me

Very truly thy Brother
George---

Aunt Ann sends oceans of Love–and is on tiptoe to welcome you---

*   *   *   *   *   *

[George L. Brown to Edward S. Aldrich]
Savannah, [Georgia, to Newnansville, Florida]
February 12, 1843

My Dear Edward

Owing to the Steamboat <u>Gen'l</u> <u>Clinch</u>'s breaking her shaft, I am detained in this city (of my abomination) until the departure of the <u>Wm</u> <u>Seabrook</u> next Monday.[16] This however, will make no difference about my returning. I shall be at Black Creek on the 27th certainly. I am stopping with Dumas whose family I found all well. Tell Louis [Aldrich] if he comes down for me at the Creek to stop at Mr. [Amaziah] Coy's where he will find tight rooms, good beds, a good establishment, & two fat daughters.[17] Also, should he be unable to come I want you to hire a buggy of old Light Townsend, or someone, and send Owen down with it, as I shall have several light articles that I would like to come up with me.

I sent by last boat yesterday to Care of S[olomon] Morgan, Black Creek, two cast iron ploughs, <u>not</u> <u>stocked</u>. The stocked ones cost near as much again & the freight is three times as much as those without stocks. If I can get any stocked ones low in Charleston I will purchase them also. If you stand in immediate need of a plough you had better take one of the above—and get [Jessee] Hagan or Wm Brown to stock it. Tell Prevat that the other is from Captain L. C. Ellis. Tell Prevat to be sure and have [Simeon] Harvey's waggon at the Creek on the 20th–as I shall have goods sufficient to load both there on that day. Dr. Griffin (U. S. A.) was a passenger from Black Creek to Savannah. He regrets very much not seeing you in Florida. I delivered your articles to Turner all right. I also saw a box in front of Turner's store (on the Bay Street) marked for you, and, I presume it was sent to you by the <u>St. Matthew</u>, which boat left here yesterday on her regular trip. Eliza Bynum's trunk I discovered in possession of the agent. He had it marked "G. L. Brown" and sent with the other things.

I stopped about ten minutes at St. Mary's. Found both George and Whipple [Edward's brothers] buried in medical books; both going to be Doctors! Your father told me he wanted to say something to me, but before he could begin, the steamboat was off; I suppose he will let me know what it was when I pass by going home. . . . St. Mary's looks as though it was under the effects of mesmerism. Dull! Dull! Ought to have been in church today but got excused on account of my ragged condition. "The foundations of the great deep are broken up" as the boy told his mother when he tore away the seat of his breeches. Tell Louis & Cushing not to kill their horses visiting Reinhardt. Making flying Dutchmen of themselves as it were. Labour in vain.

Mrs. Baldwin died last Friday morning very suddenly and will be buried to day. I regret that I cannot appear decent enough to attend her funeral. . . . May write you from Charleston if I think a letter would reach Newnansville before I did myself.

Dumas wife, Eliza, & Mrs. [Fell] (Helena)
all send love to you & Corinna.

Yours Truly,
George L. B.

P. S. I cannot help saying what a satisfaction it is to me to be away from you and know that all will go smoothly at home. Formerly, I was worried constantly during my journeys, fearful that something would happen or go wrong, and yet almost sickened at the thought of returning to Alachua—Now I think of you with pleasure and shall be glad when I again land at Black Creek. The credit for this change (under Providence) is due to you and your manly determination to abstain from exciting drinks–and I will give the same pledge if I have a chance in Charleston. I wish you god speed in this and all other good plans, and will help all in my power. Again, yrs,

George

* * * * * *

[George L. Brown to Edward S. Aldrich]
[Newnansville, Florida, to St. Augustine, Florida]
April 20, 1844

Dear Edward-

From what you said about Mr. Bell last evening, I concluded that you might have some talk with him about the house. I must however request you to decline doing so, as under my present arrangements with Mrs. Watson it will be impossible to give up the house to anyone—as for the rent, I will guarantee the payment from Watson, and if Bell is disposed to buy, I will pay for the house whatever he will offer.

If you have committed yourself to Bell any way, you can excuse yourself by the above previous arrangement of mine.

Yrs George L B

* * * * * *

[George L. Brown to Edward S. Aldrich]
Newnansville [Florida, to St. Augustine, Florida]
June 17, 1844

Dear Edw-

I sent to Black Creek today by [Thomas] Barnes's waggon several
articles of furniture. Aunt Anne will follow next Saturday. I intended
to send Charles by the waggon today but the scoundrel ran away this
morning without known cause. I shall catch him, no doubt, by next
trip of waggon and will have him sent ready <u>dressed</u>. I would advise
you by all means to <u>sell</u> him at any price; he is a worthless rascal, no
favour will make him do well; he has been stupid with liquor ever
since my return, and will not (if he continues) be worth keeping in
a year or two — I advise you to sell or exchange him without delay.
I reached home safe with my goods. — business pretty fair—Mrs.
Watson I presume will take the house next week. I send this letter per
<u>brother</u> Benning; will write a longer letter by mail —

How many segars do you ask to pull a tooth? Don't be <u>coy</u> in your
answer—love to Corinna—Truly yrs
Geo L. Brown

*   *   *   *   *   *

[George L. Brown to Edward S. Aldrich]
Newnansville E[ast]. F[lorida]. [to St. Augustine, Florida]
June 28, 1844

Dear Edward:

I received your letter (dated on board <u>Santee</u> last evening) most
sincerely do I regret your indecision as regards a location. I was very
sanguine from what I had heard that you would do well at St. Augustine. Several of your friends represented to me, that your prospects
there would be excellent. Dr. [Valentine] Conway in particular, was
very decided about it. I do not think you have given the place a
proper trial, and should advise you to hold on there awhile longer. I
even had a dislike to Jacksonville, but it may be better than St A. Of
this you must judge. I hope whatever you decide on will be for your
best interest—.

I sent the remainder of your articles to Black Creek on Monday also with instructions to have them shipped to Picolata. Mr. [Solomon] Morgan has them in care. Aunt Anne was to have followed tomorrow, but will now want <u>further</u> <u>orders</u>. Your <u>beautiful</u> <u>boy</u> Charles, was to have gone in Barnes's waggon, but for some unknown reason, he ran away the morning it started and is still in parts unknown. But for this I would send you Tom and the buggy. Charles is a most infamous scoundrel, and I warn you, nay I entreat you for your own good either to sell, swap, or give him away. I would not take him for a gift. He ran away this time for no earthly cause. He has been treated kindly, nor has he voiced any objections to going to St. A. I will make an example of him when I catch him. I brought on Charlotte [a slave] from St Marys and we get along very well at old Bachelor's Hall–Mrs. Watson is waiting to move as soon as Aunt Anne leaves. They would like to come in whilst Aunt A & Elisa are here, but I won't let them, out of spite.

. . . Keil & family have returned from Fort King, quit it in disgust. Says he has dug seven wells without getting water, says Mr. [D.] Reinhardt is very sick and talks of <u>quitting</u> for good (or bad). You did well <u>not</u> to go there however dull you may find it where you are–

I certainly would advise you to try St Augustine well before you give it up. In a place of such population (in number) there must be practice, and most assuredly you will get a lion's share–

Give my love to all at home when you reach there. I will write to Corinna today if I have time.

Truly Yrs
George L.B.

*   *   *   *   *   *

[George L. Brown to Edward S. Aldrich]
Newnansville [Florida, to St. Augustine, Florida]
July 4, 1844

Dear Edward

Your several letters and one from Corinna came duly to hand; I should have answered them last mail but I was absent from town Saturday & Sunday. The relation to account of your father's, (in extenuation of my writing to him for payment) I would say, that the bill of goods sold him were <u>staple</u> <u>articles</u>, by <u>the</u> <u>piece</u>, and at no profit at all. I only charged him the expenses; in addition, there was a piece of cloth (at 11$) which he declined taking and which I <u>gave</u> to George [Edward's younger brother]. So I was in all a loser; the goods too I have paid for in cash last April as I was short of ready money and shall be until cotton comes in, I did not hesitate to write to him. Had I however been aware that you had informed him of settling forty dollars of it I should not have written. I have made the matter straight by since writing to your father. I told him (in substance) that you and I had some conversations some months since, when you were about making a similar arrangement but being called off did not quite conclude it, that I presumed you thought it settled and that it had escaped my memory. I concluded by telling him I would take the forty dolls on you. I will pay myself from the first money collected here for you.

I would gladly send you Tom and the buggy but I fear <u>he</u> would not <u>hold</u> <u>out</u> the journey- On my return from Charleston, I found Tom a used up horse. My driver used him in the team in his return from Black Creek after you left him there, and either there or by some subsequent hard journey he broke his mind-and you cannot now ride him without his rearing and puffing like a steamboat at sea—besides this failing he is irrecoverably poor and it seems that corn and fodder could not fatten him. I have been trying to swap him and the buggy for a good saddle horse for you and if possible will do so. If not I shall get rid of him to the best advantage-or he will some day die in my hands. At present he is a perfect encumbrance - I would send him were I not certain that you would not even use him in a cart. I will try and make some trade to get you a saddle horse. Please say to Mr. [Bernardo] Segui that I called on Shriver for his money, and that Shriver says he is going to St. A. himself next week. Should he not go I will get the money and send it down the last of next week by my team.

I think Mr. Reinhardt will pay up in full before quitting Florida— I advised him to send for his accts. last mail, as I thought from letters that I had secured from him that he would pay his debts — — —

[Jacob] Summerlin, [Benjamin A.] Putnam, [Isiah] Hart & [John] Scott (who's Polk?) are the whig senators.[18] The convention made perfect mincemeat of their ticket by leaving out Col. F. R. Sanchez.

He would have carried two thirds of the loco foco[19] tickets here and in Columbia. As it is it will be a tight race.–[Lemuel] Wilson, [James B.] Blanton, are the candidates for Reps — — —

Mr., Mrs, and the younger Watsons are and have been at Worthington Springs; if only dogs and chickens were there too, I should report myself well and flourishing. We are with these exceptions. One complaint (<u>the chickens</u>) grow less every day, and the dogs need tremble.

The Worthington Springs are quite Saratogaish. The Dells, Sanchez, & Olmsted families and the numerous bipeds, ycleped.[20] Methodist parsons, lend their aid to give them <u>ton</u>.[21] I am not of them. Col. [William. F.] Dell has been quite ill but as usual is getting better. Give my love to Corinna & Aunt Anne–Louis visits with me and desires me to say that he will write this next mail certain. Truly Yrs George Brown

* * * * * *

[George L. Brown to Edward S. Aldrich]
Newnansville, E[ast]. F[lorida]. [to St. Augustine, Florida]
July 6, 1844

Dear Edward

I feel quite satisfied at the contents of your last letter; your decision in favour of St. Augustine is nicely done; as to Jacksonville, you would scarce have fixed yourself ere you would have been moving elsewhere. In St. Augustine your success seems to me sure. There must be practice to induce at least one first rate physician to remain there. You ought to make up your mind <u>decidedly</u> to remain two years or more, <u>and not think</u> of any other places. Even if you do not clear expenses the first year, no matter. <u>Stick to</u> it, and you will surely come out right at last. If cotton crop continues <u>good</u>, I shall after this fall "go ahead," and cheerfully at the end of the year, help you to make <u>both ends</u> meet, tho' I trust you will not need any of my steam to keep you going —

I have started <u>Charles</u> to Black Creek this morning on foot, as he preferred (I presume) this way of traveling, to riding when he had a chance———Louis, Aunt Anne, Elisa will leave this noon per buggy for St. Augustine. Louis is a delegate (loco foco) to Pilatka. He may and may not visit you. I presume not as he is rather busy. Louis delivered quite an excellent oration on the Fourth. Lem Wilson read the declaration of Independence, but could not rest satisfied with the part assigned him without leading off the declaration with a <u>few</u> <u>introductory</u> <u>remarks!</u> A quiet dinner finished the day's proceedings —— .

Aunt Anne will tell you all the news-wishing you all success—I am

truly yours
and Corinna's

George L.B

P.S. keep clear of Territorial politics, they are too contemptible for a busy man's attention. If you feel like talking at any time, go in on Clay & Frelinghuysen.[22]

* * * * * *

[George L. Brown to Edward S. Aldrich]
[Newnansville, Florida, to St. Augustine, Florida]
September 7, 1844

Dear Edward,

Your last letter to me came duly to hand. My last to you enclosed 20$ on account of [Elijah] Barrow the rest of your accounts here will, I expect be collected after the cotton crops come in—At least you will stand a much better chance–the article of "shine"[23] is very scarce in these parts.

Louis left here last Tuesday to see [Samuel B.] Colding, I hope he will get rid of the negroes finally; I have given him "full powers" and he will do all that can be done in the premises. I presume Louis will visit St. Mary's before he returns, as he has [R. G.] Livingston's sulky and a pretty tolerable house, which will look quite like an "Establishment" at home. I am surprised that Colding has not disposed of the negroes; though I have every reason to suppose him honest. Livingston has been quite sick since his return from St. Augustine, he rode from Palatka in a tremendous rain and was taken down immediately on his arrival here. [Dr. James] Kelly being drunk and Livingston not putting any confidence in Dr. . . . . I sent to Micanopy for Prevatt; he is now doing well and will in a few days move his bones about. Kelly, who was with him the first day of his sickness, salivated him dreadfully.[24] I believe there is no other case of serious sickness, except with children and babies. . . .

I calculate to leave home for Charleston early next month, should no yellow fever be reported. I will give you a call going or coming. Say to your friend Mr. Bernardo Segui that I noticed his request in your letter some weeks since; I postponed taking the pony from Shriver as he promised daily to go to St. Augustine himself; day after day he still remained until I concluded that he was as near St. A. as he would ever get. I have now taken the pony from [. . .] and placed him in charge of Mr. Segui's friend F. Sanchez who will keep him on his plantation until an opportunity comes to send him home.

You have heard no doubt of Leonidus McNeal's[25] performance; shooting Ashley Ganey—he shot <u>nine</u> buckshot into him; 5 near the heart, 2 in the neck, and one in the chin!—either of the shots in his heart would have killed him–cause of quarrel, <u>a bunch of hogs.</u>

Give my love to Corinna and Aunt A—
I hope to see your headquarters.
Yrs truly George

＊　　＊　　＊　　＊　　＊　　＊

[George L. Brown to Edward S. Aldrich]
Newnansville [Florida, to St. Augustine, Florida]
December 29, 1844

Dear Edward,

You and Corinna must excuse my silence since my return to Newnansville,[26] for I have not had a chance to write except in my books since my return. I have two months posting to do, & my yearly bills to make, a month's job at least. The very night I came home Prevatt took sick and was confined to his bed until last Friday—so I was in a perfect stew for the first three days; then came court week and I trotted without cessation from Monday morning to Saturday night; since last week, I have been deluged with settling of accounts and yearly & other settlements. This is the first day I have breathed free.

My leg since my return has improved, I discharged my crutch at

Black Creek—the <u>scab</u> has not come [off] yet, though it is beginning to do so; until it does, I do not feel safe to sport myself with my usual activity. My leg at night appears weak and slightly swelled at the ankle and foot. . . said it would - Do you not think some linament would benefit it . . . ? I hope to be able to walk straight shortly. Your young man Charles arrived here last Friday. As regards Pendarvis' horse Louis could not make the arrangement. L[ouis] came from Fort King last night, and went to Alligator this morning.

I have told Charles to wait here until the last of the coming week– meantime I will see what I can do for a horse for you — I have no doubt I will either get you one now, or in a short time. If I do not suc- ceed this week, I will send Charles home by my wagon, and send you a horse as soon as I can. Pendarvis' horse <u>is</u> <u>not</u> a good horse, though he asks all outdoors for him—his mind is not good, and when travel- ling in a trot; he breathes like a blacksmith's bellows.

I regret having disappointed you and Corinna so often in my promises to visit you, but I could not control the . . . events which prevented my fulfilling them. I shall go to Charleston as early in Feb- ruary as I possibly can, and either going or returning, I will be at St. Augustine—next summer, or soon after April courts, I intend spend- ing a long time with you.

Tom Aldrich[27] has a notion of coming back to Florida to practice!? He awaits instructions from me—today I write him and such a pack of lies as I have concocted to <u>deter</u> him <u>from</u> coming would aston- ish you–For god's sake and mine write him yourself and give him as dismal a picture as you can of Newnansville practice. I want no such encumbrance to annoy me. If he was decent & respectful, I could bear him, he is neither and I am sure I should insult him and cut him after his arrival here–he would only annoy myself and Louis. I tell him in my letter that we have four doctors here! And Louis is about locating in Georgia!

I have a proposition to make to you for your house here. It is now going to ruin and unless repaired will soon be worthless. I have hired Clytus of your father and intend to put it in repairs, if I can buy it from you. It will be a waste to put expense on myself unless I can reap the benefit of it —— My proposition is this–

Your account on my books is something above $500 dollars

including 60 or 70 paid to Colding at different times–I will give you this account and a good horse (sometime during the winter or as early as possible) for the house and two lots in this place. This is a big price, but in making it I remember my past indebtedness to you and shall consider I am well paid. I would not attempt to buy it of you if a purchaser could be had who would give you anything like its value or any price in cash — but there is none—and unless the house is kept in repair and new fences it will soon be of no value—let me hear about this as early as you can as I expect Clytus shortly. Give my love to Corinna & Aunt Anne. Tell C. I will write her next week.

Yrs very truly
George

*   *   *   *   *   *

[George L. Brown to Edward S. Aldrich]
Newnansville [Florida, to St. Augustine, Florida]
Jan 3, 1845

Dear Edward:

I have succeeded in purchasing for you a horse (mare) but cannot have possession of the property before next week. I shall therefore be compelled to keep Charles still another week - his detention here will probably be some inconvenience to you but I have argued to myself that you would rather lose his services for a few days than to miss getting a "critter." How you will like the animal I cannot tell. Her present owner gave 150 dollars for her, or that value. I got her considerably less- horse judges say she is 7 years old, . . . and a good horse—her present appearance is rather poor and shaggy, but corn & care will improve her condition wonderfully.

I will send you a bridle - I have no saddles on hand, but the most ordinary kind —

Prevatt sold all my good saddles before I returned from Charleston. I have seen Mrs. [Delilah] Gibbons about her note— she promises to pay something on it when Mr. Livingston returns from middle Florida—he will be back in a few days.

It is a constant source of regret to me that I have not paid you a visit. If my legs get <u>walkable</u> as of old, I shall certainly go to Charleston in February, and either going or returning you <u>shall</u> <u>use</u> <u>me</u> for a week at least. I am very anxious to see you all. Jessee Standley died here last week and on Thursday last old Charley Gibbons yielded up his earthly accounts—

I wish you all many blessings. May this year be to each of you a happy one—
Yours truly, Geo. L. B.

P.S.   Louis returned yesterday from Alligator.

*   *   *   *   *   *

[George L. Brown to Edward S. Aldrich]
Newnansville Fla [to St. Augustine, Florida]
February 2, 1845

Dear Edward

Yours of the 20th with an "unfavorable horse report" is at hand. I regret that you are so disappointed; I was sorry when I undertook to purchase a horse for you, sorry when I bought him, and been sorry ever since—I am no judge of a horse and probably will get more or less cheated every time I buy one. You are, however, in error about the mare - She never belonged to Colding. She could not; to my knowledge she was brought into Florida for the first time by Mr. [D] Bruton about six weeks before I took her. Bruton sold her to [Simeon] Harvey, and I purchased her from H., giving him eighty dollars; I did not take Harvey's price but had her valued by a third, disinterested person - I did not discover any lameness in her myself. She is an animal that I can dispose of here for what I gave for her, and if she still looks as bad as ever, I wish you would let Charles take her over to Pilatka and send her to Black Creek to A[lbert G.] Phillips for me; he will send her up. I will make one trial more to get you a horse, and can use the mare in swapping-I will let old [Thomas] Barnes take her and go in the country. We will, I think get a good animal somehow. Pendarvis said something to me about the "Hog account" some time since. If you have a bill against him send it up to me, and I will square the account if there is any balance due him - I told him when he spoke to me that I would attend to the matter. It had since escaped my memory.

Your account on Col Sanchez could be obtained by suing — it would distress him some but other people sue him and get their money. His crop did not pay his account with me this year. The Col. is now very sick and has been so several weeks. It would be useless to sue [Samuel] Russell as he has no property liable. I think too that he will soon be able to pay, he & [John] Parsons have each a claim for dry goods against U.S. for extra services in Land Office, which will be allowed them beyond doubt.

My leg is quite well again; it gives out on a long walk, but even then has its advantage as I said <u>doing</u> <u>road</u> <u>duty!</u> I hope to leave here the last of this month for Charleston. I cannot say exactly whether I will <u>call</u> going or returning; Louis & myself are making arrangements to be with you together; we have not made it fit exactly yet, will let you know —

I hope Corinna is better than your last letters advised me—give my love to her & Aunt Anne. A letter in an envelope directed to "St. Aldrich," Fla. has been passing backwards & forwards a mail or two past; Prevatt directed my attention to it last Thursday, and I immediately opened the package and found a letter from Ellen directed to Corinna at St. Aldrich for St Augustine—the letter will be forwarded this mail.

I have not heard from Doctor Tom [Aldrich]. I expect he curses me, soundly; I had rather have his oath than his "tediousness." I am truly sorry for Tom, and was he a decent man, or regarded his reputation . . . in some reasonable degree I would gladly help him—but what credit he got here would be by mistakes of people supposing Tom was you, and he in fact <u>would</u> <u>be</u> <u>you</u> to all strangers—I shall have a row with him I expect when I visit Charleston - I would advise him however to swallow his wrath, for if called upon, I shall deliver an unvarnished tale of "Tom as he would be in Florida" to his family to exonerate myself; he may not see through my drift.–yrs truly George——

❧ 3 ❧

"Man Is Born for Disappointment"

(1845)

In the first few months of 1845, George Brown reunited with his family in St. Augustine. James and Ellen Anderson and their children, Edward Willoughby and new baby Corinna Georgia, arrived in St. Augustine from New York early in the year. By that time, Dr. Aldrich had established his medical practice with Dr. J. E. Peck, the son of the recently deceased eminent physician Dr. Seth Peck, who had settled in St. Augustine in 1834.[1] Edward and Corinna welcomed the Andersons and George to their spacious house. James returned to Buffalo Barracks in March, leaving Ellen and the children in St. Augustine with the Aldriches. Ellen remained in St. Augustine for nearly a year, leaving in May to join her husband in Buffalo. In September, the family was transferred to another posting at Fort Gratiot, Michigan.

Meanwhile, Florida's existence as a territory was fast approaching its end. On March 3, President John Tyler signed a bill admitting Florida into the Union as a state, and Gov. John Branch called for an election of new state officials to be held in the upcoming months. George would have learned of this event in Charleston. On the last day of February, he boarded the steam packet *St. Matthews* at Palatka and arrived in Savannah, where he switched and caught the steam packet *Charleston* to Charleston via Hilton Head and Beaufort.[2] George's business kept him nearly a month in the city, but he no doubt visited numerous taverns and eating establishments. He might have enjoyed the theater and rambles through the old streets with their great houses. Alexander Mackay, a Scottish lawyer and newspaperman who visited Charleston in 1845, thought that in comparison with New York, Philadelphia, and Boston (cities that George knew well), Charleston was a "pleasing looking town, but by no means a striking one." The site was flat and "unimposing." On the day he arrived, it was hot and sultry. There was "not a breath of air stirring, and the waters of the bay were as calm and unruffled as a mill-pond," Mackay writes. "Before me lay a city baking, as it were, in the fierce sunshine. . . . Like Philadelphia, it presents one front to the harbor, which screens the rest of the city from view." Mackay found the "interior of the city . . . both pretty and peculiar." Its "grandeur and substantiality" did not meet the levels of other great American cities, but Mackay appreciated the practicality of its architecture:

> [It was] designed to obviate the inconveniences of [Charleston's] climate. A tolerably large portion of it is built of brick, the bulk of the town however being constructed of wood. The private dwellings are almost all wooden edifices, not lofty, but elegant, being in most cases provided with light, airy and graceful verandas, extending in some instances to the roof. They are generally painted of a dazzling white, with green Venetian blinds, the verandas being sometimes adorned with vines, and at others merely painted green. In the suburbs particularly they are embowered in foliage, with which the spotless white of the walls forms a cool and pleasing contrast.

Mackay thought the city hall and the exchange building the "finest edifices" of the city. He praised the numerous excellent hotels, some "being on a scale inferior to none elsewhere, even in Boston, New York, or New Orleans. . . . It is their vastness and excellent management that strikes the stranger with astonishment."[3]

When George visited in 1845, Charleston contained roughly 32,000 persons, with black residents slightly outnumbering white. Planters from surrounding areas made up a sizable percentage of the population. "It is from this landed gentry, who prided themselves on their aristocratic standard of conduct," one historian notes, "that the popular image of Charleston as a quiet city of culture and refinement has been largely derived. Despite this reputation, the South Carolina metropolis in fact retained a predominantly commercial character" throughout the antebellum era.

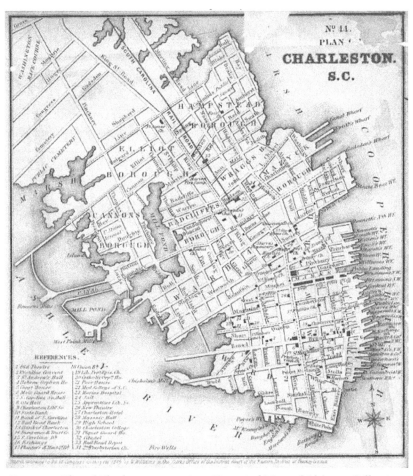

Figure 3.1. Plan of Charleston, circa 1849, Historical Maps of Alabama Collection, University of Alabama Department of Geography.

The city was a "distributing center through which almost all the business of the state and much of the hinterland beyond was channeled. Accordingly, merchants and factors consistently comprised a high percentage of the population when compared to other urban areas." In most years, at least one thousand people were involved in trade.[4] In fact, the historian continues, despite a tendency toward "social prejudice against business interests," the city enjoyed a kind of merchant renaissance beginning in 1840.[5]

During the years when George visited Charleston, the city was experiencing a transformation. Not only were many white people leaving the city for the Old Southwest frontiers of Alabama, Mississippi, or the Territory of Florida, but many newcomers from abroad were also reshaping the culture, habits, and mores of the city. Historian Barbara Bellows writes that after the Panic of 1837, many recent immigrants (most of them from Ireland and the German States) made a second or third migration by "boarding the coastwise packets and schooners heading south. The steady stream of newcomers so altered the lineaments of the urban population by 1840" that white workers were replacing slaves as laborers.[6]

Louis Fitzgerald Tasistro, New York newspaperman and aspiring actor, visited Charleston in 1842 on a theatrical excursion. Of Irish and Italian extraction, Tasistro was a keen observer of the many layers of social strata in the city. He asserted that in "no city in the Union were the gradations in the great social system so distinctly marked as in Charleston; each class seems to shun the other as a moral leprosy; there is less amalgamation of the orders than anywhere else." He divided Charleston into three "great families or separate communities, the mercantile, the literary, and the aristocratic." He asserted that the mercantile, which he defined as "all those engaged in trade, from the extensive cotton broker to the retail dealer in pickled herrings and brown sugar," was the most important, and it was to "this class that a stranger must look for hospitality and the exercise of kindness." Many were Scotsmen; others were Irish. Of the aristocracy, Tasistro noted that they were "famed all over the world for gentility of blood, high descent, and chivalrous bearing." Even so, he admitted that the "aristocracy of the present day is not exactly as it was fifty years ago: the live generation is indolent, and but little given to intellectual, or even plausible pursuits." They were to his lights the "unproductive classes; unless, indeed, the rice grown on their plantation, where they vegetate for a considerable portion of the year, may be taken as an equivalent for their want of personal industry." Tasistro described the aristocratic class in detail:

[They were] distinguished from all the rest of all mankind by their flowing locks, well oiled, brushed, and curled—fantastic goatish beards with whiskers and mustaches to match; all which forms their principal stock in trade. If the avocations of these "capillary Peripatetics" be not of very ennobling taste, and are quite on a par with the most refined English gentlemen in external polish and address. Their propensity for aping European Continental manners renders them extremely obnoxious to the more sedate and sensible portion of the community; as they lounge along the streets by fours and sixes, with that peculiar swagger which renders it impossible to conceive that the town is not their own.[7]

If George encountered any of these "aristocrats," he probably would have paid them little mind other than to wonder at their wealth rather than their status. George was most attuned to the mundane pursuits of making a living, even if he did enjoy the pleasures of Charleston. While there, he sent Edward this quick note:

[George L. Brown to Edward S. Aldrich]
[Charleston, South Carolina, to St. Augustine, Florida]
[March 6, 1845]

Dear Edward,

I am so far in possession of good health, and trust I will retain it–I have scarcely more time than to say that I shall leave here <u>next</u> <u>week</u> for Florida–and nothing to prevent, I shall be in St. Augustine a week from next Monday. Major [John] Beard & his two sons are here and will probably be my fellow travellers–

Give my love to Corinna & Ell & Aunt Anne–I am to day shipping goods for tomorrow's Boat for Savannah; of course I am stirring—
Yrs truly
Geo L. B.

A few days after George returned to Newnansville, he wrote again to Edward in St. Augustine:

[George L. Brown to Edward S. Aldrich]
[Newnansville, Florida, to St. Augustine, Florida]
[March 30, 1845]

Dear Edward:

I reached home last Wednesday by the usual route safe & sound — My fellow traveler in the stage from Black Creek to Newnansville was Capt. John Mackay of Washington. I found him a fine companion, and I was inclined to think a just man. He spoke of your account against his brother, and said he intended to pay it before he left Florida, providing he could collect money from Capt. [John] L'Engle-says he got a letter from you lately, and would have answered it, but did not care to do so until he went to Suwannee — he will be back this way next stage.

My Lieut. "Crab arse" took to his bed with the bellyache as soon as I reached home as usual— and there he is quite sick. I am so hurried by this mishap that I must be brief. Give my love to all the family, remember me to Dr. Peck.

Yrs truly George B

P.S. [Maj. Sylvester] Churchill & [Richard Pindel] Hammond are here. I will write you more leisurely next week

yrs G

*   *   *   *   *   *

[George L. Brown to Edward S. Aldrich]
Newnansville [Florida, to St. Augustine, Florida]
April 12, 1845

Dear Edward

I have to write you another very brief letter, owing to the continued sickness of Prevatt, and my many petty engagements . . . I find the amount of your account due me as per ledger is 403 31/100 Dollars, this does not include the value of "Betsy Baker"—You will please make out a bill of sale of the house with a deed to Louis for Five Hundred Dollars–The difference I will pay to Corinna with Betsy Baker thrown into the bargain.

I am anxious to hear from you what decision you have made about remaining in St. Augustine. I cannot but advise you to persevere there one year more, and give it good trial. We do not know what favorable thing might occur, and you are so comfortably fixed, that the difference of any practice in a new place to St. A. will not repay you for the sacrifices a move will cause. The arrangement in Charleston I spoke of for you, I will still make as soon as you finally decide—In short, you need not give yourself any uneasiness about making both ends meet at the close of the year. [William] Forward, [John M.] Fontane, [David] Levy, [A. H.] Cole, & [William Wing] Loring passed through here on Friday on their way to the Madison Convention.[8]

Doctor [Benjamin] Hopkins is here with a view to locate Negroes. We now have four "D.D's" or, whatever in Bill Critchton's language.

Tell Corin & Ell I will write to them, the first leisure moment. Give my love to them and Aunt Anne. –

Let me hear from you particularly about your purposes. Louis & John Wesley & family are well.

Very Truly Yours,
George L. Brown

P.S. I do not like your house very much in Augustine and would suggest that you change residences if you can better yourself at the same rate.

*   *   *   *   *   *

[George L. Brown to Edward S. Aldrich]
San Felasco [to St. Augustine, Florida]
July 4, 1845

Dear Edward:

I happened down here this morning to escape the usual <u>uproar</u> and din, consequent upon the day, which usually takes place in large cities like Newnansville. Here I must send Olmsted who is about saddling up for St. Augustine. I have offered, and he has partly consented to take Charles along with him as desired. Should he not find his load too heavy, he will take him at Newnansville as he goes through. If Mr. Olmsted does not take him I will run him down in my wagon on Monday next —

I wrote you last mail that your mare had arrived in good order; I spoke too soon; on further examination I found she was quite lame from her journey, though now much improved. I will make sure disposition of her either sell, swap, or let her run on the prairie — You do not say in your letter whether you wish <u>another</u> horse or not, and from your silence on this subject I am undecided what to do- I have a fine horse in my team, you may recollect "Barnes racing Bay." He is now rather out of order from hard work but will be good again shortly. Should you wish him I will make an exchange with you, as I intend to change all of my horses to mules. I cannot deliver him to you under a month or six weeks, as he at present belongs to <u>an estate.</u> I shall have them all valued and sold (nominally) as soon as I get letters of administration. I also thought, in relation to this horse that you might not wish to have one with you under any circumstances, or at least under <u>present</u> circumstances. A letter from you will put me right on this matter. I will have the racing nag "stall fed" until I hear from you; I can send him to Black Creek and you can send over from Augustine for him, thus saving Charles another journey up here.

The glorious Fourth will be anything but a jolly one to me. Louis is away to Colombia, and most of the towns people are to be at a barbeque at Mr. Marshal Blanton's[9] <u>seat</u> Crocket Springs. Our weather is still intolerably hot and dry. Crops very inferior. Times rather dull. I sincerely wish to be where cool breezes blow and where blue pills are not to be taken. I stuck one into my gullet night before last as big as a plum. We work them up with "moffits" as the going pill is termed. Mr. Olmsted & family contemplate spending the summer at St Augustine; his family at any rate; he will probably return here. . . . I have not heard from Anderson or any of them. I wish they would remember that Newnansville has not turned into a "big sink" yet. My love to Aunt Anne. say to her peaches are not ripe; 1 will try and get a box of ripe ones to her for the <u>fried</u>-<u>mullet</u> route-

Afftly yrs,
George B.

*   *   *   *   *   *

[George L. Brown to Edward S. Aldrich]
Newnansville [Florida, to St. Augustine, Florida]
July 7, 1845

Dear Edward

I wrote you per Olmsted on the 4th advising you that Charles would return with him in his carriage. Mr. Olmsted endeavored to get him as he passed through, and sent for him as he was not at the house. Master Charles however took his time, and did not make his appearance until after Olmsted left.

I must beg you if you have occasion to send here again to get David or some other Negro. Charles is a perfect pest to everybody. I have had at least a half dozen complaints about him from different people during the short stay he has made—he goes visiting to the different kitchens after the people have retired, and plays the very devil with other negroes. On the morning he was to have gone with Olmsted I told him if he drank any liquor during the day I would beat it out of him at night: he took the liquor and I kept my promise.

Your mare seems to improve some though still a little lame. I am in hopes to make a trade off with someone either for a good horse or mule. If I get a mule I will supply you with a horse. — — — — I shall send down Charles by my wagon tomorrow — — — —

Our fourth passed off very quickly. Blanton made some sky Rockets for the evening's entertainments, but unfortunately they were determined to be ground rockets for they would not rise over ten or twelve feet. They did pretty well for squibs.

I have no other news this mail.

Yrs truly

G. L. B.

* * * * * *

[George L. Brown to Ann Dearing]

Newnansville [Florida, to St. Augustine, Florida]

August 25, 1845

Dear Aunt Ann:

I received last mail a letter from Major Beard offering me 300 dollars for the place of Charles & yours on the St. Johns River. And I have written him in reply, that I will make the sale providing you give your assent. The price I consider very fair under all circumstances; to be sure, it <u>cost</u> more, but as it stands it is of no use to you, and probably <u>never</u> <u>will</u> <u>be</u>, and should the house get destroyed by fire, or accident, as it certainly will unless occupied, the place will be worth nothing, as the <u>land</u> is of no <u>value</u>. I advise <u>you</u> <u>by</u> <u>all</u> <u>means</u> <u>to</u> <u>sell</u>, but consult your <u>own</u> <u>wishes</u> entirely, as you are mostly interested in the matter. Should you sell, the money could be invested for you much more profitably than where it is now sunk. You could invest in Bank shares, or I would take it—and give you liberal interest; or I could buy you a little negro that could <u>grow</u> <u>worth</u> <u>more</u> every day, unlike a house, which diminishes in value. Please let the Doctor know what you decide and he will inform <u>Miss</u> <u>Beard</u>, the matter now stands until you say yes or no.

I don't know whether I ever told you that I owe you thirty Dollars, or more, being for your half of the cattle sold on St. John's River; I don't know if I did, but if anything should happen to me, you will find that much, & interest credited you on my ledger. So much for business.

We of Newnansville remain about the same old thing as when you were here, save your kind offices which are missed exceedingly. The Buttons off my shirts, and the <u>holy</u> stockings remind me of you every night & morning. I hope this letter will find you well and happy; if you are now enjoying sea breezes you have much to be thankful for, hot, and dry, and dusty, is the air of Alachua. I wish much to visit you but my business still prevents. I shall certainly see you this fall, if not sooner.

Miss [Elizabeth] Sanchez you know is married.[10] My friends have consoled me for my loss. Man is born for disappointment and disappointment comes in many shapes, sometimes good and sometimes bad luck. Among the faces which I saw in St. Augustine none struck me particularly but the young <u>Miss</u> [Sarah] <u>Drysdale</u>.[11] I only saw her in the streets—I would like to see her again—and shall try to do so–I wish you would write me a letter, and give me more about how you are. I know just enough of it to want to know more. Very affectionately yours, George L. B.

❦ 4 ❦

"To Transform a 'Yankee' to a 'Southern Cracker'"

(1846–1849)

IN 1846, GEORGE BROWN's personal prospects continued to brighten, especially as he became better known to farmers and tradesmen in the area. His trips to Charleston became more frequent, and his business contacts in that city, Savannah, and surrounding areas grew. As time went on, George took advantage of commercial opportunities that presented themselves. For example, in 1846, George became an agent for the Vance & Burns manufacturing company from St. Marys, Georgia. The company had produced a new and improved version of the roller horse gin for cleaning long staple cotton, and its advertisements listed George L. Brown of Newnansville and several others in Camden County as agents for purchase of the new machine.[1]

In 1845, cotton prices were low and several international factors created a volatile market for the commodity. The uncertainly involving America's tilt toward war with Mexico was perhaps related to Florida's declining production of cotton between 1845 and 1846. Florida's total cotton production fell between 1845 and 1846 by nearly 45,000 bales. In 1846, the total stood at 141,184 bales. In 1847, the total output dipped to 127,852 bales. Most of the cotton left the state via the Middle Florida ports of St. Marks and Apalachicola Bay, but the St. Johns River trade grew steadily. In 1847, Charleston received 1,435 bales of Florida cotton and Savannah received

559 bales.[2] In 1846, Ireland's potato crop failed, and Britain spent excessively on food that year. In 1847, things picked up, but the 1848 revolutions, the abdication of Louis Philippe, and war threats between Prussia and Denmark created more volatility. The resolution of these crises stabilized life to the point that from 1849 up to the outbreak of the Civil War, cotton prices continued to increase.[3] In 1849, Florida enjoyed its largest production total in history, with more than 200,000 bales.[4]

For the next several years, Mannevillette Brown remained in Europe studying art and painting. George and his other family members continually pleaded with him to come home while keeping him informed of their movements.[5] Once the war clouds with Mexico grew more intense, their pleadings became more pronounced. M.E.D. Brown finally returned from Europe early in 1849. He soon established an art studio in Utica, New York, where he eventually prospered.

George's friendship with Louis Aldrich continued, but Louis's election to the legislative council in 1846 meant that he would spend more time away from Newnansville. Louis won a subsequent election to the Florida House in 1847, and in 1848, he won a seat in the Florida Senate, only to resign soon after to leave for San Francisco, California, lured west by gold discoveries there. Though he was saddened by Louis's departure, George's primary concerns in 1846 consisted of the growing tensions between the United States and Mexico and what war might mean for his business and also for his sister Ellen's family. Since the beginning of the year, relations between the United States and Mexico had continued to worsen over the acquisition of Texas and President James K. Polk's campaign promise to acquire California. Once American efforts to purchase California were unsuccessful, Polk sent an American force under Zachary Taylor to what he considered the boundary between Texas and Mexico. In April, a Mexican force attacked Taylor's troops in the disputed territory. Polk responded by asking Congress for a declaration of war, and two days later, on May 13, 1846, Congress acquiesced.

George witnessed numerous volunteer units being raised throughout Alachua County and the surrounding region. By January 1847, Gov. William D. Mosely had called for volunteers to fight in Mexico. In Newnansville, leaders formed a company of volunteers. One source predicted that they would "do credit to their name, and render more efficient service to their county than a dozen companies of our regular troops, who experience has shown are no match for Indian foes however they may be against

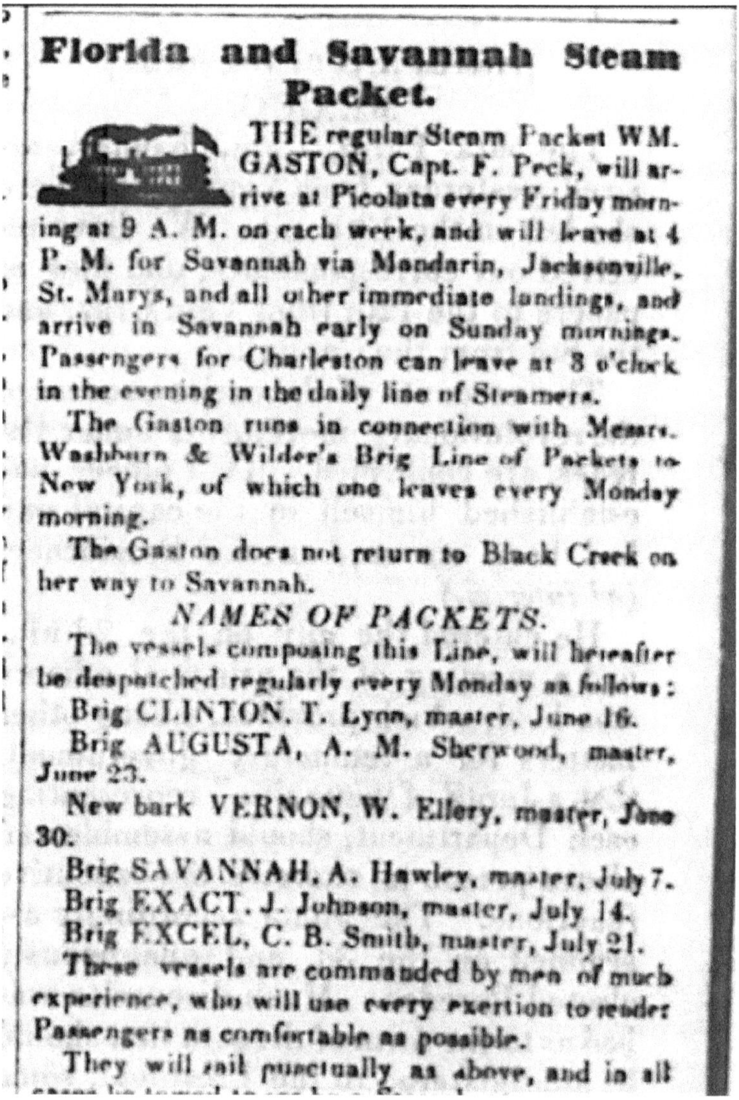

Florida and Savannah Steam Packet.

THE regular Steam Packet WM. GASTON, Capt. F. Peck, will arrive at Picolata every Friday morning at 9 A. M. on each week, and will leave at 4 P. M. for Savannah via Mandarin, Jacksonville, St. Marys, and all other immediate landings, and arrive in Savannah early on Sunday mornings. Passengers for Charleston can leave at 3 o'clock in the evening in the daily line of Steamers.

The Gaston runs in connection with Messrs. Washburn & Wilder's Brig Line of Packets to New York, of which one leaves every Monday morning.

The Gaston does not return to Black Creek on her way to Savannah.

NAMES OF PACKETS.

The vessels composing this Line, will hereafter be despatched regularly every Monday as follows:

Brig CLINTON. T. Lyon, master, June 16.
Brig AUGUSTA, A. M. Sherwood, master, June 23.
New bark VERNON, W. Ellery, master, June 30.
Brig SAVANNAH, A. Hawley, master, July 7.
Brig EXACT. J. Johnson, master, July 14.
Brig EXCEL, C. B. Smith, master, July 21.

These vessels are commanded by men of much experience, who will use every exertion to render Passengers as comfortable as possible.

They will sail punctually as above, and in all

Figure 4.1. "Florida and Savannah steam packet," *Wm. Gaston. Jacksonville Florida News,* January 30, 1846.

Mexicans." George's lawyer friend Robert Livingston of Newnansville offered to raise a company of mounted men. Writing from Newnansville on February 20, Livingston announced that those who wished to serve as "mounted men" under him as colonel could sign up at Newnansville, Black Creek, Jacksonville, St. Augustine, Alligator, Ocala, and Micanopy.[6]

At that time, Captain James Anderson, his wife, Ellen, and their children, Edward Willoughby, Corinna Georgia, and newborn baby girl Ellen Mannevillette, were at Fort Gratiot in Michigan. With the outbreak of the Mexican War, Anderson's Second Infantry, mobilized for war, descended the Mississippi for Mexico. After his departure in July, Ellen, the children, and Anderson's sister Virginia traveled to Florida via Norfolk and Charleston, where George met them and escorted them by the steam packet *Wm. Gaston* the rest of the way.[7] By that time, Edward, Corinna, and Anne had relocated to Pensacola, and Ellen's family soon joined them. The gulf port town offered a far better vantage point than St. Augustine for following the movements of the army.

As he was making his way to the front, James confided to his wife his gratitude for George's assistance to his family: "I feel very grateful to George for his kindness—had he not given you his protections & aid at the time he did (I do not know what you would have done), for I feared you were not equal to undertaking alone & knew that you feel somewhat uneasy at the undertaking yourself. I assure you, I consider myself fortunate to have such relations as Corinna, George, & the Doctor. God knows what would have been our present situation without their kindness & attention."[8] In March 1847, the Second Infantry participated in Gen. Winfield Scott's successful amphibious assault on Veracruz. By May, Scott's forces had moved forward toward Mexico City. By June, the separation of the U.S. Army from the coast was almost complete. While James and his comrades prepared for their final drive toward Mexico City, Ellen, the Aldriches, and George in Newnansville waited anxiously for information from the front.

In June, George wrote to Ellen as she and James were preparing to leave Fort Gratiot.

[George L. Brown to Ellen Brown Anderson]
Newnansville to [Fort Gratiot, Michigan]
June 29, 1846

Dear sister,

I acknowledge my indebtedness to you for two letters and not only to you but to a dozen others at least. It is a failing I have to be behind with all my correspondents, save business. It is something in my favour to say that it is my punctual attention to the one sort that causes my tardiness to the other. Your letter of May 19th was rec. during

my absence in Charleston, from which today I returned a short time
since. My trips to C. are frequent taking up nearly one third of my
time. I am pleased to know of the continued good health of yourself and Anderson & the juveniles. I would like to see your children
there — though I do not wish my eyes to be gladdened at your or
Anderson's detriment, for I certainly should consider it such did you
visit Florida consequent upon the Captain's being ordered to Texas. I
am anxious as himself for his military fame and promotions, but not
in such a war–Mean, contemptible, and unworthy as the motives are
which brought on the fray; the end will be still more so, unless speedily brought to a close. I honor the unfortunate brave men who have
suffered in the cause, but to our President Mr. Polk (the <u>pronuncia-
tion</u> of his name indicates his breed and his brains) and his admirers
will be meted a different reward - - -

The negro question we hear, is no longer a question; that it will
soon be settled on just and amicable terms — this is my earnest wish.
I am opposed to war when it can be avoided by any fair compromise.
I am also against such commotions from a selfish view. A war falls
heaviest on those who buy and sell merchandise — I am one, and do
not wish to be ruined from an excess of "American patriots." It will do
well for those who are at ease in their possessions, or for those who
have something to lose, to sing such <u>patriotic</u> strains—but for us who
are struggling in the world, peace, and peace only is to be desired;
and I think we love our land as dearly as the noisy brawler who
spouts his nonsense from every bar-room that will give him credit.

I have ever been a strong opponent of Mr. J. C. Calhoun. I retract
all my harsh words and hail him as his country's best friend.[9] Have
you read Genl. Scott & Mr. Secretary [of War William L.] Marcy's
correspondence? The Genl. you will recollect commences one of his
letters by saying that he had recd. one of Mr. Marcy's just as [he] was
sitting down to a hasty <u>plate of soup</u>, hence he is called "Marshall
Fearless"—Mr. Marcy and the whole tribe in Washington can do
nothing to injure Genl. Scott, the people know his history, and <u>theirs</u>.
They will make him president with a little more abuse.[10]

Our village is progressing a little by the aid of <u>saw mills</u>. Mrs.
[Zilphia] <u>Standley</u> is building a large prime hotel, which will be quite
a house — the old lady still drives ahead "point blank" and has too, a
new piano in town, the tum te tum therefrom can be heard all hours

of the day. My old bachelors establishment is badly in want of a fair spirit for its minister. I certainly shall [fix] myself to somebody before long. I have had an adventure of late which I will tell you of, if you will remind me when I <u>see</u> <u>you</u>—I cannot trust it upon paper.

I hear from Corinna often. She seems pleased with Pensacola; I trust [she] remains so. She amuses me as usual with Aunt Anne's whims and oddities—I suppose you hear the same—a curious old lady our Aunt; yet Corinna could scarcely do without her—like [Saw Slick's] clocks they become fixtures and necessaries by their daily associations. Give my love and best wishes to Anderson, Miss Virginia, and the "wee things."

Affectionately Yrs,
George L. Brown

*   *   *   *   *   *

[George L. Brown to Mannevillette E. D. Brown]
Newnansville [Florida, to Paris, France]
July 18, 1846

My Dear Brother,

After a long silence, I feel it my absolute duty, as well as a sincere pleasure, to write you again. I received not long ago a letter from Sister Corinna, stating to me that you stood in need of some funds, and that she was at present unable to meet your wishes, and requested that I would act for her. I immediately wrote to your agents, Messrs. Corning & Co.[11] stating that I wished to make you a remittance, and asking of them advice as to the mode and of your location. I recd. from Messrs. C & C a reply that they would cheerfully attend to any trust placed in their care, but that they were without certain information as to your residence. They also advised me of a small account of theirs against you for forwarding etc. which I have promised to settle for you and will do so. I must now beg of you to answer me as soon as this letter reaches you stating what funds you wish, and I will by the return post place the money in Corning & Co's hands. You will have little hesitation to call upon me, as I am indebted to you I think near two hundred dollars. I wrote to you on this subject of my debt to you long since but never recd. any answer. I have myself too keenly felt the want of money in former days, to delay attention to any call of my relatives and I assure you that my anxiety will be much relieved by your letters. You had better write me duplicates by different steamers, as this place is hard to find even by the United States mail—<u>penetrating</u> as it is ——

. . . . Corinna & Dr. Aldrich and Aunt Anne are now living at Pensacola, some 300 miles from Newnansville — they are all well and happy. Dr. Aldrich has there a good practice and is very popular with the people of P. so says a gentleman from there. Ellen & Captain Anderson are at Fort Gratiot, Michigan. Ellen is the mother of three children. She will have a dozen if nothing unfortunate occurs — Capt. Anderson is daily expecting orders to Texas and Mexico in which case, she and her juveniles will visit Corinna at Pensacola.

The war in Mexico, I presume, astonishes the <u>natives</u> of Europe. It is indeed a shameful affair, but now commenced, must be carried on with energy. I hope it will soon terminate. The Oregon Treaty with Great Britain, carried out by last steamer to Liverpool, by Gen'l [Robert A.] Armstrong,[12] gives much joy to the inhabitants of the U.S. of all parties. It was so unexpected, that the transition from gloom to brightness was perceptible in every face. I dreaded the prospect of a long and tedious war with England. I am as patriotic as my neighbors, still my amor patris[13] is not so very extensive as to lead me to sacrifice my life and the means whereby I live in a foolish unholy and unnecessary quarrel. War ever falls heaviest on those that buy and sell merchandise.

Why do you not visit us—we are not changed in hearts and mind, however time may have made inroads on our phizes. We are all very anxious that you should return home. You need have no apprehensions as to pecuniary matters and you can find, what you can boast of, <u>three</u> homes here, with me; or Corinna; or Ellen.— Indeed, if you wish to see us all again, you ought to return this year — for another season may make the small number of us left, still less — life is of little certainty in a southern climate, and though I still keep in excellent health, I have seen those more robust than I, snatched away by a blighting fever, without scarcely a warning. Write me without fail on receiving this, and I will let you hear from me afterwards. I am

most affectionately thy brother
George L. B.

*   *   *   *   *   *

[George L. Brown to Ellen Brown Anderson]
Newnansville to [Fort Gratiot, Michigan]
September 12, 1846

Dear Ellen

You must have made a rapid journey from Fort Gratiot to Norfolk. Your letter from Fort G. which apprised me of your contemplated travels was received in good time and duly acknowledged. I wrote immediately to you advising you how to act and who to call upon when you reach New York - I also wrote to my commission agent in N.Y. to attend to all your wishes - you must have left before my letter reached F[ort] G[ratiot].

I regret that it will be out of my power to come to Norfolk for you. I shall leave here the last week in September and be in Charleston some eight or ten days; say from the first to the 10th of October; I may remain a little longer — I hope this letter will reach you in time for you to be in C. If you are not then I shall wait until the 15th of Oct.[14] You had better stop at Stewart's Carolina Hotel— it is not the best house, yet you will find more solid comfort, and much better society than at either of the other Hotels. When we get together we will debate and decide on the most quick, and most agreeable route to Pensacola ————

Should you by your "force of miracles" get to Charleston before me, you will find Mr. Robt. Aldrich's family kind and attentive, he forwarded your letter with dispatch. I must advise you to keep out of Florida as long as you can, for the Doctor's all say that the season will be a sickly one; promising that it will from the incessant rain, during the three or four months past. As yet we all keep well in the villages; in the suburbs fever prevails to some extent. Could you jump to Pensacola without passing through Middle Florida you would escape all sickness. Hoping to meet you soon.

Affectionately, thy Brother
Geo. L. B.

* * * * * *

[George L. Brown to Mannevillette E. D. Brown]
Newnansville [Florida, to Paris, France]
July 26, 1847[15]

Dear Brother Mann

I am gratified beyond expression to receive a letter from you <u>at</u> <u>last</u>. I have written to you three times during the past twelve months and was about giving up all hope of ever hearing from you when I recd., per last mail, your letter of May 14th ult.— Let me answer, in the first place your request for payment of certain funds which I am owing you, as I know from experience how important such wants are. I shall leave here in the course of three or four weeks for Charleston S.C. when I will purchase, and send you from thence a bill of exchange either on London or Paris. I would send funds now for that purpose, but it is not in my power. At this season of the year I am always out, and am not in funds until the cotton crops come in, when I collect for most of my sales during the year. I can always though obtain a bank discount in September, on the strength of my coming shipments of cotton. I cannot say now exactly how much I will send you, but it shall cover all my dues at any rate, and if possible more. The steamers have so shortened the distance between the U. States and Europe that I hope to be able to have the funds in your hands by October 1st or early in that month. I certainly shall calculate on your return home as soon as you hear from me from Charleston. We have looked for you year after year until hope is nearly exhausted. You will find here warm hearts, to bid you welcome home, beating with love toward you, such as a brother and sister only can show. Should you come this fall you will find us all in Florida. Corinna still resides at Pensacola, Dr. Aldrich is doing a good practice there. Ellen and her family (3 children) are with her, but her stay there depends on the <u>war</u> in Mexico. Capt. Anderson is there fighting his best. He was in the "battle of Cerro Gordo" in Genl. [David E.] Twiggs command. Genl T. was in the hottest part of the battle. Most earnestly do I hope for the termination of the war. It is a disgrace to the United States, however glorious may seem the victories. It is a war of Mr. Polk's and if not ended sooner will end with his administration, which will as surely fall at the next election, as that the sun will set.

General [Zachary] Taylor seems to be the man now to whom all look for redemption from misrule and weakness; though I still hope for Henry Clay, my first, last, and only choice. You will be somewhat amused, should you ever venture your body in the Town of Newnansville. You will see in the person of your brother, how easy it is to transform a "Yankee" to a southern "Cracker" — Living in loghouses and eating "hog and hominy" transforms a person almost as soon as the light does the colour of a chamelion. Yet let the outward man change as it may, my <u>insides</u> are the same as when I last saw you, years, long years ago.

The crops in this country will be very large this season, abundant enough to supply all Europe, should it again be afflicted with short crops, as it was last year. So, you can tell your <u>empty</u> <u>gulleted</u> friends if any you have, that we can ram them full of Indian meal, and flour for the next eighteen months.

I will write you again soon. Let me hear from you often — though I trust our correspondence will soon cease by our being brought together.

affectionately your brother,
George L. Brown

On August 20, 1847, James Anderson was killed in Winfield Scott's final assault on Mexico City.[16] With mail cut off from Mexico, the family in Florida most likely first learned of Anderson's death from newspaper accounts. The loss of George's brother-in-law brought profound changes to his life as he, Edward, and Mannevillette committed themselves to Ellen and her children's support. In the spring of 1849, George provided his brother with an update on the family's activities in Florida:

[George L. Brown to Mannevillette E. D. Brown]
Newnansville [Florida, to Utica, New York]
April 5, 1849

My Dear Brother

I am much relieved by receiving your letter acknowledging the receipt of mine with the draft on New York. The long time your first letter remained here unanswered, during my absence in Charleston, together with the uncertainty of the mails <u>in</u> <u>Florida</u>, made me apprehensive that you would be longer without the needful than is comfortable.[17] I am pleased too to see that your good spirits have not deserted you. I hope you will go on flourishing; I know that you will do so as soon as you can <u>take</u> <u>root</u>. For many summers past I have promised myself a trip to New England, but have each succeeding summer given up the journey; I have now some inducement to go, and it is possible that I may drop down where you are sometime during the hot weather. I look forward with much pleasure to the time when we will meet again. I doubt if you would recognize in me the youth you left in Boston, years ago. Yet, in spite of southern miasma, and fever and ague, I still keep a little of the colour I carried in New England. I measure "five feet, ten and a half" and weigh a plum one hundred and fifty, and carry a big pair of whiskers.

I cannot advise you to come south before the Fall, not to Florida. Certainly in good time I will give you an idea how to penetrate into this wilderness. Corinna and Ellen are at present residing at Marietta, in the northern part of Georgia. My impression is that Dr. Aldrich will remove to Key West, a key or island on the Gulf side of the Florida coast famous for "wreckers" & containing some 1500 inhabitants, a sterile, dreary spot, depending for its maintenance entirely on the misfortunes of others—a good place however for a Physician.

I have rec'd letters from Corinna & Ellen since your return brimful of joy on the occasion. They want to fly to you. They too are changed although they have not grown much larger, nor do they wear whiskers, which makes the alteration less in their cases than mine — we are all indeed changed <u>outside</u>, but our "in'ards" are as trim as ever, still beating with strong brotherly & sisterly affection for you. Poor Ellen has met with much affliction in the loss of her husband in Mexico. Anderson was a noble and brave officer and a man in every walk of life. She has three little children pretty and interesting. I rec'd a letter from her little boy (about 6 years old) which reminded me of my futile efforts at letter writing to Aunt Ann when she resided at Great Falls. I saw one of them in her possession a year or two since and I rather think little "Willoughby" beats me in composition.

Florida as a residence is not a very desirable country, although I ought to speak well of my adopted state, for I have done better here probably than I would have done at the north. My business has prospered well up to 1847. The past year or so, though I have not

UNITED STATES MAIL.

Florida and Savannah packet, via Picola a, Black Creek, Mandarin, Jacksonville, St. John's Beach, St. Mary's, Brunswick, and Darien. Carrying the U. Mail to the above places.

The regular packet steamer St. Matthews, has been thoroughly overhauled, her decks and cabins rebuilt and handsomely furnished and painted, and her machinery much improved. As for accomodation and comfort, she cannot be surpassed by any boat on the route. This boat will arrive at Savannah every Thursday morning, before the departure of the daily line of steamers for Charleston, which leave every evening.

Also passengers wishing to take passage in the brig or barque line which leaves Savannah every Thursday and Saturday for New York, after the arrival of the St. Matthews from Florida.

Passengers, with their baggage, wil be put on board of either line, if required.

The above boat will leave as follows :
Leave Palatka every Tuesday a. m. 9 ool'k.

Passengers, with their baggage, wil be put on board of either line, if required.

The above boat will leave as follows :

Leave Palatka every Tuesday, a. m.		9	oel'k.
Picolata	"	" 11	"
Black Creek	"	p. m. 3	"
Jacksonville	"	night 12	"

For freight or passage, apply to Captain McNelty, on board, or to

WOOD & CLAGHORN,
Agents, Savannah.
FERNANDEZ & BISBEE.
Agents. Jacksonville.
JOHN H GUNBY,
Agent. Black Creek.
J. P. HAWKINS,
Agent, Palatka.

☞ The steamer Sarah Spalding, runs in connection with this boat, to Enterprize on Lake Monroe.

June 21, 1846.

LIVER COMPLAINTS, DYSPEPSIA

Figure 4.2. Steamers such as the *St. Matthews* carried the U.S. Mail. *Palatka Whig Banner*, July 7, 1846.

gone behind, still, the rapid decline in cotton in 1848 (thanks to the French revolution for that hit) with a large lot on hand, and the very low price this year has swept off all the profits, and given me the <u>cramp</u> in a delicate place — the pocket. I lost about 3000 dollars in 1848 — You are the only man however but myself that knows the fact. The prospects for the arriving season are very favourable, and with an unblemished credit in the market, and with a reputation with my creditors flattering to myself, I anticipate an increase to my prosperity. My assets far exceed my debts; the difficulty lies in realizing from my assets when I need them. I have no fears for the future after standing erect through the two past <u>hard</u> years.

I am an old Bachelor. I came very near being married year before last to a lady in Charleston, though <u>never</u> engaged. For reasons too lengthy to tell now, I backed out. When we meet I will "relate the story of my love." At present my ideas all centre on a single life, though I am not to be trusted if exposed to temptation. Wishing <u>you</u> well married with all the other blessings, I must "saw off." Communication having been opened with us, let us keep it so—

Truly, affectionately your Brother
Geo. L. B.

*   *   *   *   *   *

[George L. Brown to Mannevillette E. D. Brown]
Newnansville Fla [to Utica, New York]
June 3, 1849

My dear Brother:

The recent visit of Corinna & Ellen, and Dr. Aldrich, to New York appears to me something like a dream. I was apprehensive of their intended trip up to the time they reached Washington. A letter from Corinna from W was the first intimation I had of their absence from Georgia. I am really glad that they took the trip and only regret that I was not one of the party when you met at the Howard House. I would have enjoyed it well. I trust, however, that it will not be long, before I take a shake of your paw - - - I have not heard from the folks since they left New York, but presume by this they are at Key West. I wrote to them at that place last week, by way of my neighbour, who was on a journey thither. I have recently met with a Captain [Farnham

Z.] Tucker, a resident of Key West who spoke of the coming of Dr. Aldrich to reside with them as quite an event. He is well known (Dr. A) through Florida and enjoys deservedly an excellent professional reputation. Yet nature has implanted in him such a <u>roving</u> disposition that he has not made his talents as profitable as he could have done. I wish he had a dozen children; they would act like an anchor on him. Roving runs in Aldrich's family. His Brother, Louis Aldrich, my roommate here for some years, recently left Florida <u>for California</u>, abandoning a home where he commanded the good wishes of everyone, and a good law practice. Had he remained, he would in all probability have been one of the candidates for Congress next election. These inducements all failed to stop his propensity for a change. Save these faults, if faults they can be called, Dr. Aldrich and his brother also are as fine specimens of the genus "man" as one would wish to know, kind, generous, and polite, they have ever possessed my highest esteem. — — —

I am glad you have seen Ellen's interesting little family–they seem to give a promise that the race will not be extinct in the present generation. Losing their father, poor Anderson, cannot be made up to them, yet you and I, Heaven aiding us dear brother, will raise them up in the world, as he would wish them to have been raised. Before his death, I felt like an old bachelor who was satisfied to knock along through life, content if, when death called, I could square up with all and go. Now I feel these little children acting on me continually to heap up something where rust doth corrupt.[18] In short, I feel like a "man of family."

Times with us "are very tolerable and not to be endured" that is, they are very dull, but this is our <u>dull</u> season, and what we have, is just what we looked for during this summer. The late frosts so injurious to the cotton crops of So. Carolina & Georgia did not damage us to a serious extent. With good seasons, a continuation of such as we had had since the first, will give us our usual cotton picking in the Fall. We raise what is known as "Planter" or "main" cotton, a rather coarse or <u>long staple</u> worth now almost 15cts. per pound. This cotton I think stands cold weather better than the "green seed" or "upland" cotton.

The summer days in Florida are <u>damned</u> <u>hot</u>. I know no less emphatic way to speak of them. At this moment, notwithstanding a cold bath recently taken, I feel as a turkey is to feel on a roaster. With the day, however, ends the evil for our nights are invariably cool and pleasant. The change at sunset is very sudden—like going from upstairs to the cellar. You feel it all over!

I am shocked at the late riots in New York, sorry for the loss of life, yet I would have grieved still more had the civil authorities allowed the mob to rule. Better to have shot a thousand.[19]

I am pleased to see you in good spirits—may good luck attend you, give my best wishes to all who love you—write often.

Affectionately yr. brother,
George L. Brown

* * * * * *

[George L. Brown to Ellen Brown Anderson]
Newnansville [Florida, to Key West, Florida]
July 3, 1849

Dear Ellen,

Your letter of June 21st, and yours and Corinna's of an earlier date have all reached me. I am pleased to learn from the general tone of your letters that Key West is a tolerable place, and that there is some probability of your remaining some time. Mosquitoes, when too thick, are certainly very annoying, but could I exchange every flea that daily crawls and many are now "going it" over my "damnation body," for a mosquito flying around it, I should make them "jump at the chance" — A flea steals upon you ere you are aware, and when you put your finger on him, he has done his mischief and gone. A mosquito, on the contrary, heralds his approach and gives you a chance to carry into execution the threat of the bitten Irishman — "to knock the devil twice his length." Besides this advantage in the daytime, a good net secures you at night — so you see you have the advantage over us, as far as this "annoyance of bills" is concerned. Save the one complaint, Key West must be a pleasant summer residence. The rolling ocean, a sight I ever loved, and still wish for, is far more pleasant to me than the forest. No waving woods, or fruitful fields, can dim my hope that I may yet have a home by the sea-side.

I would give "a pound of flesh"[20] if I could feel this evening, tomorrow being the fourth of July — as I once felt in my juvenile

days on the near approach of the nation's birth day. I care little now
whether it brings a sunshine or a rainy day—nor could any amount of
crackers and squibs or rattails, burn they ever so brightly, now change
the dull current of my blood—We all feel alike here save one poor
fool Jimmy Pettit—do you remember him? He was once a soldier of
Anderson's. He watches for the coming day with all possible joy. He is
now at my elbow, begging some powder to salute me in the morning
with what he calls his blunderbush. Last 4 of July Jimmy got drunk
before breakfast, and went to sleep in the jam of some fence, and did
not awake till the day had nigh passed — it was a theme of self-accu-
sation for months — he vows he will not be caught so again.

I would like to see your little children — and I surely will as soon
as I can do so with a clear conscience. At present my business requires all my attention. I hope it will give me some playtime after a
while. Meantime it affords me much pleasure to know that they are
improving in mind and body — take much care of the first — everything depends upon a mother's watchfulness, and the impressions
now made upon them, and the lessons they learn will make or mar
their future happiness. If well trained, and cultured, they will prove
a fortune to you, the like of which a thousand Californias could not
yield.

Say to the Doctor that I have not heard from him since he left New
Orleans — he started from that City in the Steamer <u>Col</u>. <u>Stanton</u> on
the 5th of June. I may hear from him by tomorrow's mail — — I miss
Louis [Aldrich] very much, and would still if I kept up my Bachelor's
Hall. What once resounded with fresh play, and virtuous proceedings
is now a mere sleeping place of a Newnansville shop-keeper. I still
miss him in my daily walks and will until I am myself changed —
though I know not an enemy, I do not at the same time permit myself
to have many friends - he was one of the few I knew and put faith in,
and his loss cannot be replaced — May he make 10,000 $ a year — —

I have only time to reply to a part of Corinna's letter, where she
says that she hears I am to be married and ventures the young lady's
name. It is a mistake — some good meaning, but thick-headed person has imposed upon her — never listen to such things you hear of
me, for I promise whenever such an event takes place, you will not
only be the first to know of it, but my choice will be gladly welcomed
by you. New reports are often circulated about me, and arise from

the fact that I always pay much attention to females. I act towards the sisters of others, as I expect all men to act towards mine. Many stupid people, like your informer, don't and are not expected to have such qualities. Give my love to Corin, Edward, Virginia, Kiss your little ones for me.

Affectionately yours,
George L. B.

＊　＊　＊　＊　＊　＊

[George L. Brown to Corinna Brown Aldrich
and Ellen Brown Anderson]
Newnansville, Florida, [to Key West, Florida]
July 27, 1849

My Dear Sisters,

I have to send you a single letter for your double barreled epistle rec'd last mail (Friday Evening). My friend and fellow Bachelor, James A. Peden and myself sitting together that evening conversing with much good humour on the subject of matrimony, and had just come to the conclusion, with great laughter, that there probably were not two persons living who were less likely to be married soon, from all appearances, than ourselves & when my letters were handed to me, and I immediately opened and read yours and Ellen's. What a contrast between your opinion of my condition, and my own expressed not a moment before! You with all a sister's affection advising me to avoid forming a connection which would produce only unhappiness, and showing a lively fear lest your advice should be "too late"! And, I here, with my legs and feet stuck "a feet" above my head, with a segar in my mouth, and Peden by my side, not having a fancy or an affection for a single woman in creation (save you all)— Someone, my good sisters, has stuffed you with a story. There is no lady answering your <u>de-scription</u> here! Nor have I made advances to find fair form since my performance in Charleston long ago. In short to relieve any anxiety you feel on the subject I will say that I am not engaged to be married to any one, nor have I at this time the least notion who will be my future sleeping partner. When next you hear such news of me, listen to it, because it would be impolite not to, and no doubt the informer means well, but let the matter go out of your other ear and think no more of it. I would repeat what I said in a recent letter, "that in event I should engage myself, you will first hear of it from me["]— trust no floating stories, for during the past year, I have been engaged <u>according</u> to <u>report</u> to nearly every lady of my acquaintance — nor need you apprehend anything from my choice — I am passed[21] the day when a pretty face would be chiefly sought for. She, whoever she may be who is to share my lot through life, must have a <u>mind</u> — <u>this</u> <u>can</u> be found out before marriage. The temper, habits, & etc. of a lady are like the secrets of the Hall of Eblis,[22] only to be known when it is too late to retreat from the consequences. I could bear well with most any failing in a wife, save an empty head. I would take one as ugly as Parson Peabody and as big as Sheriff Oates, if she had the talents of the one and the good nature of the last, providing those qualities could not be obtained on other terms. I have not concluded to quit the world, and retire in this wilderness, and hope yet in my travels to light upon some damsel worthy to be loved, and to be loved by; but failing in this, I will be content to continue—

> "To pull my head like a terrapin, under the coverlid
> "Shivering & freezing by myself, all alone"—

A letter from "Mann" last mail — he was well, says he sent Edward a box . . . by steamer to Key West and requests me to advise you to that effect and to look out for the box.

We have some bad Indians news today. They have killed a Mr. [William] Barker at Indian River, and wounded Mr. [James] Russell the collector at Charlotte harbour — and broken up the Indian River settlement. Whether it is a small party only, or the beginning of another "war" I cannot yet say, as we only have the express news. I trust however that it will end by the apprehension and punishment of the rascals concerned.[23] Speaking of Indians do you remember "Old [John] Tucker" the parson, who used to appoint future preachings "the Lord willing and no Indian Scouts to go on." He was recently preaching in Levy County. He began the services by reading the hymn "How tedious and tasteless the hours, when Jesus no longer I see etc." "You will sing this hymn" said he "to common metre" and off started the congregation in full blast to "common metre." They had scarcely got half through the first line when Old Tucker barked out "A—stop! Stop a minit, I want to say something to you before I forget it. An old man living down near long pond has lost his plough mare. She is rather young, has a <u>blased</u>[24] face and two white feet. If any of the people hear of the mare and will let it be known, I will be much obleeged to 'em, the man is a poor man, and it will be an act of charity. Now you can go on with the Hymn!"

With much love to the Doctor, Miss Virginia,
the little ones and yourselves, I am
affectionately yours

George L. B.

Say to Edward I will write him soon (as usual). I sent Miss Congure the "man made of money" last mail.[25] Have not heard from Louis since he left New Orleans. I will hardly go north this season, would like to, but must stay at home. Mr. [John] Parsons, left here for Portsmouth last week, he almost "persuaded me to be a christian," that is, to go with him out of the wilderness, only I wrestled with my wishes and prevailed, and am here, G.L.B.

*   *   *   *   *   *

[George L. Brown to Mannevillette E. D. Brown]
Newnansville [Florida, to Utica, New York]
July 27, 1849

Dear Brother

I have seen your letter of July 11th. I really did not think so much time had passed since my last to you. It is not "cholera," nor "choleric" that has caused my pen to lay up, but calorie. This is not a warm region, it is hot! and this the hottest day I have felt the season through. How I wish I was with you, or at some down East place where I could smell and feel a fresh breeze. A more comfortable state of things exists towards Evening. One of my amusements here is shooting "bull-bats" on the wing—they are the same bird you know at the north called "night-hawks." They commence flying about an hour before sunset over and around the houses of the village, in considerable numbers, darting in every direction after the small flies and gnats. Myself and others, take our stations and pop away till dark. I kill about two birds of those shot, a good average on the wing — These bull bats are very fat, and taste like a nice bird — nice Eating—

This is summer shooting. In winter game is very abundant, and should you venture to Florida, you can indulge your old propensity to a full extent. Ducks, wild geese, and turkies are plenty, and not far to go for them. We also have a bird nearly like the wild pigeon, called the "field dove." They are not quite as large, but their habits, and plumage are the same. They flock during the months of Jan'y & Feb'y and afford fine sport. We only have to go to the fields in the neighborhood to find them by hundreds — Deer abound, but to me hunting them appears like hard work — as hunting and shooting is all the fun I can promise you, I thought I would enlighten you a little on the subject.

We are likely to have some shooting of a more serious sort. By express last evening we learn that the Indians have committed some outrages at Indian River, some 60 miles south of St. Augustine — they killed one man, and wounded another, Mr. Russell, the collector at Charlotte's Harbour. They then robbed the houses and done other mischief. All the settlers in that vicinity have abandoned their plantations. It is not known how many Indians were concerned. It may be the commencement of a "war," though we hope it is only a small party, whose conduct will be discountenanced by the chiefs — should they be discovered and given up the matter will end by their punishment; if not, much trouble will follow. Our citizens, have already formed an independent horse company to await the Governor's orders — I trust, if they do commence another war that "old Zachary" will send men enough to make a sweep of them. He knows the Indians well having exchanged invitations to "ball" with them at O-ce-cho-bee.[26] We will soon know what we are to have, and I presume that you will get the information as soon as I, through the papers. . . .[27]

I have just seen a gentleman from Key West. He left Corine & Ellen & the Doctor and all are well, says they are comfortably fixed and that the doctor will do well if he will remain settled. I hope he will.

I don't think I will see you this summer — I wish to come — would sacrifice a great deal to quit here for a month, but my business will not permit me. I hope to manage matters so the coming season that I may do as I please hereafter. We have good cotton crops, and with a fair price this fall I will make excellent collections. One of my neighbors, Major John Parsons, (born in Rye N. H.) late receiver of public monies, left here for <u>Portsmouth</u> last week. He made a dead set at me to start with him and I had a dozen minds on the subject before I decided that it would be impossible. We will certainly get together one of these days, because if I find in the course of time that I cannot come to you, I shall insist upon your journeying south. I will mention to Dr. Aldrich your shipment to him the first letter I write.

I enclose you a letter from Ellen's little boy to me, thinking you may not have rec'd a like Epistle. Speaking of "Boys" I have two negro women about my premises — one of them had a "boy" last week, and today the other is "in the straw" with another little "nigger." They are mine, though not <u>shoots</u> <u>from</u> <u>my</u> <u>root</u>, as they are as black as Egyptian darkness — A fine state of things for a bachelor's establishment![28]

—affectionately yours, George L. B.

*   *   *   *   *   *

[George L. Brown to Mannevillette E. D. Brown]
Newnansville, Florida [to Utica, New York]
Aug 12, 1849

My Dear Brother

In my last letter to you, I stated that we had in prospect another Florida "Indian War," and I supposed by this time, I should have a long list of bloody tales to relate, of "homes and plantations destroyed, and all their inhabitants murdered by the savages" — but to my surprise, and to the astonishment of all the "oldest inhabitants" — men tried in Indian warfare and knowing all their ways — no depredations have been committed since the first attacks at Pease Creek and Charlotte's Harbour. What the Indians intend to do;—whether the late barbarous acts were done by the whole tribe's consent, or only by a band of outlawed Indians under <u>Hapaltha</u>[29]; of these and other matters we are all in the dark. Our latest advice (yesterday) from the south left everything quiet — I apprehend, however, that the Indians will now have to go, or fight. <u>Gov.</u> [<u>William</u> <u>D.</u>] <u>Mosely</u>—<u>Our</u> <u>Governor</u>, has ordered, six companies of mounted volunteers, and some infantry, to serve for twelve months. These for the field, and Uncle Sam's "grey backs" for the Forts and posts—will make hot work for a while if the "Red Brethren" do not place themselves . . . . If they scatter and hide, we have another "seven year's war" before us, the result of which will be that the state of Florida as a residence will be about as comfortable as hell to a sinner. I hope the war will not be. If it comes, I shall, like a good dog, "growl and hold on."

The elements, as well as the Indians, are assisting to make <u>hot</u> work for us, for never during my residence south have I known the sun in August to pour down such intolerable rays. We used to have much rain by day, and cool breezes through the night. Now the "man of the weather" lets things get out of gear so, I don't understand but presume it is to benefit the cotton crop. The bolls under the influence of the sun ripen and burst open beautifully.

I have just heard a "good 'un." A friend at my elbow was speaking of a lady being in St. Mary's Ga, and remarked "that he knew her "like a book" — "like a book!" replies [James] Peden—a lawyer, "[then] you must have opened her!"

By last mail I rec'd letters from Ellen & Dr. Aldrich — they were all well — and the Mosquito nuisance abating. Did you see Miss Virginia Anderson? How would she do for a bed fellow? Not that I have any idea of straddling her at present, but surely want your opinion.

I feel pretty well today — the late cotton news, with the prospect of a <u>short</u> crop — no mistake this time — promising well for me—I sold some Florida cotton last week for 16 cents. 2 cents better than the same kind sold in July, our crops will not be so short, because we are so far south that the injury done by frost is not great. . . .

Affectionately yours,
George L. B.

❦ 5 ❦

"Wreathed in Perpetual Smiles"

(1850–1852)

AS THE NEW DECADE EMERGED, George Brown could look to the future with optimism. In 1849, Florida had produced its largest cotton crop ever, and with more and more acreage of Florida lands going into the production, there was every reason to believe that production and profits would grow as time went on. In 1850, about 2,100 of Florida's total output of roughly 181,000 bales reached the ports of Charleston and Savannah.[1] Although East Florida's cotton crop was miniscule compared with Middle Florida's, the potential for growth in the region was more pronounced, as were profits, because most of what East Florida produced was Sea Island cotton, which carried far higher prices.

According to a Jacksonville newspaper, "'better times' are evidently approaching. At no period within our recollections, have we witnessed the same . . . unmistakable evidences of prosperity, as those by which we are now surrounded." The St. Johns had come alive with traffic: "Numerous vessels, freighted with merchandise, crowd our waters, furnishing the necessary 'trade' for the rapidly increasing population, and carrying off in return our lumber, turpentine, sugar, cotton and tobacco. Our rich lands in the interior are 'filling up.'" The writer pointed to an increasing competition between Charleston and Savannah for the Florida trade.[2] The same journal noted a month or so later that since "perhaps over half of the products of East Florida will be made by native Carolinians who will naturally prefer a connection with Charleston to any other market out of state," Savannah should not take the Florida trade for granted.[3] Nor did elements in Charleston fail to appreciate the opportunities in the Florida market. Indeed, as the *Charleston Mercury* noted, "the fertile districts of Florida which find their outlet in the St. Johns. . .[are] rapidly filling up with an industrious and enterprising population, a large portion of which is from our own state, and the trade and travel, already considerable, is rapidly increasing, and will furnish a considerable addition to our articles for export in its cotton, sugar, tobacco, and fruit, which will be paid for in the dry goods, hardware, &c. of our storekeepers."[4] George no doubt appreciated these facts. As he prospered, his stature as a respected member of the business community continued to grow. On October 11, 1849, he was elected an Alachua County commissioner, polling second in a race that included fourteen candidates. On January 14, 1850, he and fellow commissioners John B. Standley, Samuel B. Colding, Charles Fitchett, and David Mizell authorized that a new courthouse be built on the public square in Newnansville on the same plan as the one that had been built in Columbia County. After receiving proposals for construction of the new structure, George and the other commissioners selected Samuel W. Burnett's bid.[5] With the military presence now practically nonexistent, the commissioners understood that the town's continued viability depended upon its status as a county seat. Even though by 1850 the town boasted its second hotel, the Galpin House, there were already signs that the town's importance as a frontier crossroads was diminishing. Even so, few took much notice of the fact. When the court was in session, the town was full of visitors, and business activity quickened. That January, town folk witnessed a sensational murder trial at the courthouse, in which three men had been concerned in the murder of Ocala planter Elliotson Mobley.[6] Also residents debated the merits of congressional candidates Edward Cabell (Whig) and John Beard (Dem.), who themselves debated the merits of the compromise bills before Congress.[7] Running simultaneously with the political hustings, the town hosted a Methodist Church revival. According to Rev. John M. Hendry, the sixteen-day event "resulted in an accession of forty-eight whites and one colored to the church."[8]

The new decade also brought many changes to the Aldrich and Anderson families, even as George continued his mercantile operation in Newnansville. The loss of James Anderson weighed heavily on Ellen and her three children, who remained in the Aldrich household in Key West,

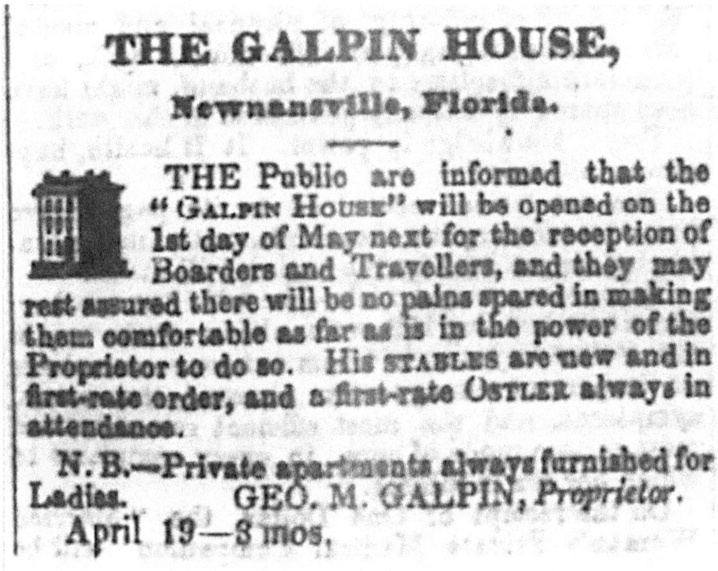

THE GALPIN HOUSE,
Newnansville, Florida.

THE Public are informed that the "GALPIN HOUSE" will be opened on the 1st day of May next for the reception of Boarders and Travellers, and they may rest assured there will be no pains spared in making them comfortable as far as is in the power of the Proprietor to do so. His STABLES are new and in first-rate order, and a first-rate OSTLER always in attendance.

N. B.—Private apartments always furnished for Ladies.   GEO. M. GALPIN, *Proprietor*.
April 19—3 mos.

Figure 5.1. The Galpin House, along with Zilphia Standley's boardinghouse, was one of two hotels in Newnansville by the 1850s. *Jacksonville Republican*, May 17, 1849.

where they had been since the summer of 1849. George's increasing prosperity put him in a position to offer financial support to his grieving sister and her children—and he did.

> [George L. Brown to Ellen Brown Anderson]
> [Newnansville, Florida, to Key West, Florida]
> January 26, 1850

Dear Ellen,

I acknowledge, if it will better the matter, that I am a very mean sort of a fellow, for not writing you more frequently, but it is a fixed fact that I am a tardy correspondent, nor do I hope for any improvement in this respect. You will probably get a longer letter from me today than usual for the reason that I am laid up today with a sprained ankle, brought about by rather too extensive an attempt at activity. Lady Ambition as well as height, has its bitter end, and had I been content to pass for an ordinary jumper my left foot would now look less like an attack of the gout, and not feel as bad as it does. Save this halt in my health I have a very hearty survival to look upon.

I will attend to your wants, and let you know what the fixing cost if you will be curious. This, and any other thing I can do for you in Charleston or Savannah will not only be done cheerfully, but having something to do for you will be more satisfactory than for me to reflect that I could serve you and lacked the opportunity because you would not ask me.

I have not been neglectful of the various suggestions about what you wished to do for yourself in your last letters. If I had been silent upon the subject it is because I knew the plans that I would suggest to you would differ from your own. It is time however that I should say something, and I will give you my candid advice and assistance. I approach the matter though, with much hesitation — You say that you are dissatisfied with Key West as a place of residence, and that you are desirous to do something somewhere for your support. Now as to your first wish, we must decide where you will go. I could never consent to allow you and your children to live at Newnansville. I love you and them too much to entertain such a thought. I wish them to grow up in health and wisdom–and here they must fail to have either. Your life would be a life of care and dullness.–I will do better than bury you here if life is spared me. I have thought that I would write to Manne and ascertain how much it would cost for you to live in your own house at Utica. What kind of place it was for a home–and get his opinion of the same. I also thought you might like to live at Portsmouth N.H. and there raise your children and find them men and women when they get to the age of manhood–or I have thought you might select your residence in any Northern town or village, where you could find good health, good schools, and good people. My preference would be one of the first named places.

Now as to the means of support I know how you feel, and your great desire to be independent. I don't blame you for this, and when you get fixed to suit you, if you will do this or that, you can, but my dear sister, here again I must differ from you. I wish to furnish the means required myself. I can do it, and will do it, if you will let me. Nor is it any great act for a brother to perform. You have only to decide what you will do,—where you will go,—and I will see to all the rest. Let me hear from you about my notions.

One thing remains. I am most decided. Do not think again of settling here. I would be glad to see you, still better would I like to

live where you may live. But when I think of the mere possibility of
the turns of fortune bringing you to this wretched hole for a place to
live, I lose all patience, and I am sure that–to send so dread a calamity to you and your little family, I would fairly quit this place forever.
Do not think I write without reflection. It is for your happiness that
I speak so I may not be mistaken. I think much about you Ellen
and a day seldom passes but you and yours are part of my thoughts.
Wrapped up here in a business that confines me to constant petty
occupations, I am illy fitted after the day's work to place my thoughts
to paper, and the convenient "next mail" offers a ready put off. You
now know my wishes regarding yourself and it remains with you to
act upon them. I can only say that to any and every proposal of your
own, save the one I have railed so against, I will give my constant
attention and assistance. My offers are warm from the heart and you
will find them cheerfully performed—God Bless you, George L. B.

Say to Edward that Jno. Sanchez rec'd a letter from Louis last
mail from the diggings. Louis & Roman Sanchez were digging gold
and doing about as well as their neighbors—his letter was far from
encouraging although they had hopes of better "washing." What a
bubble California is! And what a burst will take place in a year or
two!! Give my love to Edward & Miss Virginia. I will try and see you
all this spring if you are get-at-able. G. L. B.

On March 21, Corinna wrote to Mannevillette from Key West that her
husband was moving the family temporarily to St. Marys, Georgia, and
that Ellen and her children would join them while Edward explored opportunities in California. St. Marys was Edward's birthplace and his father
and other relations were in the area. Corinna was pleased that George
could make frequent visits on his way back and forth from Charleston:
"Edward has promised, if we go to St. Mary's, to get us a house & we will
ship from here our bedding & such articles of furniture etc. as is advis-
able." Corinna would travel to New York with Edward to see "him comfortably off." Corinna explained that she would get whatever things they
need in New York and that George had promised to supply them with
groceries from Charleston.[9] Ellen and Corinna's stay in St. Marys turned
out to be brief. From the beginning of their time there, they seemed to
be dissatisfied with the place—their brief residence with Edward's family

did not go well. By the end of the year, the sisters had decided to move to
New York City.

[George L. Brown to Mannevillette E. D. Brown]
Newnansville, Fla [to Utica, New York]
April 22, 1850

Dear Mann:

I leave here today for St Mary's Ga to see Ellen and make some arrangements for her future comfort. I expect she will probably settle
at St. Mary's for a while. You no doubt have heard from Corinna
that Dr. Aldrich had decided on a trip to California. In fact they are
now on their way to New York to take a steamer for San Francisco.
Corinna will return after Edward's departure to the South. At least, I
presume she will. This state of affairs, Manne, will prevent me from
rendering you any funds at present. The money I would have sent
you, must go to Ellen. I am determined she shall not work as long as
I can help it. I will take care of her and her children until your affairs
enable you to do your part, which I know you will cheerfully do as
soon as the world wags well with you. In addition if any accident
should happen to Aldrich, and he is bound on an uncertain journey,
Corinna will claim our <u>protection</u>.

   You will see them both in N. York and I envy them the pleasure
they will enjoy in your company. I had made every arrangement to
go <u>north</u> this summer, and I intended to take you by surprise, but
this California move has upset all my plans and forced me to save the
pennies I planned to scatter in New England.

   I have said that I could not furnish you any funds from the forego-
ing circumstances, but should you <u>need</u> them let me know and I will
do what I can for you - I have <u>means</u> but not money. The business I
do keeps me well <u>cramped.</u>

   Let me hear from you oftener. I cannot interest you with Florida
news, but news <u>from</u> New York is always acceptable.

I am affectionately
Your brother,
G. L. B.

*   *   *   *   *   *

[George L. Brown to Mannevillette E. D. Brown]
Newnansville [to Utica, New York]
August 18, 1850

Dear Brother,

I haven't heard from you for a coon's age save through Corinna and Ellen. Where are you and why don't you write me? I had laid out my plans to visit New York this summer and pass a month or two in New England to refresh myself with pure air and hunt up the scenes and companions of old. But my fate prevents the consummation. Business chains me to the oar and I must tug away be it summer or winter, hot or cold. Perhaps it is well that I have not left Florida. The pleasure of a summer at the North is I am well aware, only by anticipation. I remember, and would look to find, (albeit against any good sense) Portsmouth & Boston & Philadelphia the same, and find the same people as I left them. I should be disappointed, and gladly hasten back to the land of Hammocks. As things are, I feast myself upon the joys of a summer's day until the time arrives, and then I philosophize in the above vein, making myself very contented. Now, a trip to you, brother, would be another affair, and when you can spare the time, just pack up and make for this section, and I will show you some things not to be seen in Yankee land nor Europe.

How do you get on and how are your friends? I wrote you in my last that my increased expenses were such that I could not help you. Still you can always tell me your conditions, and sometime or another, I hope to have the amount for your wants.

Ellen claims you know artists at Bridgeport, Conn. They give a favorable account of the place and I trust will continue to have. I wish Ellen's little family to live where they can have health, and chances of a good education, but one of these small towns is far preferable to New York or any of the larger cities.

I keep in good health and intend to be a "stout individual." I was cut out for a big-bellied citizen, and would show a respectable corpulence was my wardrobe a city one, where I could get my fill of Roast Beef & other solids. Here, "Pork and grits" and the like keep my ribs from expanding–I have the frame for an alderman but will have a lean "Cassius" look as long as I stick to "Alachua" diet.[10]

You wrote me of being married. I have a notion of the kind myself! When it would be I cannot say. My <u>flame</u> is now in the upper part of Georgia, in <u>tolerable</u> bad health, and it will be some time, if ever, I jump into such a state–state matrimonial, I mean, not state of Georgia. Should such be the case, one of these days and with the lady I have selected, I will furnish you with a very loveable sister-in-law— Not pretty, but kind, affectionate, and one to mean well, with the manners and feelings of a lady—Let me hear from you and believe me

Very truly your brother,
George L. B.

*   *   *   *   *   *

[George L. Brown to Mannevillette E. D. Brown]
Newnansville Fla [to Utica, New York]
October 22, 1850

Dear Brother:

I have to day written to Ellen and Corinna stating to them that sometime in December (partly waiting their movements) I expected to take to myself a wife! And that if they had concluded to come south this winter that I would be glad to see them here in time to witness my <u>absorption</u>. And that I intended to write to you, and ask you to come south with them if your affairs permitted. I can only say, once married, that if you can conveniently come I would be glad to see you. It is a long time since we met and probably this will be the only chance for years to come. Still, however great the pleasure might be to both of us, I cannot ask you to make too great sacrifices for this purpose. I know your purse is light, and that the trip will be expensive. Could I offer you some professional inducements here I would not hesitate to be urgent - you might get some work - I could get you to paint the mugs of myself and my girl and that might stir up others to do the same thing.

If you can, write to sisters about it and come together. If your purse interferes with your decision your draft on Messrs. Boston & Gunby[11] of Savannah to be charged to me will be duly honoured. I have written in a former letter to you that my many outgoes in the way of cash kept my finances at rather low tide. I do not mean by that that my supply was entirely cut off, or that I had not a ready hand and heart for you whenever there was <u>need</u> of my assistance, let me hear from you, and I would repeat I should be heartily glad to see you.

I have little else to write that would interest you. I heard from Edward Aldrich last week. He was settled at San Francisco but I do not think he will stay there. I would not be surprised to see him home at any day.

I was in Charleston last month and took a spell of the "Broken Bone" fever, an epidemic prevailing at the time. It screws a man up like a thousand vices. I was considerably under the weather, but have come out and am now as well as usual, which is well enough.

A recent move was made to annex a part of one of the adjoining counties to this. One of the residents of the former refused to join the petition for annexation because he considered Alachua County <u>sickly</u>! Much of intellect!

With many good wishes I am affectionately yr. brother

George L. Brown

Matilda Stewart, George's fiancée, was the twenty-two-year-old daughter of Daniel M. and Eliza Stewart of Columbia County. Matilda's father (born in 1791) was descended from the prominent Georgia Revolutionary War general Daniel Stewart, who had married Eliza Eichelberger in Glynn County, Georgia, in 1824; they had eleven children.[12] The Stewarts migrated to Florida from Camden County, Georgia, in 1845, just after the birth of their youngest child, and established the Liberty Bluff plantation at the confluence of the Santa Fe and Suwanee Rivers, approximately forty miles from Newnansville. In 1850, the Stewarts owned more than eighty slaves and, with more than $34,000 in assessed property, were the wealthiest family in Columbia County.[13] Despite their wealth, violence and death assailed the Stewarts. Two of Matilda's brothers, Daniel and George W., served in Robert G. Livingston's volunteer company (Daniel as second in command and George as corporal.) Daniel Stewart died in Vera Cruz at the age of twenty-two on November 3, 1847.[14] Matilda's father died on January 8, 1848. Then, on May 9, 1850, twenty-four-year-old William Stewart died unexpectedly at the Stewart plantation.[15] When Matilda

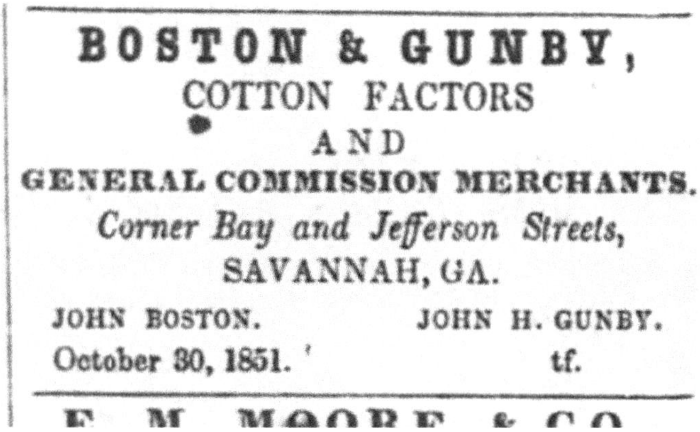

BOSTON & GUNBY,
COTTON FACTORS
AND
GENERAL COMMISSION MERCHANTS.
Corner Bay and Jefferson Streets,
SAVANNAH, GA.

JOHN BOSTON.   JOHN H. GUNBY.
October 30, 1851. '   tf.

Figure 5.2. Boston & Gunby, Cotton Factors and General Commission Merchants in Savannah frequently handled George Brown's
credit and financial transactions. *Jacksonville Republican*, April 29, 1852.

married George, the widowed Eliza Stewart was forty-six years of age and
lived with her eight children at the Liberty Bluff plantation.[16]

It is uncertain how George and Matilda met, but newspaper notices
list Louis Aldrich as Eliza's attorney in settling Daniel Stewart's estate.
George might have accompanied Louis to the Stewart plantation, or there
may have been a chance meeting of the two in Newnansville. Whatever
the circumstances, George married into one of the richest families in East
Florida.[17]

Funds from George gave Corinna, Ellen, and her children the opportunity to attend the wedding and enjoy an extended stay at the Stewart
plantation. No letters that George might have written in 1851 survive,
but several of his sisters' extant letters describe the wedding, the Stewart
plantation, and the family, and the sisters comment on the experience of
returning to Newnansville. Unfortunately, Mannevillette could not join
them in Florida, but in the letter below, Ellen provides him with a vivid
picture of the event:

January 11, 1851
[Ellen Brown Anderson to Mannevillette E. D. Brown]
Newnansville [Florida, to Utica, New York]

My Dear Mann:

I am in doubt whether I should date my letter at Felicity, Paradise, or
the Garden of Eden, but certainly I feel as if some such uncommon

caption should be at the head of the chapter. George is, if we may judge from appearance, in a state very uncommon to a man, viz. in a state of abundant satisfaction. His face is wreathed in perpetual smiles. His lady is an amiable, cheerful, and altogether very loveable person. Her name is Matilda.

Mrs. Matilda's family connections are among the most highly respectable in the Southern country and among her near relatives, her mother and brothers and sisters, there is not an unsound heart or head in the lot. You may depend, that is no small item in a man's comfort in getting married. I suppose you will be getting married next, and I hope I may take as great a fancy to your bride and her folks, as I have to George's and hers.

Neither Corine nor I have written to you, I think, since we left New York, and indeed we have been so situated that it would have been quite a task to have done so. But you could hardly comprehend this unless you had been here to see. When Corine and I arrived at Mrs. Stewart's (which is about three days before the wedding), we (figuratively speaking) rolled up our shirt-sleeves and commenced making ourselves part of the family. Mrs. S. resides on a plantation in the country, a day's ride from Newnansville, which is the most get-at-able place in the vicinity. Of course all guests have to make her house their home, and of course all those who came to the wedding had to be there all the time, and truly they seemed in more hurry to come than to go; for they all stayed until the bride and groom left which was three days after the wedding, and I did not leave then. I remained with Mrs. Stewart another week and tried my best to soften her the pain of a parting daughter. Last Friday I came in town, and since then have done nothing but entertain company until today. Today we have had our calls, but as the weather is unpleasant and as the folks have all come who are to come I think I shall get through my epistle and tomorrow being mail day I shall send it off. . . . George has come home to his dinner and is hugging his cara sposa,[18] and I have threatened to tell you how they behave, if it is only to make your mouth water. . . .

Corine, Matilda, and George have gone to dance. They have two a week here, regularly. I have not been to any yet, although I sometimes feel tempted, as I am very fond of the exercise of dancing, and do not believe there is any harm in it. On the contrary I think it beneficial. .

. . George has some very pleasant associates here in the shape of gentlemen, but the ladies, as usual, in these remote places, are not very promising. So Corine and I rise up into distinguished belleships. I really think we could get a beau apiece if we were marketable. Matilda has a sister [Adelaide] who takes my fancy, but she is too young for you being only ten years old, but the time is coming when she will give somebody the heartache. . . .

Yours, Ellen M. A.

In the two letters below, Corinna provides her own perspective on Liberty Bluff and on being back in Newnansville.

[Corinna Brown Aldrich to Mannevillette E. D. Brown]
February 1, 1851
Newnansville [Florida, to Utica, New York]

Dear Mann:

I sent you per express, my very Dear Brother, about three weeks since a little pine box, containing two slices of the wedding cake. . . . I should have written you at the time, but it was next to impossible. . . . We have come to no positive determination as yet [about where we will settle]. That is, Ell & I. I will tell you what we think may happen. To begin from the present, George will in a few days leave for Charleston to purchase his usual spring goods. He will be absent two or three weeks, and that time we have all (his wife, whose name is Matilda, Ell and her retinue, with myself) promised to spend with old Mrs. Stewart, about thirty-eight miles from here on the Santa Fe River. One of the most lonely and desolate places on Earth & but for the family which is large and interesting, I would not live there a week for "a pretty" as the children say. Indeed I think they would be glad to move, but have a large force of negroes, and the planting must be done. Mrs. Stewart has offered the plantation for sale, and may find a fool big enough to purchase, since her husband was so far attracted by its fine hunting grounds as to redeem it from the wilderness! Although you, I fancy, would scarcely think that much done! And my dear brother, one should come to a new country once, if but to appreciate the comforts of the old. Although cultivated in mind, and heart, the larger portion of such communities in the arts, and even necessaries of life, are barely civilized. I never was greatly attracted to Newnansville, but after travelling through Florida, I returned to my old log cabin with great satisfaction. George has kept everything in good order & even, much improved the grounds. But although the trees I planted are bearing fruit, the nurseries grown to orchards, and clips from an armbouquet[19] grown to large bushes, still it looks like home to me, and brings to mind the days of 'lang syne.' In this house I first assumed a matron's cares; here I first learned that, which, possibly has been of more service to me, than any practical knowledge obtained in the wide circle I have since ranged; and this the knowledge of housekeeping. I think I may add, the most important lesson of an America woman's life. One she must learn voluntarily, or by bitter experience. I know of no sure worthy object of our sympathy with a young housekeeper. Only those who have passed the ordeal, however can feel for them. Ah how many a sweet temper has been soured, how many a cheerful spirit broken by the daily troubles, the continual vexations of an inexperienced housekeeper —

And what is all this about you ask? & well you may dear; but I have been led inadvertently into the subject from association. Ell & I talk of little else when alone. We are all here, but E. & I are not comfortable, far from it. Not but George would do anything for us & his wife is very amiable, almost too amiable if such can be. The servants are at fault. They have long had their own way. We don't like to complain. It is not our place. I worked until my hands were like claws (but what can avail against bad servants). I saw it was useless. I argued with Matilda. She sees the evil, but is unwilling to pursue the only cause to set matters straight — That is to lay the matter before George, ship the darkies and begin with a new set. She has negroes and could easily do it, but puts it off. We at last concluded if we were out of the way, she would have to tell G. her troubles, and I believe, he would at once set all right. So Ell has made an agreement to remain with Mrs. Stewart, and teach her younger children, until spring, for our own and her children's board. Then, if she chooses she can either quit, or claim a salary. Until then I shall visit about. I have promised a week around to all my old friends. Occasionally I shall come & stay with George and Matilda to see how they get on, making it headquarters, you understand. And in that time, I am in hopes Matilda will get through her trials, get over her squeamishness, and having a little experience will get under full sail. Gladly would I keep house for her, if I thought it would be agreeable. But I don't think it would. In May, if I live, I shall go to New York, and if Ell concludes to stay at Mrs. Stewart's for the balance of the year, I may go on to California and Edward. And if after I get there, we deem it wise to remain, I shall go to housekeeping & send for Ellen & the little ones. But all this is open to further consideration. . . . Now I must close. I will write you punctually hereafter dear. God bless you. Ever your fond sister, Cora.

*   *   *   *   *   *

[Corinna Brown Aldrich to Mannevillette E. D. Brown]
March 10, 1851
Liberty Bluff [Florida, to Utica, New York]

My Dear Brother:

You must not blame me that you have not received an answer to yours containing the draft for 50 dollars, earlier. It was received from Newnansville in company with one advising him of your having sent it, last evening. I am still here in the woods—40 miles from any Post Office and it being planting time—tis next to impossible to send to town—George sent a boy out on foot yesterday, and by him I return this & such other letters as I have time to scribble, to the Office at Newnansville. It is a great source of vexation to me to be so situated, no matter how important my letter may be, it is only by chance I can reply! You will say, why stay here? Well, you know, I don't like to be ugly—I came while George went to Charleston, because it seemed the wish of all that I should & now I can't get away. I did go in town with Mrs. Stewart three weeks since, but was obliged to return. When George returned he came via Alligator, and took his wife with him next day—promising to send for me in a few days—Two weeks have now elapsed and here I am. If I could hire a vehicle to take me in I would but no such thing is to be had—so I must bide my time—patiently if I can. . . .

Ell's children are smart and pretty and I am sorry you did not make a paint sketch of them, when in N.Y. If you should fall in with them again—you must not fail. . . . I shall leave them this summer because it seems for the best. But I shall not remain long away from them if I go to California—I shall either send for them or hasten my return & if I do not go, I shall return to wherever they are this winter. I shall probably go to Newnansville in another week. . . .

It should not surprise me if George & his lady should take a trip North this summer—But he is a man of few words, it is impossible to find out what his intentions are—I never knew his like, for secretiveness. He took the right pledge when he became a mason!

The two Mrs. Stewarts are just come home & I must hurry. I wish they had waited a little. . . . Ell & and the little ones are gone to school. They have a log cabin, about a furlong from the house right among the Pine trees, where the young ideas are sown, and cultivated. You ask if they grow—I used to think them large until they were among this giant race! Now they seem small—Georgia is not as large as Mrs. Stewart's youngest daughter [Mary] who "they say" is younger than Villette. . . .

All send much love—Adieu, ever yrs, Cora

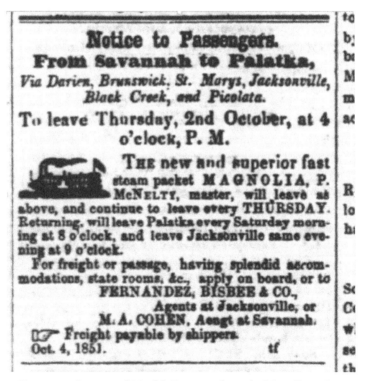

Figure 5.3. George and Matilda Brown rode on the *Magnolia* in 1851. *Jacksonville Florida News*, October 4, 1851.

(a)

(b)

Figure 5.4. George Long (a) and Matilda Stewart
Brown (b) about the time of their wedding in 1852.
Courtesy Elizabeth Traynor.

In April, Ellen and Corinna left Alachua County for New York City. George, Matilda, and her sixteen-year-old brother, James, accompanied them as far as Charleston, and then they were back in Jacksonville on board the <u>Magnolia</u> by May 4.[20] For the next two and a half years, Ellen's and Corinna's lives in New York would be consumed with providing for the children and looking after their educational needs. Edward's progress in making a place for them in San Francisco was also of primary concern. Ellen and Corinna's living arrangements were unsettled, as they moved frequently from boardinghouse to boardinghouse. George (in Newnansville), Mannevillette (in Utica), and Edward (in San Francisco) continued their financial support—even as they strategized about how to bring the family together. No doubt the strains of this existence wore on Ellen and Corinna. As Ellen commented to her brother Mannevillette not long after they arrived in New York City, "The uncertainty of life is proverbial, but, I think, the uncertainty of our lives beats the proverb."[21] Each sister coped with this stress in her own way. Ellen's outlet was her children and her writing. Corinna, as events will show, coped with her loneliness in ways that would ultimately lead to her undoing.

❧ 6 ❧

"Picking Steadily Along"

(1852–1857)

When George and Matilda began their life together in Newnansville, the county seat was still the most significant inland community in East Florida. However, few who packed the new courthouse on September 14, 1852, to hear Whig gubernatorial candidate George T. Ward and Democratic candidate for Congress Augustus Maxwell debate the issues—local, state, and national—would have realized that their "city in the wilderness" would soon face a series of challenges. Both Ward and Maxwell lost their elections.[1] Within four years, Newnansville would lose its status as a county seat and the Alachua County commissioners would order that the courthouse be sold at auction.[2] George probably did not attend the proceedings that day. He had business affairs to attend to. Sea Island cotton was selling at its highest price ever: forty-two and a half cents a pound.[3]

Although Newnansville's prospects were on the decline, East Florida was poised to grow and prosper. Newcomers from nearby states, but mostly South Carolina, were pouring in. This immigration, according to one source, "added to the capital and productive industry of the country." There was no question, according to this commentator, that this growth and prosperity were dependent on slave labor: "These newcomers belong principally to the class of planters owning small gangs of Negroes [who are] accustomed to the management of their own plantations [and] devoting their personal supervision to their crops." These "respectable and experienced agriculturists . . . bring with them the disposition to improve the country and to aid in the development of its resources." They "erect churches and establish schools . . . build better houses, put up cotton gins and saw mills. . . . We are principally indebted to South Carolina for this class of emigrants and shall welcome all who will come and cast their lot with us. Their principles are all firm and unyielding whether it be in religion, morals, or politics." The progress made since the dark days of the Second Seminole War was breathtaking: "The old battlegrounds are now ploughed fields and the tassel of the green Maize is now seen in place of the plumes of the warriors. A few years and a dense population will cover the Indian hunting grounds and the Indian war will be a legend of the distant past."[4] The message was clear: East Florida's growth and prosperity depended on slavery.

Charleston's two leading newspapers, the *Mercury* and the *Courier*, often reported on opportunities that East Florida offered even as they looked on with ambivalence at the exodus of some of their most productive citizens. Indeed, the opportunities that East Florida offered to planters were obvious. On November 21, 1853, the *Mercury* reported, "For many years the tendency of an energetic and thriving portion of our population has been to plant itself upon the virgin fields of Florida—The infusion of Carolina population has been so considerable as to form a very important element in its growth, and to have produced a corresponding tendency to form commercial connections with Charleston. . . . [A] tide of settlers is now pouring [into Florida] such as we are sorry to lose, but Florida may be proud to gain."[5] J. W. Bryant, a correspondent to the *Courier*, writing from Welaka, extolled the prospects for growing sugarcane on the lands along the St. Johns River. Long staple cotton would also bring huge profits. Corn, cow peas, pumpkins, cabbages, and sweet potatoes sold along the river brought higher prices than anywhere else. In short, Florida "presents many advantages over any other State in the Confederacy, even now, and as population increases, and the enlightened emigrants who are coming into the State influence its political, moral, and religious economy, we may confidently hope to see it, before many years, the most desirable for social life and lucrative employment." In a direct reference to the institution of slavery, Bryant continued, "There is marked difference between the population which is now filling up Florida, and that which stocks the Western States. Here we have chiefly Southern men who have property . . . and Southern sentiments."[6] As Bryant noted on another occasion, "To Charleston, East Florida is justly becoming a district of much commercial importance. The character of her produce is adapted to the Charleston market, and the sympathy between the two places is strong, from the circumstance of so many of Florida's best citizens being emigrants from South Carolina."[7]

By the 1850s, relations between George Brown and prominent men of commerce in Charleston were well established, and these relations included the buying and selling of slaves. Whether George ever visited the slave mart of Ziba Oakes, Charleston's preeminent slave dealer, on Chalmers Street is unknown, but his letters addressed to Oakes offer evidence of frequent commercial relations with the dealer on behalf of himself or prominent planters in Alachua County. Like Brown, Oakes was a New Englander, having been born in Maine in 1806. In 1817, Oakes's father brought his family to Charleston, where he became a successful grocer and merchant. After acquiring a good education, Ziba Oakes joined his father in business and by 1850 was a broker and auctioneer at his office at 7 State Street.[8] By that time, Oakes's primary endeavor involved buying and selling slaves. Oakes's trade was conducted primarily in South Carolina and Georgia, but by the early 1850s his commercial contacts reached into Florida, and George Brown dealt with him often. On one occasion, Brown wrote to Oakes that he wished to "buy one negro Boy, Black, aged about 18 to 20 years, stout and hearty, suitable for the plough; also one negro girl aged 17 or 18 for house and farm work. With or without a child—If you have negroes of the above ages and such as you can recommend please advise me of the prices, and if it would suit you to take" a note "for the amount at 4 <u>months.</u> Money will not be very plenty with us until we get cotton to market. Let me hear from you at your earliest convenience."[9] Surviving correspondence between George and Ziba Oakes suggests that George's frequent trips to Charleston often included visits to Oakes's establishment. These visits strengthened social and economic ties between the South's most sophisticated city and its southernmost developing frontier.[10]

Every month, it seemed, more and more steamers entered the St. Johns River. In 1853, the *Jacksonville Florida News* reported, "We have now four regular mail boats arriving and departing every week, from and to Savannah and Charleston, besides two river boats which ply regularly every week between Jacksonville and the upper Lakes of the St. Johns."[11] About that time, the *Florida* and the *Carolina* were introduced to the river. While the *Carolina* was the larger vessel at 176 feet long and 30 feet wide, the

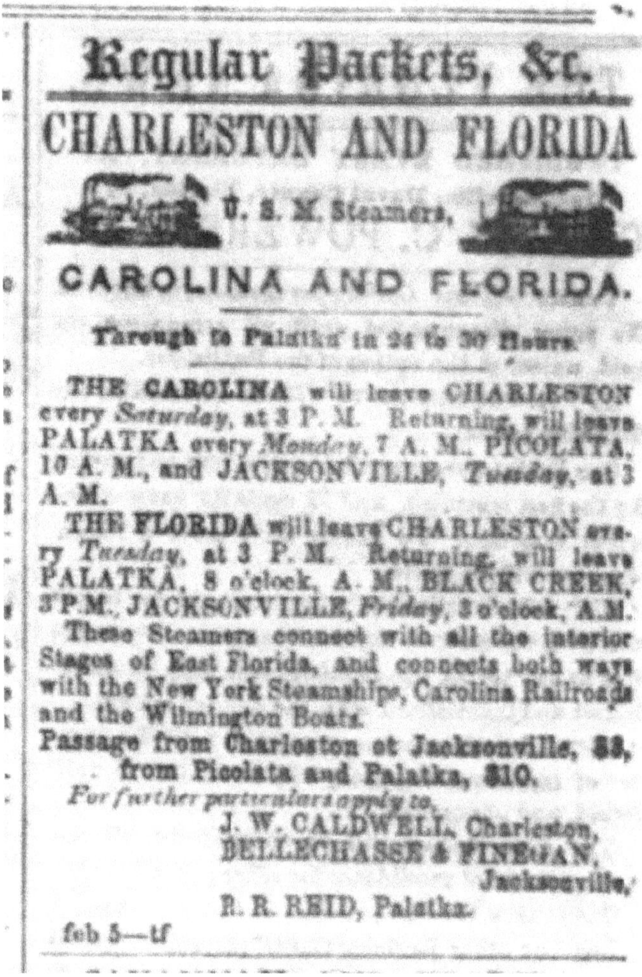

Regular Packets, &c.

CHARLESTON AND FLORIDA

U. S. M. Steamers,

CAROLINA AND FLORIDA.

Through to Palatka in 24 to 30 Hours.

THE CAROLINA will leave CHARLESTON every *Saturday*, at 3 P. M. Returning, will leave PALATKA every *Monday*, 7 A. M., PICOLATA, 10 A. M., and JACKSONVILLE, *Tuesday*, at 3 A. M.

THE FLORIDA will leave CHARLESTON every *Tuesday*, at 3 P. M. Returning, will leave PALATKA, 8 o'clock, A. M., BLACK CREEK, 3 P.M., JACKSONVILLE, *Friday*, 3 o'clock, A.M.

These Steamers connect with all the interior Stages of East Florida, and connects both ways with the New York Steamships, Carolina Railroads and the Wilmington Boats.

Passage from Charleston at Jacksonville, $8, from Picolata and Palatka, $10.

For further particulars apply to

J. W. CALDWELL, Charleston,
BELLECHASSE & FINEGAN, Jacksonville,
R. R. REID, Palatka.

feb 5—tf

Figure 6.1. By the 1850s, regular steamship service linked Black Creek with Charleston. George Brown rode on the steamship *Carolina* in 1856. *Jacksonville Florida News*, October 22, 1853.

Florida was more convenient to George and Matilda because it landed once a week at Black Creek, and from there passengers could reach Jacksonville and Charleston, where they could board steamers bound for New York. The *Florida*'s captain was Charles Willey, "who has always been and always will be successful, as he has been for twenty years on the Southern coast; he is a perfect sea dictionary for all the Keys, Islands, and Reefs, and as for weather, blow high, blow low, will ye, nil-ye, he is bound to go ahead. The boat itself is of modern construction, airy, roomy, and every-thing as snug as a biscuit, and rides the billows like a duck. She is decid-edly a favorite, and the ladies are unanimous in praise." The *Florida's* sister vessel, the *Carolina*, built by and under the command of Capt. Coxetter, the commentator observed, was as "strong as wood and iron can make a boat, and her appointments, external, internal, all of the best; large and spacious, and amply provided for all the wants of passengers." Captain Coxetter's "sea knowledge stands at No. 1. Nor should we forget 'Roux' the Purser, who always has one state-room left, and sees that your baggage is secured, be it a Valise or Big-box, hand-box, or Baby." The *Carolina* ar-rived in Jacksonville every Sunday and, like the *Florida*, connected with Charleston and New York steamships. A local newspaper reported that by the first of the year five boats—the *Darlington, Hancock, Mount Pleasant, Ocala*, and *Micanopy*—had joined the "venerable old lady *Sarah Spauld-ing*, on regular runs on the St. Johns."[12]

Although it was convenient for travel and commerce, steamboat travel carried risks. Crashes, heavy winds, boiler explosions, and other potential hazards awaited the traveler. For example, less than a year after George and Matilda rode the *Magnolia*, the steamer's boiler exploded off St. Si-mons Island while loading cotton on its run from St. Augustine to Sa-vannah, killing its captain and many others. The boat, its freight, and its baggage were all lost.[13]

Steamboats carried passengers and freight. The most valuable freight of course was cotton, but lumber increasingly took up more space. Accord-ing to one source,

> The St. John's is now the largest lumber market in the Southern States, and the erection of new mills is still going on; and it will go on, for the supply of logs on this river and its tributaries are in-exhaustible. . . . Jacksonville[,] the center of all the trade on the St. Johns[,] is keeping rapid pace with the onward progress of things around her. The population has doubled in about three years, and there are few towns in the Union that can boast that. Within the last year many handsome dwellings have been erected, and many store and ware-houses that would be an ornament to cities of much higher pretentions than our own.[14]

Jacksonville had two newspapers, more than twenty grocery and provision stores, two ready-made clothing stores, two drugstores, and more than five public boardinghouses. It also contained numerous skilled craftsmen: a watchmaker, a jeweler, a tinner, several blacksmiths and carpenters, and gun and locksmiths, as well as a tannery and an iron foundry. The town also boasted ever-expanding lumber operations. One source estimated that at least 300 vessels a year transported sawed lumber out of Jacksonville to Charleston and to points north, which in turn "bring. . .cargoes of goods and supplies from the North for the merchants."[15] Moreover, once its bar was improved, another booster noted, and a link between the Atlantic and Gulf was achieved via the contemplated railroad, "then we shall begin to count our annual increase by the thousands."[16]

Even though Jacksonville's future seemed bright, it was plagued by boom and bust cycles throughout the antebellum period. On April 5, 1854, only a few months after the report above, a fire left the entire business section of the town in ashes. That summer, the town was also struck with a yellow fever epidemic that led to a quarantine with other towns. Within a year after these twin disasters, the town was once again flourishing, only to see large sections go up in flames again in November 1856.[17]

Not only was travel by water in East Florida growing swiftly, but transportation over land, though still arduous, became easier and more certain. By 1852, a semi-weekly stage route was established from Newnansville to Black Creek (Middleburg) that would connect with mail boats. By 1855, a rival service, the Central State Line, was in place.[18] According to a correspondent to the *Jacksonville Republican* writing from Middleburg, the thirty-mile road between that town and Newnansville is "as good as any other public road in this state," and in 1854 that route was put to good use: that year, more than 2,000 bales of Sea Island cotton had been shipped from Black Creek.[19] The east-west route to Newnansville also saw advances. In 1853, J. Durrence, proprietor of the Picolata Ferry, announced improvements at the age-old St. Johns River crossing. He had procured a new set of boats and had enough hands to pass travelers of every description across the St. Johns River without delay. The road from St. Augustine to Newnansville was "well repaired" and would "be constantly kept in good repair." There were also permanent buildings on both sides of the river to accommodate travelers.[20]

Growth brought new counties in East Florida. From 1850 through 1860, Alachua, Columbia, Duval, and St. Johns Counties lost territory as new counties were created. Columbia County saw its territory reduced

NEW HACK LINE
From Alligator to Ocala, Florida.

The subscriber takes this method of informing the public that he has now in successful operation, upon this route, comfortable and safe two-horse HACKS, which run in connection with the Eastern and Western Stages from Alligator to Newnansville, and to Ocala by Micanopy, twice a week: leaving Alligator on Mondays and Thursdays, upon the arrival of the Eastern Stages, and run through to Ocala so as to connect the Stages from Palatka to Tampa Bay, on Tuesday and Friday nights.

He would, further, assure passengers who may take his line at Alligator or Ocala, that, if they desire to proceed on to Black Creek, they shall be accommodated with comfortable conveyance, at reasonable rates of fare, as if the line continued through to that point.

Every attention within his power, as to the comfort of passengers and the safety of baggage, will be rendered, and he most respectfully solicits a share of the public patronage.

CHARLES F. FITCHETT.

Newnansville, April 7, 1852.   15—3 m.

Figure 6.2. By 1852, regular stage travel was established from Alligator, Black Creek, and Newnansville to as far south as Tampa Bay and Ocala. *Jacksonville Republican*, April 15, 1852.

by two-thirds when New River (to its east) and Suwannee (to its west) were created in 1858. Also that year, Duval's size was cut in half when Clay County was created on its southern border. St. Johns County lost territory to portions of the new Putnam (1849) and Clay (1858) Counties. But it was Alachua County that suffered the greatest territorial losses. Beginning in 1843 with the creation of Benton (which later became Hernando), Alachua County ceded territory six times to Marion (1844), Levy (1845), Putnam (1849), Clay (1858), and New River (1858) Counties. By 1858, Alachua stood at approximately one fourth of its former size. Even so, its population had nearly quadrupled, from roughly 2,500 in 1850 to roughly 8,200 in 1860.[21]

These Alachua County boundary changes had the effect of reducing Newnansville's influence and its long-term viability as a county seat and commercial center. At one time or another, its superior and circuit court had served Columbia, Hillsborough, Benton, Marion, and Levy Counties, but as the population grew, each county, in turn, created its own courts. By 1850, Alachua's new boundaries found Newnansville at the northern part of the county instead of in the center as before. With the Seminole war over, soldiers no longer trudged through to buy goods or refresh themselves. Settlers pulled down Fort Gilliland, turning its timbers to other uses. By 1853, Alachua voters approved a measure by a slight majority to move the county seat to a more southerly location on the northern rim of Paynes Prairie, where the Florida Railroad's Fernandina to Cedar Key railroad surveys had been drawn.[22] The loss of its county seat and the decision to run the railroad through the new town of Gainesville instead of Newnansville were crushing blows to the village. These were ominous developments, but the end came by degrees. Even in decline, Newnansville still functioned as a significant community well into the 1860s. Numerous homesteaders from outlying areas frequently came to the town's land office to register their improvements under the Armed Occupation Act.[23] By 1854, the town boasted a new boardinghouse, and a year later when Charles Lanman visited the town during "Christmas week," he found the village alive with singing, dancing, and other types of merrymaking. "With all its discomforts," Lanman wrote, "I shall ever remember Newnansville with great distinctness and not without pleasure for having presented me with a comprehensive picture of southern life."[24] Newnansville rested on the Bellamy road, still the principle east-west thoroughfare linking St. Augustine to Tallahassee, and it remained important as a midway point between Alligator and Ocala. Even though the county seat was not officially moved to Gainesville until 1856 and the railroad was not functional until 1860, the long-term impact of the above circumstances would be obvious.

For the time being, George and Matilda Brown no doubt took in these new changes and adapted to them as well as they could. Newnansville's long-term future might have seemed in doubt, but their immediate concern was to make a living. George did his best to foster the growth and development of his town. Though he fell a few votes short of being re-elected to a seat on the county commission in 1851, he served on the board of Newnansville's and Alachua County's first educational institution.[25]

Matilda's mother, Eliza, remained on her plantation in Columbia County. Her three sons Charles C. (twenty-four), George (twenty-seven), and James M. (seventeen) assisted her in its operation, but they also employed overseers and other hands as needs arose. Claudius (nineteen) was away at school. Matilda's other younger brothers and sisters, Adelaide (twelve), Thomas (nine), and Mary (seven), also resided on the plantation.

George must have been delighted at the news of William Forward's return to East Florida. In 1853, the Florida General Assembly had elected Louis Aldrich's former law partner Judge of the Eastern Circuit of Florida. Forward settled in Jacksonville but visited Newnansville on his regular circuit.[26] Unfortunately, Forward's first visit to Newnansville in his new post would not be a pleasant one for George and Matilda, as the new judge presided over the trial of the man accused in the murder of one of Matilda's brothers. Approximately ten months after George and Matilda's marriage, a man named Stephens, who was employed as Mrs. Eliza Stewart's overseer, became involved in a dispute over some matter involving the management of the plantation. Stephens left the plantation and sent word to both George Stewart and Charles Stewart that he would meet them in Newnansville. According to one account, George and Charles went immediately to Newnansville, but several days passed; then, on October 20, George Stewart "was in a store, when he was informed that Stephens was in town. Stewart stepped out of the store on the piazza, when he saw Stephens standing about fifteen feet from him, in the street." Both men drew their pistols and fired. Both missed. By that time, the account continued, "several of Stewart's friends had arrived on the scene, including his brother Charles, who fired at Stephens and missed. When George ran across the street toward the store . . . perhaps to procure arms," Stephens shot George Stewart dead. Stephens fled but was subsequently arrested and lodged in jail.[27] Presumably, the "store" referred to in this account was George Brown's store.

One can only imagine the effect of this spectacle on George and Matilda. Not only did they have to endure the loss of a brother, but they also had to face the trial of his killer. In the May 1853 term of Judge Forward's court in Newnansville, Stephens was convicted of manslaughter, sentenced to six months in jail, and fined five hundred dollars. Judge Forward determined the jail in Newnansville to be unsafe, so he ordered Sheriff Charles Wilson to transport Stephens to Jacksonville. Charles Stewart was also prosecuted for his role in the melee: in the May 1853 term of the Alachua

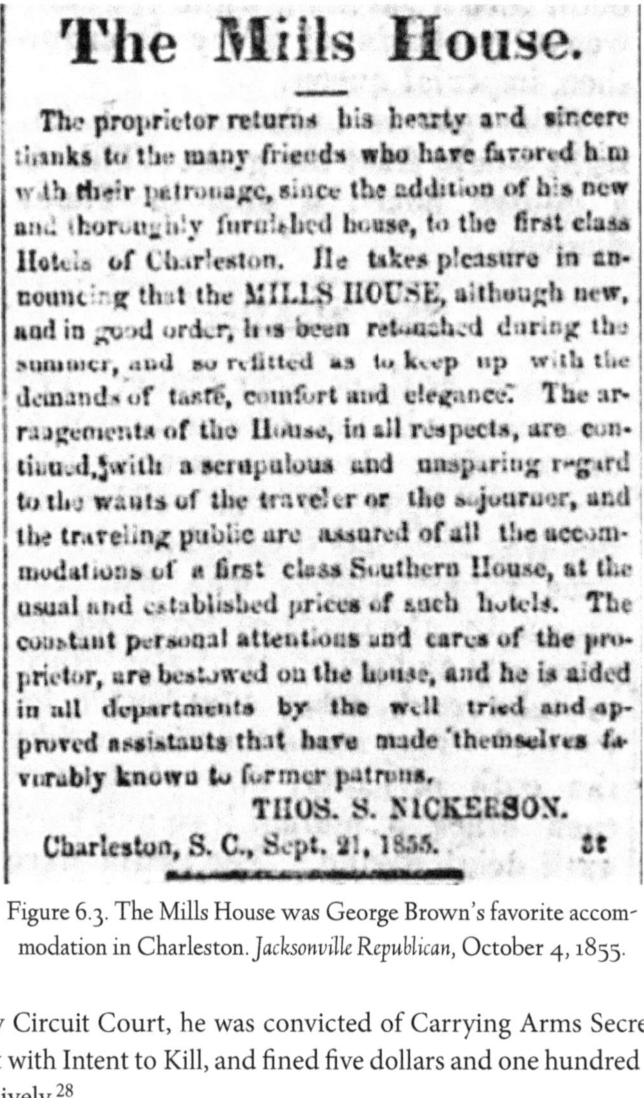

The Mills House.

The proprietor returns his hearty and sincere thanks to the many friends who have favored him with their patronage, since the addition of his new and thoroughly furnished house, to the first class Hotels of Charleston. He takes pleasure in announcing that the MILLS HOUSE, although new, and in good order, has been retouched during the summer, and so refitted as to keep up with the demands of taste, comfort and elegance. The arrangements of the House, in all respects, are continued, with a scrupulous and unsparing regard to the wants of the traveler or the sojourner, and the traveling public are assured of all the accommodations of a first class Southern House, at the usual and established prices of such hotels. The constant personal attentions and cares of the proprietor, are bestowed on the house, and he is aided in all departments by the well tried and approved assistants that have made themselves favorably known to former patrons.

                        THOS. S. NICKERSON.
Charleston, S. C., Sept. 21, 1855.   3t

Figure 6.3. The Mills House was George Brown's favorite accommodation in Charleston. *Jacksonville Republican*, October 4, 1855.

County Circuit Court, he was convicted of Carrying Arms Secretly and Assault with Intent to Kill, and fined five dollars and one hundred dollars, respectively.[28]

Not long after this family tragedy, Matilda's twenty-one-year-old brother Claudius returned to the area after years away at school. Claudius would soon be admitted to the bar, and his future looked bright. Eliza Stewart eventually sold her plantation in Columbia, sold many of her slaves, and bought a plantation in Alachua County closer to George and Matilda.[29] Meanwhile, Edward Aldrich was still striving to secure a financial footing in the San Francisco area. By 1851, he had established a medical practice in San Francisco, but due to a fire, his failed attempts to receive a medical appointment, and a series of other setbacks, success eluded him.[30]

George continued his frequent visits to Charleston, and when he traveled there he stayed at the town's best hotel, the Mills House on the corner of Meeting and Queen Streets. Opened in 1853, the Mills House was noted for its excellent cuisine, wine cellar, and elegant furniture.[31] By the mid-1850s, George had many friends and business associates in Charleston.

Despite a brief uptick in the early part of the 1850s, Charleston's economic vitality weakened. As it had from 1830 to 1840, the city lost population between 1850 and 1860. With decline came tensions.[32] As historian Philip Racine put it, in the early 1850s, Charleston was increasingly becoming "[a]cauldron of competing factions: the gentleman planters who wanted to return to genteel tradition; a competitive commercial and general business class seeking to increase manufacturing, shipping, commerce, and banking; a frightened free black community forced into trying to save itself from losing its freedoms and work; and a fast-growing underclass of immigrants, seamen, and working class people whose opportunities were shrinking as the general welfare of the city declined."[33] The political rise of George's friend William Porcher Miles epitomized these competing forces. A professor at the College of Charleston, Miles was elected mayor of Charleston in 1855 in large part owing to the political support of Irish and other new immigrant groups. Friendly to the commercial-business class, Miles bridged the gap between the old patrician class and the politicians more attuned to commerce and the need to operate cities on a more scientific, systematic basis. Miles also instituted measures to restore the city's credit and improve public health.[34]

No letters written by George in 1851 survive, and only two survive from 1852. Perhaps he was too preoccupied with his wife and her family to maintain the steady writing of the years immediately before his marriage. However, in August 1852, he wrote to Mannevillette and then to Corinna to share his good news:

> [George L. Brown to Mannevillette E. D. Brown]
> Newnansville, Fla. [to Utica, New York]
> Aug. 17, 1852
>
> Dear Brother Manne,
>
> I have waited about a year and a half for something extraordinary to happen to communicate to you. It has come at last. My wife last

Wednesday night presented me with a fat little daughter, which is a perfect facsimile of its Daddy! Having in particular perfection his nose and toes. As I have caught the knack of manufacturing little babies, the name of Brown will go down to posterity because, in the long run I will certainly happen on a little son. The Baby's mother is doing well. One of these summers I will bring my wife and little one or little ones to see you. I had planned to visit New York this year, but the above "come off" kept us at home. We lost a little one a year ago last spring by journey to Savannah. What shall I name the Baby? This is the great trouble of the household.

I have just seen the accounts of the awful burning of the Steamer *Henry Clay*. The infernal scoundrels, the owners and officers of the steamer should be hung up without the benefit of a trial. Lynch law is too mild for men who will jeopardize the lives of hundreds of people to gratify their purses and their pride. They punish such offenders in a surer way in England. In this country cash too often shields the wealthy guilty criminal.[35]

How are you doing in the world? For myself I am picking steadily along in my usual way, sometimes losing and again making money. The article I deal mostly in (cotton) is perhaps the most changeable in price of any article of traffic. Yet, to do business at all here we are compelled to try it. Last year, I [did] very well. The year before took 2 or 3000 dollars out of my pocket, and the two years prior were just touch and go. I apprehend much from the coming cotton season as the prices scale very high. When they are up, the next curve must be down. Experience, however, has made me pretty keen.

I hope that you keep well. I see that the cholera is sending out its feelers to open a campaign. When I think of it, and your wicked steamboats, and railroad accidents, I feel satisfied with my home in the woods, where we are exempt from epidemics and all accidents save a toss from a horse's back.

I would be glad to see you my Brother, but as I cannot soon expect to look upon you, unless you will come this way, shall be glad to get a letter from you. With my best wishes, and my wife's also. I am very truly, thy Brother

Geo L. Brown

*   *   *   *   *   *

[George L. Brown to Corinna Brown Aldrich]
Newnansville [Florida, to New York City]
August 21, 1852

Dear Sister,

I hear post and hasten to reply [to your last letter]–Tilda's sickness; The confusion of having a baby–and my impression that any time in August will answer your purpose is the reason I have delayed sending you the 25 dollars. To make amends for tardiness, I will add interest and send 30$ which you will find enclosed. I hope it will arrive in good time. I am pleased to hear of Edward's [arrangements] in [San Francisco] with [a man by] the name of Valentine as you say names often go far.

You say that Edward thinks of sending for you in December next– my advice to you and Ellen is to be governed entirely by his advice. He is there and knows and will recommend what is best for you. The opinions of others from California are not to be depended on at all; some are favorable; others are adverse. I would not ask for informa- tion–only from Edward–You and Ellen ought to keep together where ever [you go.]

If you go to California, go together . . . [and] stay together. I will continue to send you the 25$ per month as long as you stay in New York and after you leave there if it is necessary. I urge upon you and Ellen both not to separate from each other (I have no reason for thinking you will) for the reason that I deem it the only wise course and I trust my simple apprehension that you might live apart will only bind you closer together.

Tilda is doing well, still confined to her room–The little baby girl is hearty. I think of naming her Adelaide. Adelaide Brown will be a name filled with many pleasant recollections.[36]

Truly yours
Geo. L. B

* * * * * *

[George L. Brown to Ellen Brown Anderson]
Newnansville [Florida, to New York City]
January 11, 1853

Dear Sister,

Above you have a draft on Savannah for Fifty Dollars. Do not allow a <u>Broker</u> to <u>shave</u> <u>it</u>, but ask Messrs. Rushton, Clarke, & Co to advance you the amount, with a reasonable discount, and assure them, the draft will be honoured on presentation.[37]

I have not heard from St Marys about your parcels there, but will advise you as soon as I do. You are surprised that so long a time should have elapsed without your being informed of the Old Doctor's death. I heard of it on my way to Charleston last Fall and would have written to you about it on my return home, but when I came home, I found <u>Geo</u> <u>Stewart</u> <u>dead</u> and I forgot that there was such a place as St Marys or any of its inhabitants.

In the confusion following this <u>sad</u> <u>event</u>, I could not remember what I had or had not written you. I have no doubt all your things are safe—<u>Whipple</u> <u>Aldrich</u> heard of his Father's death for the <u>first</u> <u>time</u> <u>from</u> <u>me</u> <u>today</u>!—

Charles Stewart is married to Miss [Sarah Ann] Pelot, daughter of Jno C Pelot, niece of the Doctor's. Mrs. Stewart and family, are well. So is Matilda, and <u>Adelaide</u> and myself.

With much love to you all
I am affectionately your Brother
Geo L. B.

＊　＊　＊　＊　＊　＊

[George L. Brown to Edward S. Aldrich]
Newnansville [Florida, to San Francisco]
January 22, 1853

Dear Edward,

Your letters of Sept 30th and Nov. 14th, strange to say, were received two Mondays two weeks from each other. Your requests in relation to Corinna and Ellen's journey to California would have received my prompt assistance. I had made arrangements for the amount you desired and I may, or may not, be in time to stop it, in accordance with your last letter. When you are again ready to make a move give me notice and I will do all I can. Sometimes I feel strong in favor, and again, when cotton tumbles, I am like a church rat in worldly substance.

I expect to hear of the large fire in Sacramento, and of Louis' loss.[38] He seemed to be fixed on so good a foundation for success. However disconcerting such blows appear, still it is best to console oneself that affairs might have been worse. Louis has talents of no ordinary caliber, and his manners are of a kind to win him friends under every phase of life. May success attend him.

We have few changes in Newnansville to interest you. Sam Russell is about the only "standby" you remember, and he is constantly annoyed with the rheumatism. He holds up against it well, and one could suppose from his cheerfulness that his attacks were trifling, but he suffers awfully. He often speaks of you.

I ought to write you a longer letter and will soon, with all the little items and changes in Florida life. I will do it in course of a week or so. With my best wishes. I am truly yours.

Geo L Brown

*　*　*　*　*　*

[George L. Brown to Mannevillette E. D. Brown]
Newnansville [Florida, to Utica, New York]
January 25, 1853

Dear Manne:

The great question of naming the baby being decided, I now make known to you that your niece will flourish under the name of Adelaide. I preferred some other name, but concluded on the above because Adelaide or "Ad" Brown sounded so natural, bringing up old days before me with many pleasant remembrances of poor sister and Henry, and yourself. Our little one grows finely & is a bright, intelligent child, and good looking. Its mother and myself are well. I had a small Florida fever in November last, from the usual effects of which I am now free. What do you think of the World's fair to be opened in New York on May next? Will you be there? I have almost concluded to take myself & mine north about that time, or in June. I desire above all things to see you, and I would like to see Yankee land again. A few fresh breezes might bring the colour back to my cheeks ——— Some time since, Dr. Aldrich wrote from San Francisco in relation to arrangements for Corinna & Ellen to visit him, but has changed his mind, postponing the time until Spring. They will pass the winter in New York City. Our Indian Fellow Citizens, "Billy Bowlegs," and his tribe refuse to go west. The State Legislature has determined that they shall go by force, and I presume if the Indians resist, that we will have another Florida war. Billy Bowlegs and two Seminole Indians, and

Figure 6.4. Billy Bowlegs (Holata Micco), circa 1852.
Florida State Archives.

three Indians of the "Arkansas" delegation made a visit to Washington last fall. I happened on my way to Charleston at the same time and was a fellow passenger with them from the St. Johns River to Savannah. Billy is an intelligent fellow; talks pretty good English; and looks like a hard customer to deal with. They all love Fire Water. When the Steamer arrived at the first landing, her approach was made known by a shrill <u>Steam</u> <u>Whistle</u>. Old Abram, the Indian interpreter, was considerably startled. He turned round to me and said "Well! I believe white man can make every thing except <u>gut</u>! I now hear he made gut."[39]

Our legislature is trying to drive all kinds of evil things from the state. Having passed an act to raise licenses to sell rum, etc to 300 dollars — The highest license heretofore being 25$. The spirit of the "Maine law" is even felt here.

I will send you a box of mangos next season from my own garden. I have several fine trees. They will blossom this winter. If you will manage to keep Jack Frost with you in the cold regions, I will have a fine crop. My wife joins me in sending much love to you. Little Adalaide adds "ne-yah"

Affectionally your brother
George L.B.

*   *   *   *   *   *

[George L. Brown to Corinna Brown Aldrich]
Newnansville [Florida, to New York City]
June 12, 1853

Dear Sister,

Having recently returned from a trip to Charleston, I have received your letters and Edward's in a bunch. My reply to all will be brief, but contain all that you will desire. From your letter you and Ellen (if she goes) cannot start before fall. That you have a certain amount of funds which you wish to keep on deposit until then (deposit it <u>in a good bank</u>) working out your expenses from some other source. This is right. You will therefore <u>draw on my Factors, Messrs Boston & Gundy</u> of Savannah for <u>Fifty dollars every month</u> for you and Ellen. Should you at any time want to make it a little larger do so, and when you can let me know the time you will start and the amount of money you want, I will either send it to you or bring it myself. You will understand the above, draw a draft on Boston & Gundy every month for 50 dolls, or more, until you are ready to go and then let me know (in time) how much you will need to go there comfortably. So much for money matters ———

I have thought much over your situation and Ellen's. My desire is for you all always to live together–away from each other you would not be satisfied–a trip to California is a long one, but not the uncertain voyage it once was or the hard country to live in. My mind about it is completely changed. And I know no country where an enterprising person could do better. Gold digging is a mere secondary affair in connection with the prosperity of California. Situated so as to command the whole Pacific and the trade to china and the East Indies, it is destined far to outstrip in wealth and comfort, the Eastern Coast of the United States, and were my business so I could go, I have the will to make my home there myself—events may lead to it yet.

Edward, it seems, is finally fixed there. From his own and other accounts he is doing well. It will be a great inducement for continued exertion on his part to have you all with him (for he loves you all) to cheer him in his labours and to make pleasant his leisure hours. I would write more of your trip but have to answer Edward's and several other letters. I leave your decision to your own wisdom, but must constantly urge upon you and Ellen the importance of staying together as long as you live. Edward will strive hard to make you happy.

Tilda and my little Adelaide are well, as are Mrs. Stewart and family. Miss Ada Stewart has gone to Georgia to stay some years. Col. Dell, and I believe all the rest of us are in prime health. I hoped to be at the Crystal Palace show, but as it appears to be a humbug—and uncertain when it will open I have abandoned the idea. With love to Ell, her children, and yourself,

I am affectionately yr Brother,
George—

*   *   *   *   *   *

[George L. Brown to Mannevillette E. D. Brown]
Newnansville [Florida, to Utica, New York]
June 13, 1853

Dear Brother:

Your letter of May 28th was but recently received by me, I having been absent in Charleston. I regret to have to say that I cannot be in New York by the time you mention having many things to keep me here. Should I conclude to come later in the season, I will give you timely notice to meet me in New York or if you are too much engaged to leave Utica I will soon find the way there, or to whatever city you will be abiding in. I rec'd a letter from Corinna and one from Edward Aldrich by the same mail yours came. Doctor A sent for Corinna and Ellen and wishes them to start by July. Corinna says she cannot leave before fall. I have written her and promised them all the assistance I can to aid them on their journey and during their stay in New York and if they can fix upon a time when they will leave, I will try and see them. I have felt much troubled for Ellen's situation and have a sincere wish to make her life as comfortable as possible and to leave her children well provided for. For this reason I have always urged and advised Corinna and Ellen to stick together even in California. Corinna loves her children, and so does Edward Aldrich. He will do all in his power for them. I think if one goes, all will go. Ellen has a high toned mind and is independent in her feelings and determination to help herself. This will do for one to talk about; but she cannot do it, her physical powers are not equal to it. Still if she is determined to do something for herself, California is the country for her. I regret to part with them to go so far; still, I see no avoiding it, Corinna must, and is right to go where her husband is, and Ellen and children will be better off with her there, than they could be without her in the most favoured spot on Earth.

I write hurriedly, as I am also about to write the sisters and Doctor Aldrich. I thought but to send you a few lines if no more, that you might know of my <u>non</u>-appearance in New York. My wife and Miss Adelaide are in good health. I have a little daguerreotype of her which I am almost inclined to send to you, but it is such a poor likeness of the live little one that I fear it will give you a wrong notion of her. The picture is badly done and ugly, whereas the child is pretty plump and intelligent. I will take another look at it and perhaps send it to you. It looks as though we will never get sight of each other again, I have full confidence however, that we will.

Affectionately your brother, Geo L B

*   *   *   *   *   *

[George L. Brown to Corinna Brown Aldrich]
Newnansville [Florida, to New York City]
August 3, 1853

Dear Sister

I received your letter of July 21st by yesterday's mail and am glad to learn of your recovery from recent illness. I had thought that you had taken a sudden notion to be off for California.

I returned home last week from LaGrange Georgia, for which place I left here about the 1st of July. Miss Adelaide Stewart was at school there. Hearing that the Typhoid disorder was very prevalent and fatal in Georgia, Mrs. Stewart became alarmed for Adelaide's health and I started to bring her back to Florida. I started too late— When I arrived at Lagrange I found she had been ill for some days with the same dreadful disorder and was fast worsening. She died late next morning–Mrs. Stewart's family are truly affected—this is the fifth death amongst them within a few years past.

Tilda is not well, but her sickness is more from sorrow than anything else. Our little one keeps fat and lively. She was quite unwell last week from bowel discomfort produced probably by teething. It does not affect her general health. . . . [The baby] does not favor either of us. She has dark blue eyes, light hair, and a very fair complexion. All the people here who know you say that she looks exactly like you, and I am inclined to think so myself. She has a head shaped after yours, and your eyes to a T. so much for her resemblance in looks. I think I'll be sorry to say that you and "Toozy" are otherwise alike, for she is the most destructive little piece of mortality. . . .

I had almost concluded to start for New York on the 20th . . . . I noticed a gathering of the "Sons of Portsmouth" on the 4th of July and had all but concluded to gather with them, as I might there see some old familiar faces that I would never have a chance to look upon again. My trip to LaGrange (which I had decided about some time before leaving) would not have stopped me. Miss Adelaide Stewart's death compelled me to return home to Tilda and stay with her. I regret that I could not do as I desired, still more do I regret the cause that prevented me.

Give my love to Ellen and the Children—I supposed she knew that her pension was renewed or I should have advised her of it long ago. The act was passed last Congress to renew them five years, and I have no doubt the pension will be continued from time to time at each expiration.

Affectionately your brother
George

*   *   *   *   *   *

[George L. Brown to Mannevillette E. D. Brown]
Newnansville [Florida to Utica, New York]
September 20th, 1853

Dear Brother,

I have just returned home from Charleston after an absence of some weeks, and received a letter from Ellen, to which I have today replied. I had supposed that Corinna and Ellen would go to San Francisco together, from the contents of her letter I should judge she preferred to stay, and I know now which is best for her. Under the supposition that she would not go I have today written to her and urged her to ask your assistance to select some healthy town or village in New York or New England and make herself a <u>home</u>. She has a pension for about 250 $. I have promised to send her 500 dollars a year in monthly payments making 750 $, and stated further that you would, if your purse would allow it, make up her income to 1000 $ per year. With this she certainly could live comfortably anywhere in New England. Here it would not carry a family like hers half through the year.

I wish you would write her about this and assist her to a good location. The funds I promise shall come regularly—

My wife and child and nurse are all down with our usual fever today and I write in much anxiety of mind. Did you get the little miniature? I will write you again soon. Meantime, give your attention to sister Ellen and see that she lacks for nothing to make her happy. She has been truly misfortunate—let us do our best to make the rest of her days happy and peaceful She has much to live for in her children.

Affectionately your Brother,
George L. B.

*   *   *   *   *   *

[George L. Brown to Corinna Brown Aldrich]
Newnansville [Florida, to New York City]
Dec. 9th, 1853.

Dear Sister

From your present location I presume you will not attempt a start for California before next spring. Of the time for you to go there you are the best judge. Sister Ellen and her children are oftener the subject of my thoughts than anyone would suppose from the number of my letters on the subject. In my former correspondence, I have constantly urged on her to go with you wherever fortune might lead you, that it would be best for her and for her children to be with you whether in New York or California. I fear I have been hasty in my advice. I have reflected much upon the matter, and the questions are constantly presenting themselves to me. What could she do in California with three little children? — Could she not do better. And what could she do here? — Whether she goes or remains, will be for her to decide, but under the belief that it would be best for her for the present, at least, to stay, I have to day written to her making certain propositions to her, which if she accepts will be carried out. It will be rather hard for you to separate from each other, but where a good for others is to be accomplished, one's feelings must be kept subdued. As I have to write Ellen today besides many other letters I must say goodbye.

I trust you find your home to be a home indeed, far preferable certainly to the publicity of a private boarding house. I would rather live in a log house of my own, and in my own control all my days, than live in the most splendid boarding house in New York. The privilege of kicking up one's heels when he likes without anyone to scold, is a luxury beyond turtle soup, and Brussels Carpets.

I am affectionately your Brother,
Geo. L. B.

Matilda and little "Toosy" quite well at this time. Gen'l Samuel Russell is dead[40]—Miss Kate Rice married to Doctor [Edward R.] Power. William Dell not well, quite an invalid from affliction of liver or chest.

G. L.B

*   *   *   *   *   *

George Brown to Mannevillette E. D. Brown
Newnansville [Florida, to Utica, NY]
December 30, 1853

Dear Brother,

I wrote you last mail enclosing fifty dollars for you to send to Ellen, and I will continue to send you fifty Dollars per month. I think this would be the surest way of its falling into her hand. I have written to Corinna to discontinue her draft on my factors as my account ends with them at the end of the year.

Your letter informing me of her situation is only a confirmation of Ellen's to me. I deplore the sad state she is in, and can only hope you, as you can see what is necessary, to do what you think best. I will agree to and aid any plan you may adopt for her health and benefit.[41]

I am glad you are pleased with our little baby's looks. The little tiny animal is much better looking than the daguerreotype. Why not send me a copy of your phiz? My wife is very anxious to see how you look though she would much rather see you in person.

I will have to write you once a month at least.

Affectionately Your Brother George L. B.

*   *   *   *   *   *

[George L. Brown to Mannevillette E. D. Brown]
Newnansville, Fla. [to Utica, New York]
July 4th, 1854

Dear Manne,

Inclosed I send you fifty dollars for Ellen.

I have been much perplexed and employed the past few weeks, to prevent a duel between one of my brothers-in-law, Claudius Stewart, and another lawyer residing here. My efforts were unavailing and they took a shot at each other last week near the Georgia and Florida line. Mr. Stewart was severely wounded, but is now considered out of danger,— a poor way to obtain satisfaction![42]

How different is this day to me compared with the "fourth of July" of younger days, when Brother Charles and myself used to look up to you as one of the greatest men in the world, from the abundance of the quarters and <u>China</u> <u>Crackers</u>, and <u>gunning</u>, we got out of you. I can hardly realize that I was once a little chap and lived "down east."

I write this stripped to my pants and shirt! We are undergoing a few weeks of hot weather. Our nights are cool.

I am well, and all of mine. Give my love to Ellen and Corinna.

Truly yr Brother
Geo L Brown

*   *   *   *   *   *

[George L. Brown to Mannevillette E. D. Brown]
Savannah, Ga. [to Utica, New York]
July 24, 1854

Dear Manne,

I enclose 50$ for Ellen. I ought to have sent the same amount last month, but will try and send 100$ next month. Times are very hard this season with Florida merchants. Our long cotton which sold in August and September last at 35 to 40 ¢ per lb are now selling at 18 to 20 ¢. It makes money matters tight with me. I am now on my way home. Will write you as I get there, in haste

Affectionately your Brother
Geo. L Brown

*   *   *   *   *   *

[George L. Brown to Mannevillette E. D. Brown]
Newnansville [Florida, to Utica, New York]
September 15, 1854

Dear Brother,

I have been <u>about</u> <u>starting</u> for Charleston and Savannah for several weeks past from one of which places I intended to send you fifty dollars for Ellen. I have delayed my journey from the prevalence of

Yellow fever in these Cities, and cannot say now how soon I will be there,— sometime during the month I hope. Should Ellen need the money–write her to get it from you for the present as I cannot conveniently remit from here.

Myself, wife, and little Adelaide are all well—though we are somewhat reduced in flesh from the effects of an unusually long, dry bilious summer — a good cold snap will fill us out again —

We are without any northern mail for nearly three weeks - The quarantine laws of St. Johns River having put a stop to all steam conveyance. It is doubtful if you get this for some time, for I know of no way for it to get out of Florida, unless it fortunately takes, what we call, the Macon and Tallahassee road west.

Truly your brother,
Geo. L. B.

*   *   *   *   *   *

[George L. Brown to Mannevillette E. D. Brown]
Newnansville Fla [to Utica, New York]
October 19, 1854

Dear Brother

I have delayed making my usual fall trip to Charleston and Savannah from the prevalence of Yellow fever in those cities - the disease this year has been very malignant- eight physicians having died from it in Savannah alone.[43] We are anxiously looking for a killing frost when the fever will clear. I enclose 50$ for Ellen. Will send another 50$ as soon as I can venture to Charleston.

We have had two cases of yellow fever in East Florida, <u>one here</u>, and one at Black Creek (our forwarding place) - but there is no danger of the disease <u>spreading in the country.</u>

My wife and little daughter have been quite unwell- they are now much better - I am stout and hearty, weight 164 lbs, A pretty good load to carry about with one after passing through a long, hot, dry summer.

When I go to Charleston (in course of a week or two)
I will write you again
Affectionately your brother
George

On November 14, 1854, Corinna died in the Bloomingdale Insane Asylum in New York City; the following letters express George's feelings over this loss:[44]

[George L. Brown to Mannevillette E. D. Brown]
Newnansville, Fla. [to Utica, New York]
November 30, 1854

Dear Brother

I have just returned home from a visit to Charleston and Savannah, and find your letters the last advising me of our poor sister's death. I <u>feel</u> <u>it</u>. At the same time I can look facts in the face and am contented that she has gone from us, and from her suffering. Her disease, or habit, was past cure. And however harrowing it may be to our little band left, to part with one so near to us, yet the knowledge that "all is for the best" should temper the sad event.

Take care of Ellen and her children and I will do my part in the brotherly act.

I write in haste. One of my wife's brothers, Mr. Claudius Stewart, died last week, the fourth in four years, all grown.

Truly yr. Brother, George

*   *   *   *   *   *

[George L. Brown to Ellen Brown Anderson]
Newnansville, Fla [to New York City]
November 30, 1854

Dear Ellen,

I have just returned home from Charleston, and received Mann's letter telling me of the death of poor Corinna. This event does not take me by surprise at all, yet it seems sudden and I feel that our little band will miss her much now she is gone. I grieve for her loss as much as a brother can, still I knew her situation and the facts of her case were such, that I cannot lament that she has left this earth when her days for so long a time, (and no hope for a better change) have been days of suffering. I shall remember her only as she was in times gone by. I have only time to write you this, I have hurried home, on Matilda's account. She expects soon to be confined.

Mrs. Stewart is again afflicted by the <u>death</u> of <u>Claudius</u> [Stewart].[45]
He died at Jacksonville last week while attending Court there. I did
not know of his illness until the day after his death, on my arrival at
Jacksonville in the Steamer from Savannah. I brought his body home,
and he was buried by the side of his brother George at his mother's
plantation last Sunday. So goes the world —— Trusting you and your
little ones are well. I am

Truly your Brother,
George

*   *   *   *   *   *

[George L. Brown to Mannevillette E. D. Brown]

Newnansville, Fla [to Utica, New York]
February 5, 1855

Dear Manne:

Expecting to be absent from here about three weeks, I drop a line to
say, that myself, wife, big baby and little baby are all well. My last girl
(another fine experience) I or rather my wife has named Claudia. I
do not like fancy names, and intended to call this one (if a girl as it
has turned out) Mary, Mary Brown. The only doubt I had was the
remembrance of the old song about [Giles Scroggins] who "Courted
Molly Brown."[46]

I sent Ellen last mail one hundred dollars. When I go to Charleston again, I will arrange matters so she can get her funds in New
York. <u>Our</u> mail is decidedly unsafe having a drunken Postmaster who
is almost as bad as the North Carolina one I have heard of, that measured the mail out a <u>peck</u> each, North, South, West.

We are having one of those hard times in Florida. My collections
are worse than they have been for years, yet enough to keep me jog-
ging on safe. I hear of much distress in large cities particularly in New
York. I hope it does not reach inland.

Truly your Brother
George

I forgot to say that my wife named the baby Claudia after a brother,
Claudius, recently deceased. He was a fine man in mind and looks.

He returned from the law school at Cambridge about a year since. Had a difficulty with a lawyer here which resulted in a duel, in which Claudius was severely wounded. His health declined rapidly. His wounds apparently got well, but was no doubt the cause of his sickness (inflammation) and death.

G.L.B.

*   *   *   *   *   *

[George L. Brown to Mannevillette E. D. Brown]
Newnansville [Florida, to Utica, New York]
April 20, 1855

Dear Brother:

Your letter of March 24th only reached the last mail, Florida mails are not as regular as with you. I notice what you write about Ellen's residing out of New York and perfectly agree with you. It has always been my idea, and I have often written to Corinna on the subject–Ellen knows my views, and will with your similar advice probably act accordingly—I have written to a house in Savannah, Ga. today to remit her a check for one hundred dollars, directing her letter to 1073 Broadway. I fear it may not reach her by the first of May.[47] In case she should miss my letter and the letter with the check, apply at the Post Office,— she will get it unless she has to move in on the dreaded 1st of May. I also sent Ellen 100 $ last month —— I have written her that if she moves and her expenses are more than she anticipates in moving to let me know and I will make her another remittance immediately.

Times are still pretty hard here, but we have no <u>Banks</u> to bother us, we are perfectly indifferent to the time of day, not caring for two o'clock at all.

My wife and little daughters - "Adelaide" and "Claudia" - are well. The latter are fat, lively specimens and show the half-Yankee in their red cheeks and clear complexions—One of these days I will drop in on you with my wife and a long tail of little ones, like a comet's in length—manufacturing them now-a-days puts a stopper to travelling ——

I regret to see that your opinions long since expressed about the war in Europe are likely to prove correct. If it were not for the bad

Figure 6.5. Ellen Brown Anderson, at the time of her residence
in New York City, circa 1855. Courtesy of Elizabeth Traynor.

effect on the prices of long staple cotton they might fight till there
was not a grease spot left of them. Lord Raglan and the "cold shade of
Aristocracy" get a good share of abuse, and probably deserve it.[48]

I write today with the thermometer at 96 — rather hot—but we
will get used to it by time the summer is through——with love from
all to all

Affectionately yr. Brother
George ——

*   *   *   *   *   *

[George L. Brown to Ellen Brown Anderson]
Newnansville [Florida, to New York City]
May 20, 1856

Dear Sister

I have your two last letters by Friday's mail- you say you have received from me the past year (since May last) only 250 dollars. There is some error about the mails, as I have sent you more — one or two of the remittances must have gone to the wrong pocket —

Take a particular look over my letters if you have them and let me know the exact date and amounts you have received and I will make an accounting for what is missing—

I will have to avoid this risk, and have to day written to Mr. [W.] Stevenson, of the House of Haviland Harrell & Co [Druggists][49] of Charleston to make arrangements for you to draw fifty dollars the first of each month from their House; Haviland and Risley[50] of New York will instruct you how to get it as soon as I hear from him this will make your remittances certain.

I have had suspicion about the mail in Florida for some time —

I begin to think with you that New York is about your best residence as regards the education of your children - and their education as the most important matter for you to consider of. If little Willoughby grows up a well-educated man he will be a comfort to you for Life - He has talents for mathematics, drawing, designing &c., unusual for so young a child.

I notice your boarding house troubles. But it is the repetition of everyone's experience who has to undergo the keeping of a House of the kind - you are all served alike, though you may think your case a hard one. As long as there are rascally men and mean women in the world so long will their superiors (like yourself) be imposed upon - your consolation is that though they have more money and independence, you and yours have more brains.

I notice what you say about Mrs. Watson. She has a brother at Black Creek, and one at Micanopy. I do not like to have anything to do with other peoples' affairs - or I would advise them of her situation. Her better plan would be, if she needs aid to write herself to her brothers - to whom else could she address herself? They would no doubt assist her. If she was without such a resource I would help her myself. Mr. [George W.] Watson - though no doubt a good man - does not act in the way, or has not acted in the way- that we here think a good man should. He went in debt with perfect recklessness not knowing how he could pay. When he did get money from his surveying, instead of paying those who would have stood by him in his time of need, he let his friends go in every other direction. He owes a great deal of money here now to Philip Dell and others. For myself, he paid up all but about 100 dollars.

He was offered the situation of principal in a Methodist Academy at Micanopy (during the time he was in Roxbury) and after months of delay, the trustees had to select another. The situation was a good one and no doubt obtained through the influence of Mrs. Watson's Brother. I feel sorry for Mrs. Watson's family, but at the same time must say, that Mr. Watson, if in good health, is fully able to support them handsomely — not that he has money, but that he has in his noodle, if it is not addled by Methodism, would bring him money in any state in the Union. The nest is a perfect El-dorado for a man of his capabilities, if he would get rid of his crotchets.

My youngest daughter nears five weeks old & is as perfect a specimen of a pretty, intelligent baby as I ever saw, leaving out a father's prejudices. 'Tilda & Mrs. Stewart and others have been naming her since her birth. I have let them go on with "Irene," "Claudia," and other out-of-the-way names till to day, when being appealed to, to decide, I said in a Shandy[51] stile, "let her be called Ellen" - and Ellen she will be if her name, like Tristram Shandy's is not lost between the nursery and the place of christening - with love to all

affectionately
-Geo LB-

∗   ∗   ∗   ∗   ∗   ∗

[George L. Brown to Mannevillette E. D. Brown]
Newnansville, Fla. [to Utica, New York]
June 20th, 1856

Dear Brother Manne,

I have your kind letter of May 31st. I should—and thought I did—have stated to you how much I wished to pay for the fence and monument of my little child Claudia. I will now say from 2 to 300 dollars. If this is too low advise me. I would not have troubled you in the matter, but my wife has an idea, - had an idea, that would suit her feelings better than she or I could select in Charleston or Savannah. Get up something for me that you think will do. I have no money to throw away, but enough for me and mine, including you & Ellen —— do what you think is right.

I am writing rather hastily today. My <u>Clerk</u> is off on a <u>Cow-hunt</u>. What would old Thos. Haven have said to you, years since, if you had asked leave of absence for a week to go on a cow-hunt?! We all own cattle here. I have some <u>thirty</u> cows!!

It would give me much pleasure — to visit New York this season — to see you and Ellen and her little children. It would cost me too much. Not that either, but I would have to come home again, too soon to prevent a loss to enjoy my trip — I wish you could come see me. If I do not go north this summer try and come to me next fall or winter, and your funds shall not suffer ——

affectionately
Geo L. B.

*   *   *   *   *   *

[George L. Brown to Ellen Brown Anderson]
Newnansville [Florida, to New York City]
December 11, 1856

Dear Ellen,

Your letter of Nov 21, 1856 was rec'd last mail— I am well- so is Tilda and our little children Adelaide & Ellen. The last one I think (as all parents think) the brightest child I ever saw. I congratulate you on your good sense about the <u>Big Boarding House</u> — I have never seen anyone yet give up profitable business except from <u>bad health</u>, excess of fat (as in this landlady's case), is an argument in favor of your good judgment—for as people <u>grow fat</u>, they think themselves lighter and smarter than other people.

I am glad you have got rid of Mr (the Rev) Watson & his family — I am willing to give anyone their just due but you think more of them than I do. Mr. Watson I think has acted more like Sheridan's

Marworm[52] than anyone of his class that has come under my observation. He owes, and owes, and owes in Florida - and was he here
again, he would by strong preaching, loud shouting and fanatical
musings - get more in debt — I have no further use for him, or his. I
have the same regard for religion as you have — for the church that I
was taught in — for the church that my children are christened in and
the one that I hope you and yours and all of mine will quietly leave
this world in true belief of.

I notice my friends Haviland and Risley of New York have lost
their late place of business by fire.[53] It will make no difference with
your monthly receipt. If it should, Mr. Stevenson of their Charleston
House will soon make proper arrangements for you. I would write
you more today, but I have now to go and bury (or help do so) Mr
Charles Wilson the late Sheriff of our county — he died last night -
give my love with Tilla's to all, and for yourself

affectionately your brother
Geo L. Brown

The pressures of family obligations, conducting his business in Newnansville, and travel weighed heavily on George. Records show that in 1856 and
1857, George made at least three trips from Newnansville to Charleston.[54]
Unfortunately, George died there on October 8, 1857. A Charleston city
official notified Mannevillette of his brother's death; the official cause of
his death was recorded as "congestion of the brain."[55] Matilda directed one
of her husband's business associates and her attorney Samuel B. McLin to
notify Ellen Anderson of George's death. "Your dear Brother," he wrote,
"is no more. . . . Mrs. [Matilda] Brown feels that her cup of sorrow is great
and begs me to state that she is too much afflicted to write you herself. Mr.
Brown's death has caused a great gloom to settle over the community in
which he lived; he was esteemed and beloved by all who knew him. His
remains were brought from Charleston and deposited in the family burial
ground in Newnansville. Enclosed you will find a lock of Mr. Brown's hair
which Mrs. Brown directs to be sent."[56]

Nearly a month after his death, the *Charleston Mercury* published a
lengthy obituary of George L. Brown. Though a native of Portsmouth,
New Hampshire, and a longtime resident of Newnansville, East Florida,

George had made many friends during his nearly twenty-year-long association with Charleston. George Brown, the obituary stated,

> by integrity of purpose, and great energy of character, had arrived at the point of distinction as a merchant of rare attainment. His quiet virtues and social friendliness had won the love and esteem of all who knew him, his character was retiring and unobtrusive, but made up of sterling qualities. There was nothing ostentatious in his feelings or appearance. His habits were quiet, and his whole life pleasant and cheerful. True to his promptings of all his domestic and social relations, whether as a brother, husband or father, neighbor or friend, Mr. Brown was a bright example to all who knew him, by whom his memory will be sacredly embalmed. But his days are ended—his song of life has died into an echo. While we drop the tear of sorrow, o'er his remains, may we find consolation in his unstained record, and feel that he is with his Father, far beyond the twilight judgements of this world; high above its mists and obscurities.[57]

Epilogue

NEARLY ONE YEAR AFTER her brother passed away, Ellen Anderson learned from a friend and frequent visitor to Charleston the true nature of George's debilitating condition and death:

> Everybody spoke in the highest terms of George but there was a hesitancy on the part of his intimate friends to communicate particulars in regard to his death; finally, I came across his most intimate friend in Charleston, a Mr. [William Porchet] Miles, and I asked him leading questions, informing him that I was a connection, and wished the particulars for your information. He spoke very feelingly about George—said that he attended him through his illness, and was with him when he died and then went on to tell me that to the surprise of his friends, George had drunk immensely during the last three years, but in a very quiet Manner—his business became involved in consequence, and going on from bad to worse, he . . . died at the 'Mills House' from the effects. Another reason was given out to the world, and few knew the real facts of the case. His property would not cover his liabilities, but by a law passed in Florida the widow receives one half of what her husband dies of, personal and real estate, and no claims of any nature can affect it, consequently, Matilda is left well off. . . . [Mr. Miles] said that during the spree which George was on, he sent for his book-keeper and that he informed him that George had been in the habit for nearly three years of drinking from 2 to 3 quarts of brandy a day![1]

Because George died without a will, Matilda Brown had difficulty settling his affairs. On November 2, 1857, roughly two weeks after George's death, Matilda and her attorney, Samuel McLin, appeared in probate court. She took out an $80,000 bond and was appointed administrator of her husband's estate, and the court appointed two appraisers to make a full inventory of her husband's goods, chattel, and real estate.[2] The December 1 statement found George Brown's chattel property in Newnansville (the goods in his store and his seven slaves) appraised at $37,006.26.[3] Over the course of his business career, George had also accumulated seven tracts of land totaling more than 750 acres and nine town lots in Newnansville, with six of them containing houses.[4] Matilda petitioned the court to sell George's goods and real estate to pay his debts.[5] Unfortunately, an auction netted the estate only a little over $4,800, far below the roughly $9,000 amount necessary to satisfy the current claims against the estate, whereupon the probate judge ordered Matilda to immediately hand over whatever cash had been raised to provide distribution among George's creditors.[6] On the other side of the ledger, in subsequent years Matilda and her attorney tried continually to collect debts owed to her husband, but she enjoyed little success. Claims against George's estate went on for many years. George's creditors in Charleston refused to surrender up important documents.[7]

Meanwhile Matilda moved to her plantation near Gainesville and struggled to get by the best she could.[8] The loss of her husband must have been felt even more keenly because when George died she was expecting another child. Widowed for three months, Matilda gave birth to a son, George Brown Jr., on February 17, 1858, only to lose her three-year-old daughter, Ellen, six months later.[9]

The next year found George's estate still unresolved. Matilda wrote her brother-in-law Mannevillette that her "business [was] still unsettled":

I cannot say how long it will be before every thing will be arranged satisfactorily to all parties. During my poor husband's illness in Charleston he gave all his papers of any value to one of the Creditors (whom he believed to be a friend) to take care of his business during his illness. This gentleman wrote me to that effect a short time after the death of my husband & said as soon as I sent for them, they should be given up. I got my attorney to go immediately. They then refused to let me have them saying these papers were given to them as collateral security. Their detaining these papers has been a great drawback to me in settling up the Est.

Matilda eventually sued for the papers, but the outcome is unknown. She hoped that a "final settlement with the creditors" would "get enough to live comfortably on."[10]

At the outbreak of the Civil War, Matilda and her two children, Adelaide (eight) and George (three), resided on their farm near Gainesville. Nearby was her mother Mary Eliza's plantation, where Matilda's brother Thomas (seventeen) and sister Mary (sixteen) lived. Matilda's brother James (twenty-four) resided on his own farm nearby. The 1860 census listed far fewer slaves than the number Eliza had owned on her Columbia County plantation a decade earlier.[11] During and after the war, times were hard. Matilda's brother, James M., died in 1864. By that time, the war had taken her other brother, Thomas O., to South Carolina, where he married Olivia Quattlebaum in 1864.[12] Midway through the war, Matilda's husband's estate had yet to be settled. In May 1863, stating that the dower share of her husband's estate had never been set off, Matilda petitioned the court for relief.[13]

On April 4, 1870, seventeen-year-old Adelaide wrote to her uncle Mannevillette to thank him for sending letters and a photograph to her. She explained that she, George Jr., and her mother were still living on their plantation near Gainesville but that the war had stolen their prosperity. Then, on September 20, George Jr. died from meningitis. The next year, Mannevillette traveled to Florida for the first time, visiting Matilda and Adelaide and taking an excursion down the St. Johns and Ocklawaha Rivers.[14] In 1874, Matilda and Adelaide moved to Tennessee to be near Matilda's brother Thomas and her sister Mary. On February 25, Adelaide died of heart failure.[15] By 1880, Matilda was living in Nashville with her sister Mary and her husband Leonard Dozier. Eliza Stewart died there the next year. Matilda then lived for two years with her brother Thomas's family in South Carolina. By the middle 1880s, Matilda had rejoined the Doziers in Ocala, Florida, where she spent her remaining years. Matilda Brown died in Ocala in 1914 at the age of eighty-eight.[16]

Family members continued to communicate with one another in future years as well as they could. Ellen remained in New York City until succumbing to breast cancer in August 1862, roughly two years after sending her oldest son, Edward Willoughby, to West Point, only to urge him to resign from the academy on the eve of the Civil War's outbreak. Young Anderson enlisted and fought with the Army of Northern Virginia for the duration of the war. As Ellen became ill, she wrote to Mannevillette, pleading with him to take care of her daughters should she die, and he honored her wish. Georgia and Villette Anderson never married but lived together in various places, including Utica, New York, and Hartford, Connecticut, until finally moving to Washington after the Civil War to be with their brother, Edward Willoughby Anderson, and his wife, Elizabeth. Georgia, always in frail health, died in 1874 at the age of thirty-one. Villette worked in the patent office in Washington until her death in 1891 after a visit to Florida.

As for George's family and business associates, Edward Aldrich remained in California several years after Corinna's death in New York. He finally returned east in November 1860, and by the eve of the South's secession from the Union, he was practicing medicine in Savannah.[17] Edward's cousin Alfred Aldrich, an ardent proponent of secession, was serving in the South Carolina legislature when Abraham Lincoln was elected in 1860. As chairman of the House Committee on Federal Relations, he received "telegraphic messages . . . that urged South Carolina to act promptly."[18] On April 12–14, Edward Aldrich witnessed the bombing of Fort Sumter in Charleston.[19] After the outbreak of the Civil War, Edward served irregularly as a surgeon for the Confederacy, and after that conflict, he continued his peripatetic life, establishing a medical practice in Jacksonville; by 1867, he was living in Lake City.[20] Edward's brother Louis remained in California for the rest of his life. In 1851, he became a judge in Sacramento County, and in 1855 he married Virginia Foote. He died in San Francisco in 1885.[21]

Though he was the oldest of the Brown siblings, Mannevillette Brown outlived all his brothers and sisters. He never married, but he enjoyed a long, distinguished career as an artist. From his studio in Utica, New York, he remained in touch with George's and his sister Ellen's families until his death in 1896, just after his eighty-sixth birthday. When he learned of his uncle's passing, Edward Anderson traveled to Utica to wind up his affairs. Among the numerous family items that Anderson took back to Washington with him were the many letters written from Florida's antebellum frontier by his other uncle, George Long Brown.

APPENDIX A

The Cast of Characters

George Long Brown's letters contain references to more than one hundred individuals—family, friends, neighbors, customers, and business contacts—whose lives affected Brown's personal experiences. These people also had a large part in shaping the history of Alachua and its neighboring counties in the region's earliest years. The following list offers basic information, where available, concerning these people and their interrelationships with Brown and other principle characters in the story. Fortunately, Alachua County's antebellum records are nearly complete. In addition, the pathbreaking work of Alachua County Clerk J. K. Irby and staff member Jim Powell have made many of these records available via the Alachua County Ancient Records site on the web (http://www.alachuaclerk. org/archive/). Unfortunately, the same is not the case for other counties. Antebellum court records for Columbia and Lafayette are nearly nonexistent. The story is similar in Duval County and Putnam County. St. Johns County has some records. Attempts are made here to follow individuals to their deaths, but in many cases persons may have died unrecorded deaths.

Aldrich, Alfred. Born in Charleston in 1814, the son of Robert and Ann Aldrich, Alfred Aldrich was married to Martha Anna Ayer and by 1850 they had five children. He was a graduate of the College of Charleston and admitted to the bar in 1835. He lived at "The Oaks" Plantation in Barnwell District and was often a traveling companion of William Gilmore Simms. Aldrich was a judge-politician and became an ardent secessionist. He served in the South Carolina legislature from 1858 to 1865. A journalist once described him as "the leader of the impractical, unconquered element—the men who are sullen or spiteful, the untamed fire-eaters. [. . .] He is noticeable for his long and tumbled hair, and his long full whiskers and moustache. He is able and forcible in debate, and a 'real good fellow, personally.'" Aldrich died in 1897.[1]

Aldrich, Corinna Brown. Born in 1812 in Portsmouth, New Hampshire, the sister of George Brown, Corinna came to Florida in 1835 with her sister Ellen and brother Charles. In 1837, she married Edward S. Aldrich, a physician attached to the Florida Volunteers. Corinna lived with her husband variously at Newnansville, St. Augustine, Mineral Springs, Pensacola, and Key West, Florida. In 1851, she moved with her sister to New York City. She died there in 1854. She is buried in Greenwood Cemetery.

Aldrich, Edward S. Born in 1811 in St. Marys, Georgia, to Whipple and Letitia Aldrich, Edward Aldrich graduated from the South Carolina Medical College in 1833. In 1836, he enlisted in the Florida Volunteers. In 1837, he married Corinna Brown and they lived in numerous locations before he decided to relocate to San Francisco, California, in 1850. His wife, Corinna, died while he was in the West. Aldrich eventually returned to the East about the time of the Civil War and served sporadically in the Confederate service as a physician. After the war, he practiced medicine in Savannah, and in 1870 he was living in Lake City, Florida.[2]

Aldrich, Louis. The brother of Edward Aldrich, Louis Aldrich was born in St. Marys, Georgia, in 1821 to Whipple and Letitia Aldrich. Louis Aldrich became a lawyer, moved to Newnansville, and practiced law with William Forward in the 1840s. A Democrat, Aldrich was elected to the Florida House of Representatives in 1846 and 1847 and then to the Florida Senate in 1848. In June 1849, Aldrich resigned his seat and moved to California. A Tallahassee newspaper noted that Aldrich was in

> every way one of the most conscientious and inflexibly honest and upright men whom it has ever been our pleasure to know—a politician elevated far above the tricks of political artifice—an unflinching Democrat, but one whose devotion to party was always subordinate to his regard for the interests of the State—it was with sorrow and regret that we bid him good bye as he passed through Tallahassee on his long route.

The source asserted that Florida had lost one of "her jewels." Louis prospered in California, where he eventually was elected district judge. Louis remained in California for the rest of his life. In 1851, he became a judge in Sacramento County and in 1855 was married to Virginia Foote. He died in San Francisco in 1885.[3]

Aldrich, Robert. Born in 1780 in Massachusetts, Robert Aldrich was Edward Aldrich's uncle. The 1850 Charleston County, South Carolina, Census listed Robert Aldrich as a seventy-year-old "Wharfinger" worth $2,500. He shared his household with his wife, Francis (sixty-two), Thomas, a physician (thirty-five), Caroline (thirty-two), Sarah (twenty-two), and Julia (twenty). He died in 1851 and was buried in St. Philips Cemetery in Charleston.[4]

Aldrich, Tom. Born in 1815 to Robert and Francis Aldrich in Charleston, Thomas Aldrich was Edward Aldrich's cousin. A physician, he served briefly in the Second Regiment of the East Florida Volunteers in 1837. He returned to Charleston and in 1850 was living with his parents. He eventually married Caroline Roselia Prince. He died in June 25, 1886.[5]

Aldrich, Whipple. Born in 1782 in Providence, Rhode Island. Whipple Aldrich was a physician and merchant in St. Marys, Georgia. In 1810, Aldrich married Letitia Shearman and together they had nine children, including Edward S., their first child. Aldrich owned many acres of land in Camden County, Georgia, and Duval County, Florida. After the death of his first wife, Aldrich married Jane Johnson and they had three more children. Aldrich died in 1852 and is buried in St. Marys Cemetery.[6]

Anderson, Edward Willoughby. Born in 1841, the son of James W. and Ellen Anderson, Edward Willoughby Anderson was the nephew of George Brown and Mannevillette Brown. After attending New York public schools, Edward entered West Point Military Academy in 1860, only to resign at the urging of his mother. He eventually fought in the Army of Northern Virginia and was among the officers in Gen. Robert E. Lee's army at Appomattox. After the war, Anderson attended the City College of New York and settled eventually in Washington. He became a patent attorney. In 1867, he married Elizabeth Felicia Masi, the sister of his roommate at West Point. Will and "Lizzie" had seven children and had a long life together until Lizzie's death in 1903. Anderson died in Washington in 1915.[7]

Anderson, Ellen Maria Brown. Born in 1814 in Portsmouth, New Hampshire, Ellen Anderson, George Brown's sister, came to Florida in 1835 with her sister Corinna and brother Charles. She married Lt. James W. Anderson in Newnansville in 1840 and bore three children, Edward Willoughby, Georgia, and Villette. Her husband was killed in the Mexican War, and in 1851 Ellen moved to New York City. She died there in 1862 and is buried in the Greenwood Cemetery in Brooklyn, New York.

Anderson, James Willoughby. Born in Norfolk, Virginia, in 1812, James Willoughby Anderson graduated from West Point Military Academy in 1833. In 1839, Lt. Anderson entered the Second Seminole War as a member of the Second Infantry. In 1840, Anderson married Ellen Brown, George Brown's sister. Anderson served with distinction in the war and was transferred to Fort Gratiot and Buffalo Barracks, New York. After the outbreak of the Mexican War, he participated in Winfield Scott's amphibious invasion of Vera Cruz and fought in all the battles leading up to the occupation of Mexico City. He was killed in the battle of Contreras-Churubusco in August 1847.

Anderson, Georgia. The daughter of Ellen and Capt. James Anderson, Georgia Anderson was born in 1843. The niece of George and Mannevillette Brown, she lived with her father and mother on various military postings in Florida, New York, and Michigan until her father's death in the Mexican War. Then she resided with her widowed mother and her brother, Edward, and sister, Villette, in Key West and New York. When her mother died, she and Villette lived together variously in Utica, New York, and Hartford, Connecticut, until eventually the sisters moved in with Edward in Washington, D.C. Georgia never married, and she died in 1874.

Anderson, Villette. The daughter of Ellen and Capt. James Anderson, Villette Anderson was born in 1847. She was also the niece of George and Mannevillette Brown. She lived with her father and mother on various military postings in Florida, New York, and Michigan until her father's death in the Mexican War. Then she resided with her widowed mother, her brother, Edward, and her sister, Georgia, in Key West and New York. When her mother died, she and Georgia lived together variously in Utica, New York, and Hartford, Connecticut, until eventually the sisters moved in with Edward in Washington, D.C., where she worked in the U.S. Patent Office. Villette never married, and she died in 1891.

Barnes, Thomas. Born in 1815 in Georgia, Thomas Barnes lived in Newnansville, but by 1850 he was living in Marion County. Thomas married Mary Ann Barnes in 1844. He died in 1881.[8]

Barrow, Elijah. A farmer born in Georgia, Elijah Barrow was born in 1822. He married Belinda Walker in 1848. Barrow enlisted as a private in Company H, Second Florida Cavalry Regiment, on July 15, 1863. He was mustered out on May 20, 1865.[9]

Bates, Wilson. Born in Virginia in 1795, in 1840 Wilson Bates was a farmer and lived in Fort Micanopy in Alachua County. Bates served as a private in Captain Michael Garrison's Mounted Company of the First Regiment, Second Brigade of the Florida Militia, commanded by Col. John Warren from September 22, 1836, to January 22, 1837. He also served from May 3 to November 2, 1839, in Captain Matthew Hindley's Mounted Company of the First Regiment of the Florida Volunteers, commanded by Col. John Warren. In the 1840s, he married Mary Catherine Watson. He died in 1860 in Alachua County.[10]

Beard, John. Born in 1811, John Beard was a native of Salisbury, North Carolina, and came to Leon County, Florida, in 1838 after serving in the North Carolina legislature. President John Tyler appointed him U.S. marshal for the Eastern District of Florida from 1842 to 1845. In 1845, he was selected registrar of public lands. He married Sarah Lingo of Jefferson County in 1846. A prominent Democratic politician, he ran unsuccessfully as a candidate for the U.S. Congress in 1850. In 1851, the General Assembly appointed him comptroller of the state. He died in 1856 in Jefferson County.[11]

Blanton, James J. B. A Newnansville resident in 1844, J. B. Blanton was born in North Carolina in 1813. He served as first sergeant in Captain Jonathon Tyner's Company of Florida Mounted Militia from October 7, 1839, to April 7, 1840. Blanton reenlisted in Captain C. Ellis's Company of the First Regiment, Brigade of the Florida Mounted Militia, commanded by Col. W. J. Bailey from August 17 to December 5, 1840. Blanton and his wife, Catherine, and seven children eventually relocated to Madison County. He died in 1894.[12]

Bonneville, Benjamin Louis Eulalie. Born in 1793 in France and immigrating with his family to New York during the Reign of Terror, Bonneville eventually graduated from West Point in 1815. Before coming to Florida, Bonneville made a remarkable exploration of the "Far West," and his journals were edited and published by Washington Irving in 1837. He was a captain in the Seventh Infantry and served in Florida from 1839 to 1843. He was attached to Forts Harlee and Brooke during his Florida service. After leaving Florida, he fought in the Mexican War in the battles of Contreras and Churubusco, the Battle of Molino del Rey, and the assault and capture of Chapultepec. He then served in various frontier stations in the West. In 1856, he commanded the Department of New Mexico (1856–1858); in 1857, he led the Gila Expedition. Though he retired from active service in 1861 with the rank of colonel, he spent the entire Civil War in the Union service in Missouri recruiting and performing other duties. He died in Fort Smith, Arkansas, on June 12, 1878.[13]

Bronson, Isaac H. Born in Jefferson County, New York, in 1802, Bronson practiced law in Watertown, New York, from 1822 to 1837 and was elected to Congress in 1836 as a Democrat. Martin Van Buren appointed Bronson judge of the Eastern Judicial District in 1840, and he and his wife, Sophronia, and daughters, Gertrude and Emma, lived in St. Augustine until Bronson moved to Palatka in 1846. In 1846, President James K. Polk appointed Bronson U.S. district judge, and he served in this post until his death in 1855.[14]

Brown, Adelaide. Born in 1852 in Newnansville, Florida, Adelaide Stewart Brown was the daughter of George and Matilda Brown. She resided with her widowed mother in Alachua County. On February 25, 1874, she died of heart failure in Nashville, Tennessee.[15]

Brown, Charles Burroughs. Born in 1816 in Portsmouth, New Hampshire, and brother of George L. Brown, Charles Brown migrated to Florida in 1835 with his sisters, Ellen and Corinna. He settled first in Mandarin, Florida, where he farmed a homestead adjacent to the plantation of his aunt Delia and her husband, Dr. James Hall. Eventually, Brown migrated to Newnansville, Florida, and was preparing to go into the mercantile trade with his brother George and brother-in-law Edward Aldrich when he died suddenly in Savannah in 1840.[16]

Brown, Corinna. See Aldrich, Corinna Brown.

Brown, Elihu Dearing. The father of George Brown, Elihu Dearing Brown was born in 1777. He was a prominent ship designer, builder, and privateering ship captain who lived in Portsmouth, New Hampshire. In 1806, he married Elizabeth Dearing and they had seven children. Brown commanded the *Fox* against British shipping during the War of 1812 and again sailed against Spain in the service of the Argentine revolt. In 1819, he was captured by the Spanish off the coast of Africa and he died in a prison in Cádiz, Spain.[17]

Brown, Elizabeth Dearing. The mother of George Brown, Elizabeth Dearing Brown was born in 1785 and married Capt. Elihu Dearing Brown in 1806. She and her husband had seven children and made their home in Portsmouth, New Hampshire. She died in 1832.[18]

Brown, Ellen. See Anderson, Ellen Maria Brown.

Brown, Mannevillette Elihu Dearing. Born in 1810 in Portsmouth, New Hampshire, and brother of George L. Brown, M.E.D. Brown was a notable American engraver and artist who lived in Boston and Philadelphia before training in Europe from 1838 to 1849. Brown eventually settled in Utica, New York, and became an artist of some renown. Brown enjoyed success as a painter until his death at the age of eighty-six in 1896.

Brown, Matilda Stewart. Born Matilda Stewart in 1827 in Georgia, Matilda married George L. Brown in 1852 and moved to Newnansville, Florida. She bore four children, Claudia, Ellen, Adelaide, and George. In 1857, she became a widow, left Newnansville, and moved to a farm in Alachua County and then eventually to Gainesville. After the Civil War, she relocated briefly to Tennessee. She eventually moved in with her sister Mary Dozier and her husband in Ocala. She died in Ocala in 1914.[19]

Bruton, David. Born in 1804 and a native of South Carolina, David Bruton was a very early settler of Alachua County. The 1830 Alachua County Census lists him as living in the Spring Grove settlement. In 1845, Bruton married Nancy S. Connell in Marion County, and they had three children before Bruton's death in 1853.[20]

Clarke, Saul. A merchant and Connecticut native, in 1849 Clarke lived on Drake Street in Charleston. Clarke was affiliated with S. S. & G. Clarke Fancy Goods, 151 Meeting Street. Saul Clarke's residence was the Charleston Hotel.[21]

Colding, Samuel B. Born in South Carolina in 1793, Samuel B. Colding was one of the earliest residents of Alachua County. He lived with his wife, Jemima, and their five children. He is listed in the 1830 and 1840 censuses. In 1838, the county court appointed Colding as its tax assessor. He died in 1855 and is buried in the Wacahoota Methodist Church Cemetery in Williston, Florida.[22]

Cole, Archibald H. A native of Virginia, Archibald Cole was a prominent resident of St. Augustine and relative of George W. Cole who headed the federal land office in St. Augustine. Born in 1813, Cole married Annie L. Mays of Madison on May 15, 1848, and they relocated to Putnam County; his real estate was valued at $40,000. By 1860, Cole was a banker living in Fernandina and his personal wealth had grown to $160,000. Cole served in the early years of the Civil War as an aide to Gen. Joseph E. Johnston and later attained the rank of major as a Confederate transportation official. By 1870, he was a merchant in Orange Mills, Putnam County. He died in Putnam County in 1879.[23]

Coker, Joseph B. A prominent Democrat, Coker practiced law with Bird Pearson in Newnansville. Coker fought a duel with Claudius Stewart on the Georgia line on June 19, 1854. One account noted that the cause of the duel was a misunderstanding between Coker and Stewart over Stewart's courting of a young woman. Stewart subsequently died of his wounds in November 1854. Coker married Miss A. M. Ledwith in Jacksonville in February 1855. Coker died suddenly in Newnansville on November 1, 1856.[24]

Conway, Dr. Valentine Y. Born in Stafford County, Virginia, in 1803, Conway was appointed surveyor general of Florida in 1842 by President John Tyler. He succeeded Robert Butler, who was again appointed in 1845 by President James K. Polk. He and his wife, Mary, had nine children in 1850. He died in 1881 in Stafford County, Virginia.[25]

Coy, Amaziah. A native of Massachusetts born in 1801, Amaziah Coy was a hotel keeper at Garey's Ferry. He also served as postmaster of the town from 1843 to 1849. He married Emilia Spear in 1825, and in 1850, they had sons John (21) and Amaziah Jr. (18) and daughters Maria (22) and Caroline (15) living with them at the hotel at Garey's Ferry. Coy died in 1864 and is buried in the Old City Cemetery in Jacksonville.[26]

Churchill, Sylvester. A native of Vermont and a veteran of the War of 1812, Sylvester Churchill was a journalist and author before he became a soldier. Remaining in the army after the War of 1812, Churchill served on several frontier posts before coming to Florida in 1838. In 1840, Gen. Zachary Taylor ordered Churchill to "inspect, from time to time, the militia in the service of the United States, east of the Suwanee River, and to muster militia into and out of service when necessary." In 1841, Churchill was promoted to inspector general of the army, and he remained in that capacity until his retirement in 1861. He saw combat in the Mexican War, fighting in the Battle of Buena Vista as a brigadier general. He retired in September 1861, and he died on December 7, 1862.[27]

Critchton, Dr. John P. Born in St. Marys, Georgia, in 1816, Critchton served as a mounted private for three months and twenty-five days in A. W. Critchton Detachment of the Fourth Regiment, Second Brigade of the Florida Militia, commanded by Col. Warren. from November 1835 to March 1836. Critchton practiced medicine in Newnansville until relocating to Benton (Hernando) County in the mid-1840s. He eventually migrated to Tampa, where his medical talents and public service achievements were well-respected. He was elected mayor of Tampa in 1860 and spent the Civil War years there. Critchton spent the last years of his life in Atlanta, where he died in 1888.[28]

Cushing, Charles W. Cushing was a native of Portsmouth, New Hampshire, a friend of Mannevillette Brown, and a business associate of George Brown and Edward Aldrich. He was admitted to the Alachua County bar not long after he migrated to Florida. He traveled back and forth from Alachua County to Portsmouth often. He and his wife, Ann, had four children. Cushing died on October 2, 1843. Edward Aldrich became the administrator of his estate.[29]

Dearing, Delia (Dorothy). See Hall, Delia.

Dearing, Ann. The sister of Elizabeth Dearing Brown, Ann Dearing lived in the Portsmouth household of Capt. Elihu Brown. She assisted in caring for her nephews Mannevillette, Charles, and George and nieces Corinna, Ellen, and Adelaide Brown. In 1835, she migrated to Mandarin, Florida, with her nephew Charles and nieces Corinna and Ellen Brown, joining with her sister Delia Dearing, who had recently married Dr. John

Hall, a substantial planter. In 1840, she moved to Newnansville, where she kept house for her niece Corinna Aldrich and her husband. She also helped her other niece Ellen Anderson in caring for her little children. She lived with the Aldriches variously in Newnansville, St. Augustine, and Pensacola. She died in Pensacola in 1846.

Dearing, Mary. The sister of Elizabeth Dearing Brown, Mary Dearing lived in the Portsmouth household of Capt. Elihu Brown. She assisted in caring for her nephews Mannevillette, Charles, and George and nieces Corinna, Ellen, and Adelaide Brown. In 1835, she migrated to Mandarin, Florida, with her nephew Charles and nieces Corinna an Ellen Brown, joining her sister Delia Dearing, who had recently married Dr. John Hall, a substantial planter. She died in Mandarin in 1839.

Dell, Bennett Maxey. Born in 1794 in Screven, Georgia, Bennett Dell was involved in the "Patriot" invasion of the Alachua area in 1813 and 1814. He, along with his two brothers, Simeon and James, returned to the area soon after the transfer of flags in 1821. Maxey, as he was most often referred to, originally settled in the Wanton's (Micanopy) area, but he and his brothers eventually founded the community of Dells in the early 1830s, which eventually became Newnansville. Dell was a farmer, sawmill owner, and lay preacher. He married Penelope Love (1785–1832) in 1817 in Screven, Georgia. In 1837, Dell married Eliza Dorothy Boston and they had six children. From December 29, 1840, to March 29, 1841, Dell served as Lt. Col. in the Second Regiment, Brigade of the Florida Mounted Militia, commanded by F. L. Dancy. Dell died on February 21, 1855.[30]

Dell, Philip. The son of Bennett Maxey and Penelope Dell, Philip Dell was born in Sumter, Georgia, in 1815. Dell married Mary Matilda Boston in December 13, 1838. They had two children, Henrietta and Talula. Dell was captain in the First Regiment, Brigade of the Florida Mounted Militia, commanded by Col. John Warren. He served from November 5, 1839, through May 5, 1840. Dell was appointed postmaster of the Flemington Community in Marion County in 1847. He died in 1889.[31]

Dell, William F. Born in 1824 and the son of Bennett Maxey and Penelope Dell, Dell served as a private in Capt. James Dell's company of the First Regiment of the Florida Militia, commanded by Col. John Warren. He served from March to July 1837. On June 11, 1845, he married Elizabeth Sanchez. By 1850, he had become a merchant in Newnansville, and in

1853, he was appointed the town's postmaster. He died on October 23, 1854, at his father's residence.[32]

Doggett, John L. Born in 1798 in Massachusetts, Doggett was a graduate of Brown University who became a prominent Duval County lawyer. He migrated to Florida from Massachusetts soon after the change of flags in 1822 with his wife, Maria Fairbanks. They had four children: Aristides, John L., Maria C., and Simeon T. In 1824, the legislative council granted Doggett the license to operate a ferry to cross the St. Johns River. One year earlier, he was granted a contract to build the first Duval County Courthouse. A leading Duval County Democrat, he represented the county in the legislative council from 1824 to 1827. In 1827, he served as the body's president. Doggett served as judge of the Duval County Court from 1824 until his death in 1844. On March 6, 1840, Gov. Robert Raymond Reid appointed him examiner of the Jacksonville branch of the Southern Life Insurance & Trust Company. By 1843, he was serving as collector for the Port of Jacksonville. Doggett died at his residence in Jacksonville on January 8, 1844.[33]

Douglas, Thomas. Born in 1790 in Connecticut but migrating as a young man to Indiana, Douglas and his wife, Hanna, migrated to Florida in 1826 when President James Monroe appointed him U.S. attorney for the Eastern District of Florida. He served in this post until 1845. After statehood, Douglas served as judge of the Eastern Judicial Circuit of Florida from 1845 to 1853. He also served as associate justice in the Florida Supreme Court. Douglas died in 1855.[34]

Dozier, Mary Stewart. Born on Oran Plantation on the St. Marys River on October 28, 1845, Mary Stewart was the youngest daughter of Daniel M. and Eliza Stewart. That year she migrated with her family as an infant to Columbia County, Florida. After the death of her father in 1848, she lived with her widowed mother in Columbia and Alachua Counties. She married Leonard Dozier in 1866. She lived in the Nashville, Tennessee, area before finally relocating to Ocala, Florida, with her husband. She had three children, Eugene Jackson Dozier, Lauragene Dozier, and Florence Dozier. Her widowed sister Matilda Brown lived with her and her husband in Ocala from roughly the 1880s until her mother's death in 1914.[35]

Elwes, Alfred W. H. Born in Pennsylvania in 1798, Alfred W. H. Elwes attended medical school at the University of Maryland, Baltimore, graduating in 1820. He joined the army in 1825 and was promoted to surgeon in 1836. He married Catharine Thomas in 1828 in Baltimore County, Maryland. He died in Palatka on June 12, 1842.[36]

Fontane, John M. John M. Fontane was born in Florida in 1798. He was the owner of a large tract of land south of the forks of Black Creek. He served in many leadership positions in St. Augustine, including postmaster from 1843–1844. He represented St. Johns County in the House of Representatives in 1841 and 1845. In 1846, President James K. Polk appointed Fontane receiver of the public monies at the St. Augustine land office. In 1853, Fontane served as secretary of the executive committee of the St. Johns County Democratic Party and Alderman of the City of St. Augustine. He died in 1855.[37]

Forward, William A. Born in New York in 1812, William A. Forward studied law and came to St. Augustine in 1840 as a kind of protégé to Isaac Bronson, U.S. judge of the Eastern Judicial District of Florida. On June 10, 1842, he married Mary Anita Hutchinson and they had four children in St. Augustine. In 1843, he formed a law partnership with Louis Aldrich and practiced throughout the Eastern Judicial District. A Democrat, Forward opposed statehood and favored division of the Florida Territory. In 1844, he was elected to the territorial House of Representatives and was its Speaker in 1845. He represented St. Johns County in the House again in 1847 and then was elected to the Senate in 1848 and 1850. In 1850, Forward left East Florida and formed a law partnership with Simon Towle in Tallahassee. In 1853, the General Assembly of Florida elected Forward judge of the Eastern Circuit of Florida. Residing in Jacksonville, he served until 1857, when he went into private practice with John P. Sanderson. Forward moved to Palatka and in 1859 was popularly elected to the Supreme County of Florida. He died in 1865.[38]

Gibbons, Charley. An early settler in Newnansville, Charley Gibbons served in Capt. James Piles's Company of the First Regiment, Second Brigade of the Florida Militia, commanded by Col. John Warren, from November 24 to February 23, 1837. He reenlisted from December 6, 1840, to March 6, 1841, in Matthew Hindley's company of the Second Regiment, Brigade of the Florida Foot Militia, commanded by Col. F. L. Dancy. On May 24, 1844, Charley Gibbons made a will leaving all his earthly goods, including his one hundred head of cattle and his fifty head of hogs, to Sylvester Bryant. He died in January 1845 in Newnansville.[39]

Gibbons, Delilah. Born in 1812 in Georgia, Delilah Gibbons was the widow of William Gibbons, who died in 1836 in Jacksonville. She lived in Newnansville from the 1840s through the 1860s.[40]

Goodrich, Charles. Born in New York in 1811, Goodrich served as sergeant from May 3 to November 2, 1839, in Captain Matthew Hindley's Mounted Company of the First Regiment of the Florida Volunteers, commanded by Col. John Warren. He reenlisted as a private on March 19, 1841, and served until April 6. He married Rebecca Moody on January 20, 1839, and they lived in Newnansville in 1840. By 1850, Goodrich and his wife, Rebecca, and five children were living in the Melendez settlement in Benton County. They subsequently relocated to New River (eventually Bradford) County. Goodrich died in 1888 in Volusia County.[41]

Hall, Delia Dearing. The sister of Elizabeth Dearing Brown, Ann Dearing, and Mary Dearing, Delia Dearing Hall was the first of the Portsmouth clan to migrate to territorial Florida. In 1833, after a brief business venture in St. Augustine, Delia Dearing married well-to-do planter Dr. James Hall, who owned a large estate on the St. Johns River community of Mandarin. Soon thereafter, beginning in 1835, her sisters, nephew (Charles), and her nieces (Corinna and Ellen) homesteaded on Hall's land nearby. When her husband died in 1838, Hall continued in Mandarin. She died in 1843.

Hammond, Richard Pindel. Born in Maryland but later moving with his family to Arkansas, Richard Pindal Hammond was admitted to West Point Military Academy in 1837. After graduating in July 1841, Hammond served briefly at Fort McHenry in Baltimore but came to St. Augustine in 1842 as a second lieutenant in the Third Artillery. From December 3, 1844, through August 16, 1845, Hammond assisted the inspector general in investigation claims of Florida Volunteers. He remained in Florida until his active service in the Mexican War. On May 28, 1846, he was promoted to first lieutenant of the Third Artillery and served on Brig. Gen. James Shields's staff. He participated in the march though Coahuila, in the Siege of Vera Cruz, and in the battles of Cerro Gordo, Contreras, and Churubusco, where he was recognized for gallant and meritorious conduct. He was among the troops that captured Chapultepec and participated in the final assault and capture of Mexico City. After a brief period as secretary of the city government and acting judge advocate of Mexico City and coastal survey duty, Hammond resigned his commission in 1851. Hammond migrated to California, where he became prosperous in mining and railroad enterprises. He died in San Francisco in 1891.[42]

Hart, Isaiah. Born in Georgia in 1792, Isaiah Hart came with his family to Spanish Florida in 1801, settling in the Trout Creek area of the St. Johns. Hart is associated with the founding of Cow Ford in 1821–1822 (the settlement that eventually became Jacksonville). He married Nancy Nelson in 1818, and among their children was future Florida governor Ossian Hart. A Whig, Hart represented Duval County in the legislative council from 1837 to 1845 (first in the House in 1837 and 1838 and then in the Senate from 1839 to 1845). He died in 1861.[43]

Harvey, Simeon. Born in 1820 in Georgia, Simeon Harvey was an early settler of Alachua County. Harvey married Elizabeth Goodbread on September 21, 1839. By 1850, Simeon and Elizabeth and their seven children were living in Levy County. In the Civil War, Harvey fought with the Fifth Regiment, Florida Infantry. He died in Richmond, Virginia, on November 28, 1862.[44]

Heintzelman, Samuel Peter. A native of Pennsylvania, Heintzelman graduated from West Point in 1826. He served in Missouri, Michigan, and Wisconsin before he was assigned to quartermaster duty in Florida in 1834. From 1838 to 1842, his principal duty as captain and assistant quartermaster was investigating Florida militia claims. This duty took him all over the territory. After his Florida service, Heintzelman served in Buffalo, Detroit, and Louisville primarily as a recruiter. Heintzelman served in the Mexican War with distinction. He was a member of Winfield Scott's army during the siege of Vera Cruz, and on October 9, 1847, he received the rank of brevet major for gallant and meritorious conduct at the Battle of Huamantla. After the war, Heintzelman served in California, the New Mexico territory, Texas, and other locations until the outbreak of the Civil War. He commanded volunteers as a brigadier general in the Army of the Potomac and fought in all the major battles of that army in the Eastern Theater. Heintzelman remained in the army after the Civil War, serving in various western posts in Texas. In 1869, he retired from the army and worked as an executive in the mining and life insurance business. He died in Washington in 1880 at the age of seventy-four.[45]

Heiskell, Henry Lee. A career army physician, Henry Lee Heiskell was born in 1803 in Winchester, Virginia. In 1833, Heiskell married Margaret S. Baldwin. He married Elizabeth Kortright in 1842, the granddaughter of President James Monroe, and they lived in Washington, D.C., and had two children. Promoted to the rank of surgeon in 1838, he served as Gen. Edmund P. Gaines's chief medical officer. He died on August 12, 1855.[46]

Hopkins, Benjamin F. Born in 1800 in South Carolina, Benjamin Hopkins migrated to Putnam County from Georgia in the 1840s and became one of the area's most substantial planters. In 1850, he and his wife, Susan, had six children living in their household. Also in 1850, Hopkins represented St. Johns-Putnam County in the Florida House of Representatives. In 1852, Gov. Thomas Brown appointed Hopkins major general of the Florida Militia. He died in 1862.[47]

Hopson, Nevil. A native of Kentucky, Nevil Hopson graduated from West Point in 1837. He fought in Florida from 1839 to 1843 as a member of the Seventh Infantry. Following his service in the Mexican War, he was dismissed for drunkenness.[48]

Keil, Adam. Born in 1820 in Hesse-Darmstadt, Germany, Keil migrated to the United States in the late 1830s. He was a tailor by trade. Keil married Clarissa Prevatt in 1843. Keil served in Captain C. Ellis's Company of the First Regiment of the Florida Mounted Militia, commanded by Col. W. J. Bailey, from August 17 to December 5, 1840. Keil reenlisted on December 6 and served until March 6, 1841, in Matthew Hindley's company of the Second Regiment of the Florida Foot Militia, commanded by Col. F. L. Dancy. When his wife died, Keil moved to Bellville, Illinois.[49]

Kelly, James Dr. A native of Charleston, Kelly arrived in St. Augustine in 1822, lived briefly in Palatka, and eventually moved to Alachua County, where he was employed as a physician by the Florida Association for a settlement in the county the group had established in about 1822. Kelly returned to St. Augustine, but by 1830 he was back in Alachua County in the Spring Grove settlement, where he practiced for some years before finally relocating permanently to St. Augustine.[50]

Knight, Jeptha. Born in Georgia in 1816, Knight served as corporal from May 3 to November 2, 1839, in Captain Matthew Hindley's Mounted Company of the First Regiment, Brigade of the Florida Volunteers, commanded by Col. John Warren. Knight reenlisted on November 2, 1839, and served to May 2, 1840, and then again from March 19, 1841, until April 6. He married his first wife, Eliza, on July 1, 1843. In 1851, after his wife's death, he married Mary M. Watson on June 24, 1851. During the Civil War, Knight was a member of Company A, First Regiment, Florida Infantry Reserves. He died in 1886 and was buried in Jonesville Cemetery in Newberry, Florida.[51]

L'Engle, John. Born in South Carolina in 1801, John L'Engle was admitted to West Point in 1816 and graduated in 1819. He was appointed second lieutenant of the artillery corps. He first served at Amelia Island from 1819 to 1820 before the transfer of flags, was reassigned to Charleston harbor from 1820 to 1826, and attended artillery school at Fort Monroe in Virginia; he was promoted to first lieutenant after completion in 1825. After serving briefly at Fort Monroe and Fort Constitution in New Hampshire, L'Engle was assigned to quartermaster duty in St. Augustine from 1829 to 1832. In 1830, he married Susan Fatio of Mandarin. From 1832 to 1833, L'Engle superintended repairs of roads in Florida. He remained in Florida in the quartermaster service until he resigned his commission in 1838. After leaving the military, L'Engle became successful in planting and the lumber trade in Duval County. He died on September 19, 1864, at Lake City at the age of sixty-four.[52]

Levy, David. See Yulee, David Levy.

Livingston, R. G. Born in 1820, Robert G. Livingston practiced law with Charles W. Downing in Newnansville. He led a company of volunteers in the Mexican War. He died at Puebla, Mexico, on February 9, 1848, from an accidental wound sustained while hunting a wolf near his encampment.[53]

Loring, William Wing. Born in 1818 in Hanover County, North Carolina, William Wing Loring lived a truly remarkable life. He came to St.

Augustine with his parents, Reuben and Hanna Loring, at a young age
and fought in various Florida militia units during the Second Seminole
War. Loring attended Georgetown University and returned to St. Augustine in 1840 and studied law in Judge Robert Reid's office; he was soon
admitted to the bar. He was also associated with David Levy. Known
for his impetuousness, Loring was often involved in physical conflicts.
One example was a nearly fatal affray when he and his brother Charles
fought George and John Mackay in the streets of St. Augustine. Loring
received a bullet in the shoulder and at the time of the ruckus, Loring
was member-elect of the state of Florida's first General Assembly. At the
outbreak of the Mexican War, Loring led a company of mounted volunteers as captain. He fought bravely in battles leading up to the capture of
Mexico City, losing an arm in the process. After the Mexican War, Loring
remained in the U.S. Army, serving in the New Mexico territory and
California, and he reached the rank of colonel before resigning his commission to accept a brigadier generalship in the Confederate Service. He
served in Virginia, Kentucky, and then Mississippi during the Vicksburg
Campaign. He was a division commander in the Atlanta campaign and
subsequently joined the Army of Tennessee, fighting in the battles of
Franklin and Nashville. Loring surrendered with Joseph Johnson's forces
at Durham Station, North Carolina. After the war, Loring accepted a
commission as brigade general in the Army of the Khedive of Egypt. He
served from 1869 to 1879 and received the Imperial Order of the Osma-
riah. He returned to Florida in 1879 and was an unsuccessful candidate
for the U.S. Senate. He is the author of *A Confederate Soldier in Egypt*
(1883). He died in New York City on December 30, 1886.[54]

Mackay, George. A native of Georgia and the brother of U.S. Army officer
Captain John Mackay, George was a lawyer and supplemented his legal
practice as a surveyor.[56]

Mackay, John. Born in Georgia and graduating from West Point in 1829,
John Mackay served in Georgia, Alabama, and Louisiana before coming
to Florida just before the Dade massacre in 1835 as a first lieutenant of
the Second Artillery. He served in the Seminole War from 1837 to 1839
on topographical duty. On July 7, 1838, he became captain of the Topographical Engineers. Perhaps Mackay's most important accomplishment
while in Florida was his execution of his famous "Map of the Seat of War
in Florida Compiled by Order of Bvt. Gen. Zachary Taylor, Principally

from the Surveys and Reconnaissance of the Officers of the U.S. Army," published in 1839. Also working on this map with Mackay was George Brown's brother-in-law, Lt. James Willoughby Anderson. Mackay remained in Florida until his reassignment to Texas in 1846. Soon thereafter, he went on sick leave, and he died in Savannah on May 31, 1848.[57]

McKay, Alexander. A member of the regular army, McKay was a lieutenant attached to Fort Heilman in October 1836. He left the army soon thereafter and moved to Jacksonville and then to Newnansville. He also worked as a surveyor in the late 1840s.[55]

McLin, Samuel B. Born in Tennessee in 1832, Samuel B. McLin was a lawyer. He came to Florida from Georgia in the 1850s. He married Mary Tooke in Madison County on September 5, 1855. Eventually settling in Newnansville, McLin practiced law and was in Gainesville when the Civil War broke out. On March 20, 1862, McLin enlisted as a first Lieutenant in Company C, Seventh Florida Infantry Regiment and was mustered out at Newnansville on January 25, 1863. McLin and his wife, Mary, eventually relocated to Orange County, Florida. He died in Orlando in 1879.[58]

Miles, William Porcher. Born in 1822 in Charleston, William Porcher Miles graduated from the College of Charleston in 1842. He was admitted to the bar soon thereafter. He became a professor of mathematics at the College of Charleston and was elected mayor of Charleston in 1855. In 1857, he was elected to Congress and served until 1860. He served in the Confederate Congress and on the staff of Gen. P. G. T. Beauregard. After the Civil War, he became president of the University of South Carolina in 1880, serving until 1882. He died in 1899.[59]

Morgan, Solomon. Born in 1793 in New London, Connecticut, Morgan was a merchant in Black Creek. He married Belinda Gates Budington on February 2, 1825. He died in Middleburg, Florida, in 1853.[60]

Olmsted, Woodbridge S. Born in 1802 in Connecticut, Olmsted migrated to Alachua County, Florida, at an early age. He served as a private in Garrison's Company in Warren's Florida Mounted Militia from 1836 to 1837. He married Margaret Sanchez on February 22, 1841. He served as a private in Capt. Thomas Ellis's Company of the Second Regiment of the Florida Mounted Militia, commanded by Col. F. L. Dancy, from January

12 to April 12, 1841. He served as postmaster of Newnansville from 1837 to 1838. In the 1840s, Olmsted migrated to Homosassa, Benton County, Florida, and became postmaster there in August 1846. By 1850, Olmsted and his wife were living in Hartford, Connecticut. He died there in 1871.[61]

Parsons, John. Born in Connecticut in 1810, John Parsons came to Florida in the 1830s. He served as major and brigade inspector in Brig. Gen. Leigh Read's Brigade of the Florida Militia from November 24, 1840, to February 4, 1841. Parsons was appointed receiver of the public monies at the Newnansville Land Office on August 30, 1842, by President John Tyler. He was reappointed twice to the post. In 1844, he and Samuel Russell were appointed to a tribunal before which settlers were to make proof to secure their land titles in compliance with the Armed Occupation Act.[62]

Pendarvis, James. Born in Colleton County, South Carolina, in 1809, Pendarvis was an early settler of Alachua County. He married Nancy Williams in 1830. He served in the Sixth Regiment in the Florida Militia from 1835 to 1836. He died in 1867.[63]

Peden, James A. A Democrat and a lawyer, Peden was born in 1823 in North Carolina. In 1850, he resided in Newnansville. President Franklin Pierce appointed Peden chargé d'affaires to Buenos Aires. He served abroad until 1858, when he returned to Jacksonville to practice law. He died in 1894.[64]

Pelot, John C. Born in McIntosh, Georgia, in 1809, John C. Pelot was an early settler in Columbia County. He married Sarah Ann Crews in 1827. They had seven children, including Sarah Ann, born in 1838, who married Charles Stewart in 1853 and Susan Marion, born in 1833, who married James M. Stewart. After the death of his first wife in 1853, he married Jane Ann Rawls in 1854. Pelot died in 1879 in Manatee County.[65]

Pettit, James. Pettit served in Murphey's Company of Mounted Militia in 1839 and in Captain C. Ellis's Company of the First Regiment, Brigade of the Florida Mounted Militia, commanded by Col. W. J. Bailey, from August 17 to December 5, 1840.[66]

Phillips, Albert G. Born in 1805 in Georgia, Albert Phillips was one of the earliest settlers in the Black Creek area. He married Margaret Ann Hendricks in 1829. From November 1835 to March 1836, Phillips served as a private in Captain James Dell's company of the Fourth Regiment, Second Brigade of the Florida Militia, commanded by Col. Warren. By 1850, Phillips and his family were living in Jacksonville. Albert Phillips died in 1874.[67]

Powers, Dr. Edward. A native of Ontario County, New York, Dr. Edward Powers moved to Newnansville in 1853. He joined Dr. Craven Lassiter in establishing a drugstore there. By 1860, he had relocated to Lafayette County. At the outbreak of the Civil War, Powers served briefly as a private in a volunteer company organized in Jacksonville.[68]

Prevatt, Thomas J. Born in 1803 to Thomas B. and Mary Studstill Prevatt in Georgia, Prevatt first migrated to the Florida Territory in the late 1820s. In 1830, he was living in the Lochloosa Creek settlement in Tampa Bay. In 1839, he married Elizabeth Wiles, and after her death he married Dicey Standley in 1848. He was a justice of the peace for Alachua County in the 1840s. He served as postmaster of Newnansville from 1841 to 1848. He died in April 1857 and is buried in the Newnansville Cemetery.[69]

Putnam, Benjamin A. One of Florida's most distinguished political and judicial leaders of the nineteenth century, Benjamin A. Putnam was born in Savannah in 1801. Coming to Florida with the transfer of flags in 1821, he studied law and was admitted to the bar in 1824. In 1830, he married Helen Kirby in St. Augustine. He fought as a major in the Florida militia and distinguished himself in the Second Seminole War. He was elected to the territorial house in 1835 and 1840 and to the territorial senate in 1845. In 1848, he served as Speaker of the Florida House of Representatives. He served as surveyor-general of Florida from 1845 to 1854. In 1857, he was appointed circuit judge, serving until 1865. He died in Palatka on January 25, 1869. Putnam County is named in his honor.[70]

Russell, Samuel. Samuel Russell was born in 1814 in Wilmington, North Carolina. A Democrat, Russell was active in politics and received numerous appointments to federal positions. In 1842, he was appointed registrar of the Newnansville Land Office by President John Tyler. In 1846, President James K. Polk reappointed him. In 1844, he and John Parsons were appointed to a tribunal before which settlers were to make proof of their compliance with the Armed Occupation Act. He married Mary Tison on February 27, 1845. In 1846, Russell was elected brigadier general of the Third Brigade of the Florida Volunteers. In 1851, he was elected Alachua County Clerk. In 1853, President Franklin Pierce appointed Russell receiver of the public moneys at the land office at Newnansville. He died soon thereafter in Savannah on November 2, 1853.[71]

Sanchez, Francis R. One of the largest landowners in Alachua County, Francis R. Sanchez owned the San Felasco plantation four miles from Newnansville. In 1836, he served as colonel in the Sixth Regiment of the Florida militia and later in 1839 as lieutenant colonel of the Florida Mounted Volunteers. In 1838, Gov. Richard K. Call appointed him Alachua County judge. After the death of his first wife in 1839, he married Sarah A. Houck in 1841. Sanchez died in 1845.[72]

Sanchez, George Washington. Born on July 4, 1819, into one of the oldest families in Alachua County, George Washington Sanchez served as a private in Lt. Henry Harn's detachment of the Second Regiment, Second Brigade of the East Florida Mounted Volunteers, commanded by Col. Will J. Mills, in 1837. In 1839, he reenlisted and served in Capt. Philip Dell's company of the First Regiment Brigade of the Florida Mounted Militia, commanded by Col. John Warren. He saw service a third time from December 6, 1840, to March 6, 1841, in Mathew Hindley's Company of the Second Regiment, Brigade of the Florida Foot Militia, commanded by F. L. Dancy. Sanchez married Sarah Ann Harrison in 1840. After the death of his first wife, he married Harriet Ann Davis. He died on August 10, 1903, in Trenton, Florida.[73]

Sanchez, Joseph Simeon. Born in 1797 in St. Augustine, Joseph Simeon Sanchez was the oldest son of the well-to-do Spanish Florida rancher-plantation owner Francisco Xavier Sanchez. He married Mary Lopez and they had eight children. Sanchez, a leading planter and politician in the territory and state, was a Democrat representing St. John and Mosquito Counties in the legislative council from 1827 to 1832. He served as colonel in the Second Regiment, Second Brigade of the Florida Militia from November 1835 to March 1836. He was a member of the St. Joseph Constitutional Convention in 1839. In 1841, he was elected to the Florida Senate, and in 1844 he was elected to the Florida House of Representatives. In 1837, President Martin Van Buren appointed Sanchez U.S. marshal of the Eastern Judicial District of Florida, in which capacity he served until 1842. He was reappointed by President John Tyler. From 1845 to 1847,

Sanchez served as sheriff of St. Johns County. He died on September 17, 1853.[74]

Scott, John. A resident of Palatka, John Scott was born in Kentucky in 1806. He and his wife, Sarah, eventually relocated to Marion County, where he represented the county in the House of Representatives in the General Assembly of Florida in 1847, 1848, and 1850.[75]

Segui, Bernardo. Born in 1786, Segui was a prominent merchant of Minorcan descent from St. Johns County. He represented East Florida in the territory's first legislative council in 1822. Along with William P. DuVal and James Gadsden, he was a signer of the Treaty of Moultrie Creek (1823). The large land grant provided to him in 1814 was affirmed as valid by the U.S. Supreme Court in 1836. He served as postmaster of St. Johns County from 1830 to 1834. He died on November 15, 1859.[76]

Smart, Samuel. Samuel Smart served in various Florida militia units from 1835 to 1839. The final unit from which we have record was Captain Bleach's company of Mounted Volunteers in Warren's battalion, in which Smart served as a corporal. He enrolled at Fort Harlee on May 9, 1839, and was mustered out on November 9, 1839. Smart soon joined another volunteer company and was killed near Fort Tarver on August 12, 1840. About that time, he was appointed justice of the peace by Gov. R. R. Reid.[77]

Smith, Joseph L. A native of Connecticut and a Yale graduate, Smith attended Tapping Reeve's famous Litchfield Law Academy. He married Frances "Fanny" Marion Kirby in 1807. He was a man of great talents but had a mercurial personality. Smith came to St. Augustine in 1822 when President James Monroe appointed him superior court judge of the Eastern Judicial District. He served as district judge until 1832, when he was replaced by Robert Raymond Reid of Georgia. He resumed the practice of law in St. Augustine until his death on May 24, 1846. Smith had four children, including Edmund Kirby Smith, a future Confederate general.[78]

Standley, Jessee. Born in 1790 in Liberty County, Georgia, Jessee Standley and his brother, John, migrated to the Newnansville area in the 1830s. Jessee Standley served as a private in Captain J. G. Black's Company of the Florida Mounted Volunteers, Brigade of the Florida Militia, commanded by Col. John Warren, from May 9 to November 9, 1839. He was stationed at Fort Harlee. Standley reenlisted in Captain C. Ellis's Company of the First Regiment, Brigade of the Florida Mounted Militia, commanded by W. J. Bailey, and served from August 17 to December 5, 1840. Standley died in 1844 and is buried in the Newnansville Cemetery.[79]

Standley, John. Born in Tattnall County, Georgia, in 1790, John Standley married Zelphia Townsend in 1816. In the 1820s, they migrated to Jefferson County and then with his brother Jessee and his family they migrated to Alachua County, Florida, in the 1830s. He had a substantial plantation and established one of the first trading posts and boarding-houses in Newnansville. He died suddenly in Newnansville on July 4, 1837.[80]

Standley, John B. The son of John and Zelphia Standley, born in 1818 in Tattnall County, Georgia, Standley migrated with his family to territorial Florida at an early age. He married Penelope Barrow on January 2, 1839. One of the largest property owners in Alachua County, Standley served as a private in Captain Hindley's Company in the Second Regiment, Second Brigade of East Florida Mounted Volunteers, commanded by Col. W. J. Mills, from July 20 to December 20, 1837. Standley served as a private in Capt. C. Ellis's Brigade of the Florida Mounted Militia, commanded by W. J. Bailey, from August 17 to December 5, 1840. From March 19, 1841, through April 6, 1841, Standley served as second lieutenant in Capt. Mathew Hindley's Company of the Second Regiment, Brigade of Foot Militia, commanded by Col. F. L. Dancy. In May 1840, the Seminoles burned his plantation, killing his livestock and destroying his stores of corn. The 1850 Alachua County Census valued his property at $3,000. In 1850, he represented Alachua County in the Florida House of Representatives. The next year, Standley suffered the misfortune of having his ginhouse and its 60,000 pounds of long staple cotton valued at $5,000 go up in flames. According to one source, Standley had "made the brag crop of East Florida, and it is now in ashes." Standley died in 1860.[81]

Standley, Zilphia. Born Zilphia Townsend, the daughter of Light and Phoebe Townsend, in 1795 in Liberty County, Georgia, Zilphia married John Standley in McIntosh County, Georgia, in 1816. In the 1820s, she and her husband migrated to Jefferson County, Florida, and by the 1830s they were residing in Alachua County. Among her children was John B. Standley, who was born in 1818. She was widowed in 1837. One of the largest slaveholders in Alachua County, she also operated a boarding-house in Newnansville. She died in 1855 and is buried in the Newnansville Cemetery.[82]

Stewart, Adelaide. Born in Glassy Glade, McIntosh County, Georgia, on September 8, 1839, Adelaide Stewart migrated with her parents to Columbia County, Florida, at the age of six in 1845. She attended La Grange College, in Columba, Georgia, and died in Columba on July 12, 1853.[83]

Stewart, Charles. Born in 1829 on Tuscawilla Plantation, Glynn County, Georgia, Charles Stewart was the son of Daniel M. and Eliza Stewart. He resided on the Liberty Bluff plantation in Columbia County until shortly after his father's death in 1848. Then he resided with his widowed mother in Columbia and Alachua Counties. He married Marion Pelot. He died on May 23, 1857, at Tuscawilla Plantation in Alachua County.[84]

Stewart, Claudius. Born in 1833 in Tuscawilla, Glynn County, Georgia, Claudius Stewart was the son of Daniel M. and Eliza Stewart. He resided on the Liberty Bluff plantation in Columbia County until shortly after his father's death in 1848. Then he resided with his widowed mother in Columbia and Alachua Counties. He attended Emory College in Oxford, Georgia, before studying law at Harvard University in 1853. In 1854, he returned to Alachua County and was admitted to the bar. In June 1854, Stewart fought a duel with fellow lawyer, Joseph B. Coker, and survived, but he died of his injuries on November 23 during a session of the Duval County Circuit Court.[85]

Stewart, Daniel M. Descended from the prominent Georgia Revolutionary War general of the same name, Daniel M. Stewart was born in 1791 to Daniel and Susannah Stewart in Glynn County Georgia. Stewart married Mary Eliza Eichelberger in 1824 in Glynn County, Georgia. They had eleven children. The Stewarts migrated to Florida from Camden County, Georgia, in 1845, just after the birth of their youngest child and established the Liberty Bluff plantation at the confluence of the Santa Fe and Suwanee Rivers, approximately forty miles from Newnansville. Stewart died on January 5, 1848.[86]

Stewart, Daniel M., Jr. Born in College Creek, Glynn County, Georgia, in 1824, the son of Daniel M. and Eliza Stewart, Daniel M. Stewart migrated with his parents to the Liberty Bluff plantation in Columbia County. In

1846, at the age of twenty-two, he was second in command of the Florida volunteer force in the Mexican War. He was killed in Vera Cruz on November 3, 1847.[87]

Stewart, Eliza. Born Mary Eliza Eichelberger in Georgia in 1808, she married Daniel M. Stewart in Glynn County, Georgia. She had eleven children with Stewart, including George Brown's future wife, Matilda. The Stewarts migrated to Columbia County, Florida, in 1845 from Camden County, Florida, establishing the Liberty Bluff plantation at the confluence of the Suwannee and the Santa Fe Rivers. Widowed in 1848, Eliza eventually moved to another farm in Alachua County. After the Civil War, she migrated to Tennessee and died in Nashville on February 2, 1880.[88]

Stewart, George W. Born in 1828, Stewart was the son of Daniel and Eliza Stewart and the brother of Matilda. He was killed in Newnansville in 1852 in a dispute with his widowed mother's overseer.[89]

Stewart, James M. Born in 1835 in Tuscawilla, Georgia, James M. Stewart was the son of Daniel M. and Eliza Stewart. He resided on the Liberty Bluff plantation in Columbia County until shortly after his father's death in 1848. Then he resided with his widowed mother in Columbia and Alachua Counties. He married Sarah Ann Pelot and died in 1864 at Potosi Plantation in Alachua County.[90]

Stewart, Mary. See Dozier, Mary.

Stewart, Matilda. See Brown, Matilda.

Stewart, Thomas O. Born in St. Marys, Georgia, on October 26, 1841, Thomas Stewart was the son of Daniel M. and Eliza Stewart. He resided with his widowed mother in Columbia and Alachua Counties. Stewart served in the Civil War. On February 14, 1865, he married Olivia Quattlebaum in Lexington County, South Carolina. They had three children.[91]

Stewart, William George. Born in Tuscawilla, Georgia, in 1826, William Stewart was the son of Daniel and Eliza Stewart. He served in the Mexican War as a corporal and died on the Liberty Bluff plantation on May 9, 1850.[92]

Summerlin, Jacob. Born in 1820 at Alligator, Florida, Jacob Summerlin and his father served in Captain John E. Tucker's Company of the First

Regiment, Florida Mounted Militia, commanded by Col. John Warren, from November 5, 1839, to January 31, 1840. Both men reenlisted and served from November 28, 1840, to February 28, 1841, in George E. Mc-Clellan's Company of the Second Regiment, Brigade of the Florida Militia, commanded by F. L. Dancy. In 1843, Jacob Summerlin represented Columbia County in the House of the Legislative Council. In 1845, he was elected to represent the Eastern District of Florida in the Senate. In 1844, Summerlin married Frances Knight Zipperer and homesteaded at Knights Station in present-day Hillsborough County, where he served as deputy sheriff and postmaster of Hickpocksassa. By the late 1850s, Summerlin had acquired extensive herds of cattle, owning 2,100 head by 1860. Summerlin served in the Civil War, and after the war he established a lucrative trade in cattle with Cuba. He eventually moved to the community that became Orlando and founded Punta Rassa in Charlotte Harbor as a shipping point for cattle. Known and respected widely for his philanthropy and assistance to education, Summerlin was dubbed by his contemporaries "King of the Crackers." In 1883, he returned to Orlando, where he died in 1893.[93]

Townsend, Light. Born in South Carolina in 1770, Light Townsend also lived in Georgia before migrating to Jefferson County and then Alachua County, Florida, with his wife, Phoebe. They were the parents of Zilphia, who married John Standley in Georgia in 1816 before migrating to Florida. Light Townsend served in Capt. James Niblick's Company of the Second Regiment, Second Brigade of East Florida Mounted Volunteers, commanded by Col. W. J. Mills, from June 1837 to December 18, 1837. The troops were enrolled at Fort Lancaster. Light Townsend joined Captain Matthew Hindley's Mounted Company of the First Regiment, Brigade of the Florida Volunteers, commanded by Col. John Warren, on May 3, 1839, and served for six months. Townsend reenlisted and served in Captain C. Ellis's Company of the First Regiment, Brigade of the Florida Mounted Militia, commanded by Col. W. J. Bailey, from August 17 to December 5, 1840. By the 1850s, Light Townsend had relocated to Benton County. He died in 1851.[94]

Tucker, Farnham Z. Born in 1818 and a native of Maine, Farnham Z. Tucker was listed as the shipmaster of the *Henry Clay* in Account of Vessels Entered at the Port of Tampa Bay, 1845. In 1860, Tucker and his wife,

Mary, had four children and were living in Brooklyn, New York. Tucker died in 1880 in Brooklyn and is buried in Greenwood Cemetery.[95]

Tucker, John. A farmer and lay preacher, John Tucker was born in 1785 in Tatnall County, Georgia. He married Mary Polly Carter in St. Augustine in 1805. He served as corporal in William Cason's mounted company of the First Regiment, Second Brigade of the Florida Militia, commanded by Col. John Warren, from September 1836 through January 1837. He re-enlisted and served as a private in Captain Mathew Hindley's Company of the First Regiment of Florida Mounted Volunteers from November 2, 1839, to May 2, 1840. He married Mary Geiger on June 15, 1837. He died in Hernando, Florida, in 1853.[96]

Watson, George W. Born in Maine in 1822 and a Methodist minister, Watson was active in the Newnansville district of the Methodist Church from its founding. He was married to Susan Watson and they had three children.[97]

Wilson, Charles L. Born in Maine in 1818, Charles Wilson married Mary C. Russell on December 28, 1854. A Democrat, Wilson served as sheriff of Alachua County from 1849 to 1855. First elected in 1849, Wilson was reelected in October 1851. He served until 1855 and died in 1856.[98]

Wilson, Lemuel. Born in 1815 in North Carolina, Lemuel Wilson married Rafaila Sophia Maria Sanchez Olmsted on May 26, 1842. He served as the registrar of the Land Office in Newnansville from 1850 to 1854. Lemuel Wilson died in 1872 and was buried in the Newnansville Cemetery. Rafaila Wilson died in 1887.[99]

Yulee, David Levy. David Levy Yulee was a friend to Ellen, Corinna, and Charles Brown from their arrival in the territory in 1836. The son of prosperous Jewish West Indian merchant and land speculator Moses Elias Levy, David Levy came to Florida as a boy about the time Spain ceded the territory to the United States. Levy studied law in Judge Robert Raymond Reid's law office in St. Augustine and was admitted to the bar in 1832. Levy, a Democrat, became one of the most powerful politicians of the time. He served in the legislative council from 1837 to 1838 and played a leading role in the territory's constitutional convention in 1839. A leading advocate of statehood, Levy was elected as Florida's territorial delegate to Congress in 1841 and was in this office when Florida became a state. In 1845. Levy (by this time known as David Levy Yulee) became one of Florida's first two senators. Yulee represented Florida in the U.S. Senate from 1844 to 1851 and from 1855 to 1861. Yulee's chief pursuit was planting and railroad building, and by the time of the Civil War's outbreak, he headed the Atlantic and Gulf Railroad, the line that ran from Fernandina to Cedar Key. He served in the Confederate Congress, and after the war he was briefly incarcerated. Though disenfranchised, he made use of his many political and business contacts and resumed his business activities. He died in New York City in 1886.[100]

APPENDIX B

Two Additional Letters Written
before George's Florida Venture

The first of George's surviving letters was written from Philadelphia to Mannevillette, who had moved to Paris the previous year:

> [George L. Brown to Mannevillette E. D. Brown]
> Philadelphia [to Paris, France]
> June 2, 1839

Brother Manne,

I little thought when studying my "geography" at the high school,[1] and telling how France was bounded and how Italy was surrounded that it would ever be my good fortune to have a correspondent in those countries. I can well recollect the wonder with which I first saw the first foreign letter at old Marie's store–but time which alters all things has changed my youthful feelings and I pen this epistle with the same cool indifference as I would one to Florida or "down east"— I hardly know what to write you though I have a large and interesting stock of news; at least, for home contemplation.–should I inform you of public matters, they would prove twice told tales I fear, for you probably see a plenty of American papers on your routes   I will however let you know how I came to be a resident of this city and then I will proceed in that beautiful miscellaneous order of a militia company on the march. You are aware that I left New York for Macon last Fall and arrived there safe—that, disappointed, I left M. for Charleston being persuaded at the time by very flattering inducements–but it was a will-o-the-wisp expedition and left me floundering in a bog mire–disgusted with the south I wrote to Manning Kennard who advised me by all means to come to Philadelphia and very lucky it has proved. I am very hopefully situated in a wholesale French House—Ingraham & Martin N 100 Market St. (to whose care please address me). The lesson of adversity, which I have learned during this past year will teach me to value more any present success. I have now been with them 4 months (since Feb. 1) and have no reason to think they are otherwise than pleased with me—and with health I hope yet to render a good account of myself. Say what they will of Yankees of their love of money–their bargain-downing propensity, etc. the Southern merchants are exactly the same—Cheating, gouging, meanness and amor pecunia[2] flourishes as well south of Mason Dixon's line as it does elsewhere.

I rec'd one pleasure only to repay me for my January–the gratification to find Corinna well married. Her husband–Dr. Aldrich–is a noble youth and loves her devotedly–the luckiest day she ever saw was when she dismissed that scoundrel Pomeroy. He lives here as a bookkeeper somewhere, has a wife and child with him.——I rec'd a letter from Corin yesterday. She and all the folks were well. Ell was to be with her soon. I hear occasionally from Portsmouth through James Kennard a regular list of the deaths and marriages. . . .–Marriage and death will soon cause the few remaining ties that bind me to old P–to snap asunder. You have long ceased to think of it I expect but my impressions of the village are more recent.

You must be enjoying yourself finely among the vine clad hills of France and the glorious sunsets of Italy. You must write me a <u>double</u> letter of manners and customs–your "inklings of adventure" in payment for this miserable doc ——Though I have written little to please you and less that is new. Still, I feel confident that it gladdens your heart to know that I am once again pursuing my proper business and on the high road to preferment–besides it gives me an opportunity to thank you for your kindness when I needed assistance and to assure how dear will ever be your fame and success to–very cordially and sincerely

Your affectionate Brother,
George L. Brown

Later that year, George sent another letter to Mannevillette, now in Italy, that explains his own situation and the economic circumstances that had cast doubt on his career in Philadelphia:

[George L. Brown to Mannevillette E. D. Brown]
Philadelphia [to Rome, Italy]
Nov. 14, 1839

My Dear Brother

Your Lancaster friend must have been delayed on his route for your letter dated last July was only rec'd last week via New York. I have been absent on business a few days and must beg pardon for not answering your esteemed favour instantly. Contents lost none of their value by detention being of that description which is new whenever obtained—alas! How fickle is fortune! Your congratulations for my success in Phil. Just reached me in time to witness another problem in the mercantile world. To be brief my employers Messrs Ingraham & Martin stopped payment on the 1st of October. At that time, they intended to get an extension and go on as usual, but the problem is that the gloom of the present and the uncertainty of the future or rather the uncertainty of the future misfortunes in business have induced them to give up, though the schedule of their affairs shows a clear surplus of $4000–This unlooked-for event does but throw me immediately into idleness as I shall remain with them until January. I have no hesitation in saying that then or before that time I shall obtain another situation–for under the peculiar circumstances I can carry with me to the house I may form connections with <u>the whole</u> of our trade—this qualification alone is sufficient to insure me employment in the fullest business seasons–though I trust I can bring other recommendations to my favor. I have many sincere and active friends among the merchants of Market & Front streets on whom I may with confidence rely. They all speak favorably on that subject. Still this occurrence produces unpleasant feelings. I regret it more on my employers' account than my own. I never had an unkind word from them, nor any directions on my duties–they are in short perfect gentlemen and their course of conduct toward me was more like to a son than a clerk had things gone on smoothly. In a year or two

I should have been one of the firm; this is not Egotism but Mr. Ingraham's own words. . . .

The times in this country are indeed gloomy. Our banks have suspended specie payments–trade has stopped–not knowing who to trust, Merchants look with distrust upon their former most intimate associates. When and where this state of things will lead no one can tell though all hope and tremble while they hope that things will improve in the spring. I patiently submit to whatever may happen. It seems as though Nature — so beautiful and pleasant is the Season was enjoying the contrast between her works and the operations of man. October & November so far have been delightful. Healthy breezes–bright sunny days–such as shall produce only happiness = abundant crops to gladden the poor and needy. Still what matters it that her charms combine around us if merchants are sick? Time the best physician may yet cure all.

I had a letter from Charley some days ago. He has gone to Newnansville E. F. to reside for a while and should he like it forever he intends establishing a druggist shop there–in connection with Aldrich– he (Aldrich) Chas says is gaining ground in his profession rapidly–he is surgeon for two military forts at $100 per month besides an extensive practice. Corin has secured an excellent and devoted husband in him. I know you will like the young gentleman if you have the opportunity to know him. Aunt Mary and Ann live cosily together at La Grange and Aunt Dolly <u>nigh</u> within a stone's throw of them–it is lucky her residence is not <u>within</u> the distance of it more. I should say from all accounts they might stand a chance of getting a brick bat at their heads. Ell says Aunt D is subject to fainting fits something like Mrs. Gribards when she tumbled down on a little dog once in Daller's Lane. You recollect it I guess–you were there any how.

Should you like to hear something about the down easters? . . . I have nothing to say about Philadelphia but that I like it! What could you expect from this quiet city? The Phils still keep up their quiet reputation not withstanding their misfortunes. They even have a pun on their own distress. "You have suspended and I have too" says one of the "stopped" to another–now what are we like? "Why a pair of suspenders!" Why is a man's cue[3]–says another–like the statement of my affairs? Give it up? 'cause it is a tail never known <u>before</u>! Thus we joke on through all calamities–The women complain now more than the men for how, they say, can we cuss?!

I feel much indebted to you for your letter–and regret that the paper would not admit of your being more extensive in your illustrations of the old Country. I have been reading Gallen's Roma—that part which tells of the very part where you now reside—What a change between the 6th & the 19th Century—1300 years have tolled away and a gentleman from New Hampshire treads over the ground once trod by the Emperors! And that *man* worth the whole from Augustus to Augustulus! I must give you credit for your progress in the foreign lingoes—What Italian! German! Spanish! French! In faith Manne don't forget your English–"I guess" "do tell" "I calculate" or "you don't say" will sound sweeter in your ears than the language of Tasso–of Goethe–of Cervantes–or Rousseau! Will it not? Write me very soon–I hope this will reach you. They will forward it to you I suppose. Good bye–affectionately your brother

George L Brown

NOTES

Introduction

1. George L. Brown to Mannevillette E. D. Brown, July 18, 1840, Anderson-Brown Collection, United States Military Academy, West Point, New York (hereinafter USMA).

2. See James M. Denham and Keith L. Huneycutt, eds., *Echoes from a Distant Frontier: The Brown Sisters' Correspondence from Antebellum Florida* (Columbia: University of South Carolina Press, 2004); James M. Denham and Keith L. Huneycutt, eds., "With Scott in Mexico: Letters of Captain James W. Anderson in the Mexican War, 1846–1847," *Military History of the West* 28 (Spring 1998): 19–48; James M. Denham and Keith L. Huneycutt, eds., "'Our Desired Haven': The Letters of Corinna Brown Aldrich from Antebellum Key West, 1849–50," *Florida Historical Quarterly* 78 (Spring 2001): 517–45; James M. Denham and Keith L. Huneycutt, eds., "'Everything Is Hubbub Here': Lt. James Willoughby Anderson's Second Seminole War, 1837–1842," *Florida Historical Quarterly* 82 (Winter 2004): 313–59.

3. According to baptismal records prepared by the Reverend Charles Burroughs, Rector of St. Johns Church in Portsmouth, the children of Elihu and Elizabeth Brown were Henry Alexander, born September 5, 1807; Adelaide Mary, born December 11, 1808; Mannevillette Elihu Dearing, born April 13, 1810; Corinna Elizabeth, born April 20, 1812; Ellen Maria, born April 30, 1814; Charles Burroughs, born January 30, 1816; and George Long, born November 7, 1817. George was named for his father's business partner George Long, who had invested in his privateering ventures. For Brown's privateering exploits, see Faye M. Kert, *Privateering: Patriots and Profits in the War of 1812* (Baltimore: Johns Hopkins University Press, 2015), 130–33. Also, information on George Brown's family and antecedents can be found in Denham and Huneycutt, eds., *Echoes from a Distant Frontier*, xvii–xxi, 1–7.

4. Michael Hugo-Brunt, "A History of the City of Portsmouth in New Hampshire from 1623–1839" (Ph.D. dissertation, Cornell University, 1957), 2: 116. For a discussion of Portsmouth schools in 1839, see Hugo-Brunt, "A History of the City of Portsmouth in New Hampshire from 1623–1839," 2: 114–118.

5. Elizabeth Dearing Brown to Mannevillette and Charles Brown, December 8, 1831, USMA.

6. Elizabeth Dearing Brown to Mannevillette and Charles Brown, February 2, 1832, USMA.

7. The Brown family's regular epistolary habits reflect a general increase in letter writing among Americans in the nineteenth century. As David Henkin points out, "Throughout the first third of the century, most Americans . . . neither exchanged mail nor organized their daily lives around the expectation of postal contact"; mail was irregular and slow, and "receiving a letter was, for most Americans, an event rather than a feature of ordinary importance." However, with an overall rise in literacy and various reforms to the U.S. Postal Service, correspondence became more widespread. He adds that in the 1840s and 1850s, "what emerged most generally during this period was a set of practices, discourses, and beliefs—a postal culture—that redefined the very status of mail. More specifically, Americans began producing and circulating in massive numbers something that had never before been an instrument of everyday sociability among ordinary people: the personal letter." David M. Henkin, *The Postal Age: The Emergence of Modern Communication in Nineteenth-Century America* (Chicago: University of Chicago Press, 2007), 93.

8. David Henkin explains: "Despite a long tradition associating letters with polite society, despite a continual emphasis in etiquette books on letter-writing as an act of personal self-presentation, and despite the construction of letters as windows into the soul in popular epistolary novels, Americans at mid-century understood that the prototypical letter-writer was a businessman. . . . Much of the conduct of long-distance trade took place via the post, and much of the labor associated with the mercantile economy consisted of writing, copying, and filing letters. . . . Clerks . . . were part of a new breed of white-collar employee, for whom entry-level, salaried positions . . . served as badges of middle-class status and promised upward mobility. . . . Guides to success in business emphasized the importance of composition, orthography, and penmanship, not only because those features of correspondence would be taken as reliable signs of character (especially penmanship) but also because so much of commercial life revolved around the production of letters." Henkin, *The Postal Age*, 94–95.

9. That any letters at all survive from a man who lived on Florida's antebellum frontier is itself impressive. Aside from the busy schedule that would preclude much unclaimed time for writing, the logistics of writing and delivering correspondence from the wilds of Florida were particularly difficult. As a merchant, George would have easier access to writing material of good quality than would most of his contemporaries, but mail delivery was often unreliable, as evidenced by family references to numerous sent letters that never reached their destinations. Letters were delivered on foot, on horseback, by stage, and by boat, not only by the U.S. Postal Service but also by individuals, private companies, and the military. Thomas G. Day, ed., *The United States Postal Service: An American History, 1775–2006* (Washington, D.C.: United States Postal Service, 2012), 12.

10. *St Augustine Florida Herald*, August 15, 1833; *Portsmouth (N.H.) Journal of Literature and Politics, Rockingham Gazette and State Herald*, June 15, 1833.

11. *Portsmouth (N.H.) Journal of Literature and Politics, Rockingham Gazette and State Herald*, November 16, 1833.

12. Corinna Brown Aldrich to Mannevillette E. D. Brown, August 17, 1849, USMA.

13. Anthony Rotundo, "Learning about Manhood: Gender Ideals and the Middle-Class Family in Nineteenth-Century America," in *Manliness and Morality: Middle-Class*

Morality in Britain and America, 1800–1940, ed. J. A. Mangan and James Walvin, 35–51 (New York: St. Martins, 1987), 36, 37.

14. David S. Pugh, *Sons of Liberty: The Masculine Mind in Nineteenth-Century America* (Westport, Conn.: Greenwood, 1983), 126.

15. Denham and Huneycutt, *Echoes from a Distant Frontier*, 54–55.

16. Charles T. Thrift, *The Trail of the Florida Circuit Rider* (Lakeland: Florida Southern College Press, 1944), 50–52, 74–77.

17. *Minutes of the Annual Conferences of the Methodist Episcopal Church, South for the Year*, 269–270.

18. For example, see Alachua County census. Many were signers of petitions that are listed in the Florida volumes of Clarence Carter, ed., *Territorial Papers of the United States*, Vols. 24, 25 and 26 (Washington, D.C.: U.S. Government Printing Office, 1934–62).

19. Historian Frank Byrne has noted that "the same cultural values that the Whig Party publically espoused during the 1840s—hard work, frugality, domesticity, gentility, and self-improvement—most southern merchants also held dear. Similarly, business men and Whig leaders believed that such economic policies as the Bank of the United States and federally funded internal improvements offered a political means to achieve their economic goals. . . . Finally, the Democratic Party itself, particularly under Andrew Jackson, alienated many retail and wholesale dealers across the South. The merchants' conservative faith in a social hierarchy based on merit clashed with a Jacksonian democratic ethic that celebrated egalitarianism and small government." Frank L. Byrne, *Becoming Bourgeois: Merchant Culture in the South, 1820–1865* (Lexington: University Press of Kentucky, 2006), 51.

20. *Charleston Southern Patriot*, March 13, 1833.

21. Ellen refers to Edward's uncle Robert, whom George was visiting in Charleston. Ellen Brown to Mannevillette Brown, November 20, 1838, USMA.

22. Corinna Brown Aldrich to Mannevillette E. D. Brown, October 14, 1838, USMA.

23. Edward Aldrich practiced medicine briefly in Macon, Georgia. *Macon Southern Post*, April 21, November 24, 1838.

24. Corinna Brown Aldrich to Mannevillette E. D. Brown, August 18, 1839, photocopy in possession of the authors.

25. Other sources on Newnansville are Susan Yelton, "Newnansville: A Lost Florida Settlement," *Florida Historical Quarterly* 53 (January 1975): 319–31; Denham and Huneycutt, *Echoes from a Distant Frontier*; Phillips, "A Diary of Jesse Talbot: Newnansville and Tallahassee," *Florida Historical Quarterly* 18 (October 1939): 115–26; Jacob Rhett Motte, *Journey into the Wilderness. An Army Surgeon's Account of Life in Camp and Field during the Creek and Seminole Wars, 1836–1838*, ed. James F. Sunderman (Gainesville: University of Florida Press, 1953), 90–92; E. Ashby Hammond, *The Medical Profession in 19th Century Florida: A Biographical Register* (Gainesville: George Smathers Libraries, University of Florida, 1996), 163–65.

26. See Hooper, *The Early History of Clay County: A Wilderness That Could Be Tamed* (Charleston: History Press, 2006), 136–67; Arch Fredric Blakey, *Parade of Memories: A History of Clay County, Florida* (Jacksonville: Drummond Press for the Clay County Bicentennial Steering Committee, 1976), 31–34.

27. Henry Benjamin Whipple, *Bishop Whipple's Southern Diary*, ed. Lester B. Shippee (Minneapolis: University of Minnesota Press, 1937), 71.

28. "Diary of Whitfield Brooks," December 1, 1845, College of Charleston.

29. "Magnolia House, and Mill—Black Creek, &c." *Jacksonville Florida Republican*, February 23, 1854.

30. Charles Lanman, *Adventures in the Wilds of the United States and British Provinces* (Philadelphia: John W. Moore, 1856), 2: 126–27.

31. Alachua, Columbia, and Hillsborough Counties, Minutes of the Superior Court, book 1, 233.

32. *Burlington (Vt.) Free Press*, January 25, 1836.

33. *Jacksonville Courier* quoted in *Tallahassee Floridian and Advocate*, September 17, 1836.

34. *Jacksonville Courier* quoted in *Tallahassee Floridian and Advocate*, September 17, 1836.

35. On this phase of the Second Seminole War, see C. S. Monaco, *The Second Seminole War and the Limits of American Aggression* (Baltimore: Johns Hopkins University Press, 2018), 47–63; John K. Mahon, *History of the Second Seminole War, 1835–1842* (Gainesville: University Press of Florida, 1967; revised edition, 1985), 135–89; John Missall and Mary Lou Missall, *The Seminole Wars: America's Longest Indian Conflict* (Gainesville: University Press of Florida, 2004), 93–121; John T. Sprague, *Origins, Progress, and Conclusion of the Florida War*, 1848, facsimile reprint (Tampa, Fla.: University of Tampa Press, 2000), 96–166; John K. Mahon and Brent R. Weisman, "Florida's Seminole and Miccosukee Peoples," in *The New History of Florida*, ed. Michael Gannon (Gainesville: University Press of Florida, 1996), 196–98.

36. Corinna E. Brown to Mannevillette E. D. Brown, May 27, 1836, USMA.

37. *Raleigh North Carolina Standard*, April 12, 1837.

38. Motte, *Journey into the Wilderness*, 90–91.

39. Ellen Brown to Mannevillette E. D. Brown, December 14, 1839, USMA.

40. J.D.B. DeBow, *The Seventh Census of the United States: 1850, Embracing a Statistical View of Each of the States and Territories Arranged by Counties* (Washington: Robert Armstrong, Public Printer, 1853), 400.

41. Everett W. Caudle, "Settlement Patterns in Alachua County, Florida, 1850–1860," *Florida Historical Quarterly* 67 (April 1989): 437.

42. *Compendium of the Enumeration of the Inhabitants and Statistics of the United States* [in 1840], 97–99.

43. "Census of Alachua County," in *Jacksonville Florida News*, March 6, 1845.

44. Alachua County, Fla., Census (1850), 1, 2, 16, 25, 26, 32. The census also listed six clerks: Henry Hennis, twenty-three, South Carolina native; Joshua Hawkins, thirty-three, Georgia native; Allan Hancock, twenty-one, Florida native; Thomas Winn, twenty-three, Georgia native; Isaac Carter, thirty-four, Georgia native; and George's clerk Simeon Sanchez, twenty, Florida native. See Alachua County, Fla., Census (1850), 1, 2, 25, 26.

45. Alachua County, Fla., Census (1850), 1, 25, 26.

46. Duval County, Fla., Census (1850).

47. T. Frederick Davis, *History of Jacksonville and Vicinity, 1513 to 1924* (St. Augustine:

Florida Historical Society, 1925), 74–75; Denham and Huneycutt, *Echoes from a Distant Frontier*, 35, 71.

48. "The Baptist Church, Jacksonville," *Jacksonville Republican*, April 5, 1855.

49. For Jacksonville as a business center and its attraction for northern commercial interests, see Anne Robinson Clancy, ed., *A Yankee in a Confederate Town: The Journal of Calvin L. Robinson* (Sarasota, Fla.: Pineapple, 2002); Daniel L. Schafer, *Thunder on the River: The Civil War in Northeast Florida* (Gainesville: University Press of Florida, 2010), 28–30.

50. St. Johns County, Fla., Census (1850).

51. Whitfield Brooks Diary, November 3, 1845, College of Charleston.

52. Columbia County, Fla., Census (1850).

53. Putnam County, Fla., Census (1850); Levy County, Fla., Census (1850); Madison County, Fla., Census (1850); Marion County, Fla., Census (1850).

54. Lewis E. Atherton, *The Southern Country Store, 1800–1860* (Baton Rouge: Louisiana State University Press, 1949), 15, 42–62.

55. Atherton, *The Southern Country Store, 1800–1860*, 193.

56. Woodman, *King Cotton and His Retainers: Financing and Manufacturing the Cotton Crop of the South, 1800–1925* (Columbia: University of South Carolina Press, Southern Classic Series, 1990; originally published by the University of Kentucky Press in 1968), 77–78.

57. Woodman, *King Cotton and His Retainers*, 77–79, 83.

58. Byrne, *Becoming Bourgeois*, 54, 55.

59. Edwin G. Burrows and Mike Wallace, *Gotham: A History of New York City to 1898* (New York: Oxford University Press, 1999), 336.

60. DeBow, *Seventh Census of the United States: 1850*, 407–09.

61. Shofner and Rogers, "Sea Island Cotton in Ante-bellum Florida," *Florida Historical Quarterly* 40 (January 1962): 375, 373, 377; "About Long Cotton," *St. Augustine Ancient City*, February 19, 1853. Also on the cultivation of Sea Island Cotton, see Lewis Cecil Gray, *History of Agriculture in the Southern United States to 1860*, 2 vols. (Washington, D.C.: Carnegie Institution, 1933. Reprint, Gloucester, Mass: Peter Smith, 1958), 2: 731–39; Julia Floyd Smith, *Slavery and Plantation Growth in Antebellum Florida: 1821–1860* (Gainesville: University of Florida Press, 1973), 153–55.

62. Alachua County, Fla., Census (1850).

63. Alachua County, Fla., Census (1850), 34; Alachua County, Fla., Slave Census (1850), 17.

64. Alachua County, Fla., Slave Census (1850).

65. Caudle, "Settlement Patterns," 438–40.

66. Larry Eugene Rivers, *Slavery in Florida: Territorial Days to Emancipation* (Gainesville: University Press of Florida, 2000), 68, 71.

67. DeBow, *The Seventh Census of the United States: 1850*, 47–48.

68. On the herding culture of East Florida, see James M. Denham and Canter Brown, *Cracker Times and Pioneer Lives: The Florida Reminiscences of George Gillett Keen and Sarah Pamela Williams* (Columbia: University of South Carolina Press, 2000); Joe Akerman, *Florida Cowman: A History of Florida Cattle Raising* (Kississimme: Florida

Cattleman's Association, 1976); John Solomon Otto, "Open Range Cattle-Herding in Southern Florida," *Florida Historical Quarterly* 65 (January 1987): 317–34; Dana Ste. Claire, *Cracker: The Cracker Culture in Florida History* (Daytona Beach: Museum of Arts and Sciences, 1998); James M. Denham, "The Florida Cracker before the Civil War as Seen Through Travelers' Accounts," *Florida Historical Quarterly* 72 (April 1994): 453–62; James M. Denham, "Cracker Women and their Families in Nineteenth Century Florida," in *Florida's Heritage of Diversity: Essays in the Honor of Samuel Proctor*, ed. Mark I. Greenberg, William Warren Rogers, and Canter Brown Jr., 15–27 (Tallahassee, Fla.: Sentry, 1997); Grady McWhiney and Forrest McDonald, "Celtic Origins of Southern Herding Practices," *Journal of Southern History* 51 (May 1984): 165–82; Grady McWhiney, *Cracker Culture: Celtic Ways in the Old South* (Tuscaloosa: University of Alabama Press, 1986).

69. Alachua County, Fla., Census (1850), 2, 26, 27, 32.

70. Alfred Aldrich's political activities and their relationship to Hammond is explored in Carol Bleser, ed., *Secret and Sacred: The Diaries of James Henry Hammond, a Southern Slaveholder* (New York: Oxford University Press, 1988), 151, 164–68, 235, 237, 239–42, 252–53, 308; Drew Gilpin Faust, *James Henry Hammond and the Old South: Design for Mastery* (Baton Rouge: Louisiana State University Press, 1982), 289–90; Harold S. Schultz, *Nationalism and Sectionalism in South Carolina, 1852–1860: A Study of the Movement for Southern Independence* (Durham, N.C.: Duke University Press, 1950), 32.

71. Records reveal that George traveled on the following boats: *General Clinch* (1841), *Isis* (1841), *Beaufort District* (1843), *Charleston* (1844, 1845, and 1846), *William Gaston* (1847), *William Seabrook* (1847, 1848), *St. Mathews* (1849), *Welaka* (1851), *Magnolia* (1851), *Gordon* (1856), *Carolina* (1856), and *Cecile* (1857).

72. See, for example, Harold D. Woodman, *King Cotton and His Retainers: Financing and Manufacturing the Cotton Crop of the South, 1800–1925* (Columbia: University of South Carolina Press, Southern Classic Series, 1990; originally published by the University of Kentucky Press in 1968); Atherton, *The Southern Country Store*; Woodman, "Itinerant Cotton Merchants of the Antebellum South," *Agricultural History* 40 (April 1966): 79–90; Ronald L. F. Davis, "The Southern Merchant: A Perennial Source of Discontent," in *The Southern Enigma: Essays in Race, Class, and Folk Culture*, ed. Walter J. Fraser Jr. and Winifred B. Moore Jr., 131–41 (Westport, Conn.: Greenwood, 1983. Some modern studies are Bruce W. Eelman, *Entrepreneurs in the Southern Upcountry: Commercial Culture in Spartanburg, South Carolina, 1845–1880* (Athens: University of Georgia Press, 2008); Tom Downey, *Planting a Capitalist South: Masters, Merchants, and Manufacturers in the Southern Interior, 1790–1860* (Baton Rouge: Louisiana State University Press, 2006); Jonathan Daniel Wells and Jennifer R. Green, eds., *The Southern Middle Class in the Long Nineteenth Century* (Baton Rouge: Louisiana State University Press, 2004); Jonathan Daniel Wells and Jennifer R. Green, eds., *The Southern Middle Class in the Long Nineteenth Century* (Baton Rouge: Louisiana State University Press, 2004); Byrne, *Becoming Bourgeois*. In general, studies of commerce or mercantile activity in antebellum Florida are lacking. One exception is Jerrell H. Shofner's excellent study of a Wakulla County merchant, *Daniel Ladd: Merchant Prince of Frontier Florida* (Gainesville: University Press of Florida, 1978).

73. Fletcher M. Green, *The Role of the Yankee in the Old South* (Athens: University of Georgia Press, 1972), 113.

74. Latin for "love of money."

75. George L. Brown to Mannevillette E. D. Brown, June 2, 1839, USMA.

76. Whipple, *Bishop Whipple's Southern Diary*, 73.

77. Daniel Robinson Hundley, *Social Relations in Our Southern States* (New York: Henry D. Price, 1860. Reprint, Louisiana State University Press, 1979), 102–3, 130.

78. Amanda Reece Mushal, "Bonds of Marriage and Community: Social Networks and the Development of a Commercial Middle Class in Antebellum South Carolina," in *The Southern Middle Class in the Long Nineteenth Century*, ed. Jonathan Daniel Wells and Jennifer R. Green, 62–83. Baton Rouge: Louisiana State University Press, 2011," 65. See also Green, *The Role of the Yankee in the Old South*, 112.

79. See, for example, James M. Denham and Randolph Roth, "Why Was Antebellum Florida so Murderous?: A Quantitative Analysis of Homicide in Florida, 1821–1861," *Florida Historical Quarterly* 86 (Fall 2007): 216–39.

80. For violent clashes between military and civilians in Alachua County, see James M. Denham, "'Some Prefer the Seminoles': Violence and Disorder Among Soldiers and Settlers in the Second Seminole War, 1835–1842," *Florida Historical Quarterly* 70 (July 1991): 44–45, 48–49, 53–54.

81. "$200 Reward Proclamation," May 25, 1838, in *Tallahassee Floridian and Advocate*, September 29, 1838.

82. Alachua, Hillsborough, and Columbia Counties Grand Jury Presentment, December 1841, in Alachua, Hillsborough, and Columbia Superior Court Minutes, 1838–1843, book 2, 144.

83. *St. Augustine Florida Herald and Southern Democrat*, December 31, 1840; Affidavit of Thomas Douglas, April 21, 1841, Territorial Auditors Vouchers, RG 352, Ser. 584, box 4, folio 1, Florida State Archives.

84. William H. Watson, alias James Black, shot Alachua County Sheriff William Gibbons and fled. See *Jacksonville Florida News*, April 15, May 13, June 3, 1848, January 12, 1849.

85. *Jacksonville News*, June 16, 1849; *Jacksonville Republican*, June 14, 1849; *Tallahassee Floridian and Journal*, June 16, 1849.

86. Alachua, Hillsborough, and Columbia Superior Court Minutes, 1838–1843, book 2; Alachua, Hillsborough, Benton, and Marion Counties, Minutes of the Superior and Circuit Court, 1844–1850; Alachua, Hillsborough, Benton, and Marion Counties, Superior and Circuit Court Minutes, 1840–1849; Alachua and Levy, Minutes of the Circuit Court, 1850–1857.

87. Corinna Brown Aldrich to Mannevillette E. D. Brown, September 29, 1839, USMA.

88. *St. Augustine Florida Herald and Southern Democrat*, August 22, 1839. See also *St. Augustine Florida Herald and Southern Democrat*, June 6, August 15, 1839. On Gen. Alexander Macomb's peace plan, see Monaco, *The Second Seminole War and the Limits of American Aggression*, 122–27; Mahon, *History of the Second Seminole War*, 255–63; Sprague, *Origins, Progress, and Conclusion of the Florida War*, 228–29; Missall and Missall, *The Seminole Wars*, 163–69.

89. See *Tallahassee Floridian*, March 28, 1840; Robert M. Temple, *Florida Flame: A History of the Florida Conference of the United Methodist Church* (Nashville: Parthenon, 1987), 80–81.

90. *St. Augustine Florida Herald and Southern Democrat*, May 16, 1840; *Edgefield (S.C.) Advertiser*, May 21, June 4, 1840; *Washington D.C. Madisonian*, May 14, 1840.

91. *Savannah Georgian* quoted in *Conservative and Holly Springs (Miss.) Banner*, October 9, 1840.

92. See *Tallahassee Floridian*, January 30, 1841; *St. Augustine Florida Herald and Southern Democrat*, January 29, 1841. For other attacks in the Newnansville area at that time, see *Charleston Courier* quoted in *Savannah Weekly Georgian*, May 18, 1839; *Edgefield Advertiser*, May 23, 1839; "Depredations," *St. Augustine Florida Herald and Southern Democrat*, February 5, 1840; "Indian News—Outrage Upon Outrage," *Jacksonville Advocate* quoted in *Savannah Daily Republican*, May 30, 1840; "Indian News," *Savannah Daily Republican*, August 21, 1840. One of the most sensational accounts of heroism to be reported was Newnansville area pioneer Simeon Dell's rescue of a woman and her children from an Indian attack. See "A Noble Deed," *Raleigh North Carolina Standard*, August 21, 1839.

93. In May, Indians attacked the Snowden homestead near Fort Clarke and killed Absalom Snowden and his three children. Only his wife survived. About the same time, the same party attacked Mr. Moses Cason's cabin and killed his wife and infant child. Mr. Cason escaped with two children. "The Alachua Massacre," *Savannah Republican* quoted in *Edgefield SC Advertiser*, June 8, 1842; "More Indian Murders—War Not Yet Ended," *St. Augustine News* quoted in *Washington Madisonian*, May 28, 1842.

94. On this phase of the Second Seminole War, see Monaco, *The Second Seminole War and the Limits of American Aggression*, 130–33; Mahon, *History of the Second Seminole War, 1835–1842*, 274–320; Missall and Missall, *The Seminole Wars*, 192–202; Sprague, *Origins, Progress, and Conclusion of the Florida War*, 286–493; James W. Covington, *The Seminoles of Florida* (Gainesville: University Press of Florida, 1993), 96–109; Mahon and Weisman, "Florida's Seminole and Miccosukee Peoples," 196–98; Francis Prucha, *The Sword of the Republic: The United States Army on the Frontier, 1783–1846* (New York: Macmillan, 1969), 297–303.

95. On the Armed Occupation Act, see Daniel L. Schafer, "U.S. Territory and State," in *The New History of Florida*, ed. Michael Gannon (Gainesville: University Press of Florida, 1996), 217–18; James W. Covington, "The Armed Occupation Act of 1842," *Florida Historical Quarterly* 40 (July 1961): 41–52; Sidney Walter Martin, *Florida during Territorial Days* (Athens: University of Georgia Press, 1944), 93–96; Canter Brown, *Tampa before the Civil War* (Tampa, Fla.: University of Tampa Press, 1999), 84–87; Canter Brown, *Florida's Peace River Frontier* (Orlando: University of Central Florida Press, 1991), 65–68; Memorial to Congress by the Citizens of East Florida, December 26, 1839, Clarence E. Carter, ed. Territorial Papers of the United States (Washington: U.S. Government Printing Office,1934–1962) (hereafter TP), 26: 11–13; Dorothy Dodd, "Letters from East Florida, 1843," *Florida Historical Quarterly* 15 (July 1936): 51–54.

96. "From Florida," *Richmond Enquirer*, August 1, 1843.

97. M.E.D. Brown's experiences were similar to those of other aspiring American

artists studying in Europe discussed in David McCullough's recent work. See David Mc-
Cullough, *The Greater Journey: Americans in Paris* (New York: Simon and Schuster, 2011).

98. George L. Brown to Mannevillette E. D. Brown, June 2, 1839, USMA.

99. George L. Brown to Mannevillette E. D. Brown, November 14, 1839, USMA.

Chapter 1. "I Shall Be My Own Man" (1840–1842)

1. Corinna Brown Aldrich to Mannevillette E. D. Brown, May 23, 1840, Anderson-
Brown Collection, United States Military Academy, West Point, New York (hereinafter
USMA).

2. Corinna Brown Aldrich to Mannevillette E. D. Brown, August 2, 1840, USMA.

3. Edward S. Aldrich purchased a town lot in Newnansville on June 16, 1841, for fifteen
dollars. Alachua County, Book of Records (Deeds and Lands), 1826–1846, 391–92.

4. Memorial to Congress by Citizens of East Florida, December 26, 1839, Clarence
Carter, ed., *Territorial Papers of the United States*. (Washington, D.C.: U.S. Government
Printing Office, 1934–62) (hereinafter TP), 26: 11–15.

5. Participating in this meeting were Jesse Carter (president), Charles Dell (secre-
tary), and committee members B. M. Dell, Capt. M. Hindley, Dr. E. S. Aldrich, J. M.
Bates, Thos. Colding, Thos. J. Prevatt, and Asa Clark. *St. Augustine Florida Herald and
Southern Democrat*, December 5, 1839.

6. Among those in Reid's entourage were his wife, daughters, and son-in-law Francis
L. Dancy, Joseph S. Sanchez, A. H. Cole, and David Levy of St. Augustine, and Judge John
L. Doggett and Major Critchton of Duval County. Among the official welcoming com-
mittee were Col. F. R. Sanchez, John Tucker, T. J. Prevatt, Bennett Dell, James Pendarvis,
Simeon Dell, and G. F. Olmstead. *St. Augustine Florida Herald and Southern Democrat*,
January 9, 16, 1840.

7. Aldrich's toast: "David Levy, Esq., one of the candidates for our next Delegation
to Congress—Let us begin the system of reform by voting for an honest man, without
regard to political prejudice." "Harrison Men-Look Here!" *Tallahassee Floridian and Advocate*, April 10, 1841.

8. Corinna Brown Aldrich to Mannevillette E. D. Brown, August 2, 30, 1840, USMA;
Genealogical Committee, Georgia Historical Society, *Register of Deaths in Savannah,
Georgia*. 1833–1847, 5: 136.

9. Corinna Brown Aldrich to Mannevillette E. D. Brown, October 11, 1840, USMA.

10. *Savannah Daily Georgian*, January 6, 1841.

11. *Charleston Mercury*, January 25, 1841.

12. *Savannah Daily Georgian*, May 14, 1841.

13. Alachua County Marriage Records, 1837–49, book 1, 22.

14. "Phiz" is a colloquial and archaic term meaning "a face or facial expression; coun-
tenance" (OED).

15. George Brown to Mannevillette E. D. Brown, June 12, 1841. Ah-Tah-Thi-Ki
museum.

16. French for "we will see."

17. Zilphia Standley (often spelled Stanley), a native of Liberty County, Georgia, was
born in 1795 and operated a boardinghouse in Newnansville. She died in 1855 and is

buried in the Newnansville Cemetery. Alachua County, Fla., Census (1840), 161; Alachua County, Fla., Census (1850), 32.

18. Samuel Peter Heintzelman. Diaries and Papers. Library of Congress, Washington, D.C. (1841)(hereinafter LC), June 27, 1841, 208.

19. Diaries and Papers of Samuel Peter Heintzelman (1841), LC, July 7, 1841, 219.

20. Diaries and Papers of Samuel Peter Heintzelman (1841), LC, July 9, 1841, 220–22.

21. Diaries and Papers of Samuel Peter Heintzelman (1841), LC, July 12, 15, 17, 20, 29, August 17, 30, 1841, 229, 236, 237, 244, 264.

22. Diaries and Papers of Samuel Peter Heintzelman (1841), LC, December 1, 1841, 397.

23. Diaries and Papers of Samuel Peter Heintzelman (1841), LC, December 4, 5, 6, 1841, 400, 402–4.

24. On January 1, 1842, George L. Brown secured a license to "retail spirituous liquors by the small measure in this county [Alachua] from this date for twelve months." He took out a bond of $200 to "well and truly keep peaceably, quiet and well-regulated house at all times." Alachua County, Bonds and Letters Probate, 1840–1857, book A, 99.

25. Walter Edgar, *South Carolina: A History* (Columbia: University of South Carolina Press, 1998), 291; William H.Pease and Jane H. Pease, *The Web of Progress: Private Values and Public Styles in Boston and Charleston, 1828–1843* (New York: Oxford University Press, 1985), 176–77; Walter J. Fraser, *Charleston! Charleston! The History of a Southern City* (Columbia: University of South Carolina Press), 221–22; Philip N. Racine, ed., *Gentlemen Merchants: A Charleston Family's Odyssey, 1828–1870* (Knoxville: Unversity of Tennessee Press), xvii; P. C. Coker, *Charleston's Maritime Heritage, 1670–1865: An Illustrated History* (Charleston: CokerCraft, 1987), 172. Some scholars argue that due to inadequate transportation and communication with the interior, Charleston's economy declined. See Pease and Pease, *The Web of Progress*, 176–77, 187; Barbara L. Bellows, *Benevolence among Slaveholders: Helping the Poor in Charleston, 1670–1860* (Baton Rouge: Louisiana State University Press, 1993), 67–68, 160, 162; Frederick C. Jaher, "Antebellum Charleston: Anatomy of an Economic Failure," in *Class Conflict and Consensus: Antebellum Southern Community Studies*, ed. Orville Vernon Burton and Robert C. McMath Jr., 207–31 (Westport, Conn.: Greenwood, 1982).

26. This firm was located on 26 Vendue Range. See James W. Hagy, *Charleston, South Carolina City Directories for the Years 1830–1841* (Baltimore: Clearfield, 2002), 118. Samuel S. Mills was born in New York in 1816 and was married to Mary E. Mills of Charleston County. See Charleston County, SC, Census (1850), 22. In 1852, he was a grocer at 56 Market Street. He resided at 69 Tradd Street. By 1856, he was an agent of Atlantic wharves and resided on Green St. Baggett, *Directory of City of Charleston* (1852), 88; James W. Hagy, *Charleston, South Carolina City Directories for the Years 1849, 1852, and 1855* (Baltimore: Clearfield, 2002), 87; R. S. Purse, *Charleston City Directory and Strangers Guide for 1856* (New York: J. F. Trow, 1856), 126.

27. Abbreviation for Latin *instante mense*, meaning "this month."

28. *Yard* is archaic for penis. See OED.

29. William Selden served as treasurer of the United States from 1839 to 1850 and enjoyed appointments by presidents Martin Van Buren, William Henry Harrison, John Tyler, James K. Polk, Zachary Taylor, and Millard Fillmore.

30. This is a reference to Edward Aldrich's slave Charles.

31. This obsolete meaning of "waiter" as "an attendant upon the bride (or, more recently, the bride or groom) at weddings" was still current in George's day (OED).

32. The two criminals hanged that day were Chandler Hastings, convicted of murdering Philip Rhorback, and James Greer, convicted of murdering his wife. Both were convicted in the April 1842 term of court. According to a newspaper account, both culprits "exhibited great calmness and resignation in their last moments." They made solemn and impressive addresses to the spectators and fully admitted the justice of the sentence they were about to suffer. *St. Augustine News*, June 13, 1842; *St. Augustine Florida Herald and Southern Democrat*, June 17, 1842. Alachua, Hernando, and Hillsborough County, Minutes of the Superior Court, 1838–1843, 155–58, 170–74, 190–91, 199–201.

Chapter 2. "Better to Make Money as a Cracker Merchant" (1843–1845)

1. Account of William Cason to George L. Brown, May 17–September 26, 1846, William A. Cason Papers, P. K. Yonge Library of Florida History, University of Florida.

2. Schedule of property belonging to the estate of George L. Brown taken in appraisement, December 1, 1857, Alachua County, Administrators Bonds, 1857–1869, book b, 72–77.

3. Corinna Brown Aldrich to Mannevillette E. D. Brown, March 13, 27, May 12, 1842, USMA; *St. Augustine Florida Herald and Southern Democrat*, May 27, 1842.

4. *St. Augustine News*, October 15, 22, 29, 1842; *St. Augustine Florida Herald and Southern Democrat*, November 21, 1842.

5. *St. Augustine Florida Herald and Southern Democrat*, November 21, 1842. Captain Samuel Heintzelman reported seeing Edward and Corinna often in Washington during the first week of the year. Journal of Samuel Peter Heintzelman (1843), LC, January 4, 7, 1843, p. 2.

6. *St. Augustine News*, December 19, 1842; *St. Augustine Florida Herald and Southern Democrat*, January 9, 1843.

7. See Alachua County, Inventory and Order Book, book 2, 1841–1857, 203; Alachua, Hillsborough, Benton, and Marion Counties, Superior and Circuit Court Minutes, 1844–1850, p. 15, 18, 19, 24, 25, 120, 135, 136, 139.

8. Phelps, *People of Florida Lawmaking in Florida*, 1.

9. Corinna Brown Aldrich to Mannevillette E. D. Brown, October 21, 1844, USMA.

10. French for "silver," or money.

11. For accounts of the attack, see *St. Augustine Florida Herald and Southern Democrat*, December 24, 31, 1841; *St. Augustine News*, December 25, 1841; "From Florida," *Savannah Republican* quoted in *Athens Southern Whig*, January 7, 1842; John T. Sprague, *Origins, Progress, and Conclusion of the Florida War*, 1848, facsimile reprint (Tampa, Fla.: University of Tampa Press, 2000), 400–401; Mahon, *History of the Second Seminole War, 1835–1842* (Gainesville: University Press of Florida, 1967; revised edition, 1985), 305.

12. Abbreviation for Latin *Ultimo*, meaning "of last month" (OED).

13. Sam Weller is the witty character in Charles Dickens's picaresque novel *The Pickwick Papers*, first published serially in 1836 and 1837.

14. "A bad-tempered, overbearing woman; a shrew, a scold" (OED).

15. Peter Punctilio is the titular character of Henry Mayhew's "Peter Punctilio, The Man in Black," a short story published in *Bentley's Miscellany* in 1839.

16. George eventually arrived in Charleston a few days later on board the steamer *Beaufort District* from Savannah via Hilton Head and Beaufort. *Charleston Patriot*, February 14, 1843.

17. George is referring to Maria and Caroline Coy.

18. George is repeating the slur of the Whigs after the Democrats nominated James K. Polk. The East Florida Whigs met at Fort King on July 24 and nominated B. A. Putnam of St. Johns, Jacob Summerlin of Columbia, Isaiah Hart of Duval, and John Scott of Marion County. That year the East Florida Democrats assembled in Palatka on July 9 to nominate their candidates for the legislative council. Among those delegates representing Alachua County were Louis Aldrich and Philip, Bennett, and Charles Dell. The top four vote getters were Summerlin, Putnam, Hart, and Jesse Carter, a Democrat. *St. Augustine Florida Herald and Southern Democrat*, May 14, July 30, November 19, 1844.

19. "Loco Foco" was a derogatory term for Democrats.

20. Archaic for "called."

21. "The fashion, the vogue, the mode; fashionable air or style" (OED).

22. This is a reference to Whig candidates for president and vice president in 1844, Henry Clay and Theodore Frelinghuysen.

23. George is referring to specie: gold or silver.

24. To "salivate" was to induce excessive salivation "by ingestion of mercury," a medical treatment (OED).

25. Leonidus McNeal was indicted for murder in Alachua County in December 1844. He was granted a change of venue to Duval, where he wasted away in jail until his physician predicted that he would die unless able to get "pure air." After a number of appeals, Governor William D. Moseley pardoned McNeal. See Alachua County, Minutes of the Alachua, Hillsborough, Benton, and Marion County Superior Court, 1844–1850, 85, 104–111; Pardon of Leonidus McNeal, September 19, 1846, Book of Record (Governors Proclamations), RG 156, ser. 13, book 1, no. 40, p. 30, Florida State Archives, Tallahassee.

26. George made a trip to Charleston in the fall of 1844. Newspaper sources have him arriving in town in the middle of October. He was gone approximately two months. George arrived in Charleston on board the steamer packet *Charleston* in the second week of October. *Charleston Southern Patriot*, October 14, 1844.

27. Thomas Aldrich of Charleston was Edward Aldrich's cousin.

Chapter 3. "Man Is Born for Disappointment" (1845)

1. E. Ashby Hammond, *Medical Profession in 19th Century Florida: A Biographical Register* (Gainesville: George Smathers Libraries, University of Florida, 1996), 485–86.

2. *Savannah Daily Republican*, March 1, 1845; *Charleston Southern Patriot*, March 1, 1845.

3. Alexander Mackey quoted in Thomas Clark, ed., *South Carolina: The Grand Tour, 1780–1865* (Columbia: University of South Carolina Press, 1973), 235–36.

4. Gregory Allen Greb, "Charleston, South Carolina Merchants, 1815–1860" (Ph.D. dissertation, University of California, San Diego, 1978), 23–26.

5. Greb, "Charleston, South Carolina Merchants," 38–40.

6. Barbara L. Bellows, *Benevolence among Slaveholders: Helping the Poor in Charleston, 1670–1860* (Baton Rouge: Louisiana State University Press, 1993), 105.

7. Tasistro quoted in Clark, *South Carolina*, 185–87.

8. All four were delegates from St. Johns County to the Democrat Nominating Convention in Madison for the first General Assembly of the State of Florida. Louis Aldrich and Charles Dell represented Alachua County. The convention met on April 14 and nominated William D. Moseley for governor and David Levy for Florida's lone congressional seat. *St. Augustine Florida Herald and Southern Democrat*, April 15, 22, 1845.

9. Crocket Springs was located near present-day High Springs, Florida, in northeast Alachua County. Marshal Blanton and Fernando Underwood were two of the earliest settlers there. http://www.waymarking.com/waymarks/WM39RR_High_Springs_Florida.

10. Elizabeth Sanchez, the daughter of Francis R. Sanchez, married William Dell. Alachua County Marriage Records, book 1, p. 60.

11. Sarah Drysdale was the daughter of John and Louisa Drysdale. Fifteen years old in 1845, she married F. C. Humphreys on June 18, 1847. "Drysdale," in Vertical File, St. Augustine Historical Society Library.

Chapter 4. "To Transform a 'Yankee' to a 'Southern Cracker'" (1846–1849)

1. "To Sea Island Cotton Planters," *Savannah Daily Georgian*, September 26, 1846; "Sea Island Cotton Gins," *Savannah Daily Georgian,* July 8, 1847.

2. E. J. Donnell, *Chronological and Statistical History of Cotton* (New York: James Sutton, 1872), 323, 335, 336.

3. Theodore Rosengarten, *Tombee: Portrait of a Cotton Planter* (New York: William Morrow, 1985), 85.

4. Donnell, *Chronological and Statistical History of Cotton*, 359.

5. Most of George's surviving correspondence after 1845 is directed to his siblings rather than to Edward, probably because George's business was becoming more independent from Edward so that correspondence between them became less urgent and frequent. Most likely, he also felt a stronger need to write to his siblings since he was geographically isolated now not only from Mannevillette but also from his sisters. David Henkin comments that in the mid-nineteenth century "separated kin using the post to . . . affirm family intimacy helped shape the meaning of mail in American culture." David M. Henkin, *The Postal Age: The Emergence of Modern Communication in Nineteenth-Century America* (Chicago: University of Chicago Press, 2007), 11.

6. "Volunteer Company," *Jacksonville Florida News*, January 29, 1847; "Col. R. G. Livingston" and "To the Public," *Jacksonville Florida News*, February 26, 1847. See also *Jacksonville Florida News*, June 12, 1846. Livingston's Florida Independent Rifle Company mustered in Alligator in June 1847, marched to Tallahassee, arriving on July 9, and was mustered into service of the United States there in August. From Tallahassee, the company left St. Marks for New Orleans, received training, and headed for Vera Cruz, arriving September 30, 1847. From the outset, the company was plagued by disease; many died, including Captain Livingston, but only one person died of combat wounds. The

company spent time in Jalapa and Puebla before being mustered out of service on July 8, 1848. Davis, "Florida's Part in the War with Mexico," 247–53.

7. George arrived in Charleston from Savannah on board the *Charleston* in February and was there again in June. In October, George made a third trip to Charleston, where he met Ellen and her family. Together, they boarded the steamer *Wm Gaston* and were soon in Florida. *Charleston Southern Patriot*, February 6, 1846; *Jacksonville Florida News*, June 12, October 16, 1846.

8. James Anderson to Ellen Brown Anderson, January 2, 1847, Anderson-Brown Papers, USMA.

9. George is referring to Calhoun's principled stance in opposition to war with Mexico. See Charles M. Wiltse, *John C. Calhoun, Sectionalist, 1840–1850* (New York: Russell & Russell, 1968), 282–86, 422–29; Merrill D. Peterson, *The Great Triumvirate: Webster, Clay and Calhoun* (New York: Oxford University Press, 1987), 436–37; Irving Bartlett, *John C. Calhoun: A Biography* (New York: Norton, 1993), 335–49. An extended treatment is found in Ernest Lander, *Reluctant Imperialists: Calhoun, the South Carolinians, and the Mexican War* (Baton Rouge: Louisiana State University Press, 1980).

10. George is referring here to heated correspondence between Gen. Winfield Scott and Secretary of War William Marcy. At the war's outbreak, President Polk immediately appointed Scott commander of all U.S. troops in the field. Instead of departing for Mexico immediately, Scott stayed in Washington longer than Polk thought necessary, and a heated correspondence that was published in the newspapers transpired. In one of Scott's responses, he mentioned that he had received Marcy's latest transmission while sitting down to a "hasty plate of soup." Scott's dispute with the Polk administration continued until he was finally offered command of the Veracruz operation in November 1846. Political cartoonists had a field day with the remark and soon caricatures of the general eating soup were in many of the public prints. See John Eisenhower, *Agent of Destiny: The Life and Times of General Winfield Scott* (New York: Free Press, 1997); John Eisenhower, *So Far from God: The U.S. War with Mexico, 1848–1848* (New York: Random House, 1989), 92–97; 223–31; K. Jack Bauer, *The Mexican War, 1846–1848* (New York: Macmillan, 1974), 70–74.

11. Corning and Company was a banking firm based in upstate New York. The bank failed in 1857. Irene Neu, *Erastus Corning: Merchant and Financier, 1794–1872* (Ithaca, N.Y.: Cornell University Press, 1960), 115–30; *The Bankers Journal of the Money Market and Commercial Digest*, 17 (January–December 1857), 935.

12. Gen. Robert A. Armstrong was a veteran of the Seminole War, where he commanded Tennessee volunteers and fought in the Battle of Wahoo Swamp (1836). In 1845, his fellow Tennessean President James K. Polk appointed him consul to Liverpool, England. Sprague, *The Florida War*, 161–62.

13. Latin for "love of country" or "patriotism."

14. "Mrs. Anderson and family" arrived in Jacksonville on board the *Wm Gaston* in mid-October. *Jacksonville Florida News*, October 16, 1846.

15. This is George's only extant letter from 1847; none written in 1848 survive.

16. For Anderson's entire Mexican War service, see James M. Denham and Keith L.

Huneycutt, "With Scott in Mexico: Letters of Captain James W. Anderson in the Mexican War, 1846–1847," *Military History of the West* 28 (Spring 1998): 19–48.

17. George was in Charleston by the second week of February. He boarded the *St. Mathews* at Picolata and passed through Savannah on his way to Charleston. *Savannah Daily Republican*, February 12, 1849.

18. Matthew 6:19.

19. George is referring to the Astor Place Riot that occurred on May 10, 1849. The riot left approximately twenty-five people dead and hundreds injured. The riot took place outside the Astor Opera House in Manhattan between the fans of two Shakespearian actors: Edwin Forrest (an American) and William Charles Macready (an Englishman). Both rival actors represented different groups: Forrest working-class Americans and Irish immigrants and Macready the upper classes. After the situation got out of hand, the authorities called in soldiers, who fired into the crowd to stop the rioting. Edwin G.Burrows and Mike Wallace, *Gotham: A History of New York City to 1898* (New York: Oxford University Press, 1999), 761–66.

20. George quotes Shakespeare's Shylock, who demands this payment from his debtor, Antonio, in *The Merchant of Venice* (*The Merchant of Venice*, ed. G. Blakemore Evans et al. (New York: Houghton Mifflin Company, 1997), 148–51.

21. Alternate spelling for "past" (as a preposition) that was current in the nineteenth century.

22. Eblis is the principle devil or evil spirit of Islamic belief. George may be referring to the concluding episode in William Beckford's gothic novel *Vathek* (1786), in which the hero journeys to the fabulous hall of Eblis and is doomed to eternal torture.

23. For the attack on Fort Pierce on July 12 and the attack on the Kennedy and Darling store on the Peace River five days later, see James W. Covington, *The Seminoles of Florida* (Gainesville: University Press of Florida, 1993), 115–16; James W. Covington, "The Indian Scare of 1849," *Tequesta* 21 (1961): 53–64; John Missall and Mary Lou Missell, *The Seminole Wars: America's Longest Indian Conflict* (Gainesville: University Press of Florida, 2004), 210–11; "Attack on the Indian River Settlement," *Jacksonville Republican*, July 26, 1849.

24. The preacher's reference is to a blaze, a white spot or area down the center of a horse's face.

25. George refers to Douglas Jerrold's *A Man Made of Money* (London: Punch Office, 1849). According to Stephen G. Worth, the book is "a satire against the whole world of consumerism." See Stephen G. Worth, "Douglas William Jerrold," in *Encyclopedia of British Humorists*, ed. Stephen H. Gale (New York: Garland, 1996), 1: 581.

26. Here George refers to Zachary Taylor's battle with the Seminoles at Okeechobee on Christmas Day 1837.

27. George here repeats the story he told to his sisters about the lost plough mare, but to Mannevillette he identifies the preacher as a Baptist "known as 'old hard-shell.'" He also adds that the congregation resumed singing "after this singular interruption–to me the scene was 'rich' but the brethren did not seem to think it otherwise than 'all right.'"

28. In 1850, George L. Brown owned six slaves: three men aged forty-five, thirty, and

twenty-five; two boys aged four and one; and one woman aged twenty-three. Alachua County, Slave Schedule (1850), 9.

29. George is probably referring to Holahteelmathloochee, a prominent Seminole leader in the Peace River Region.

Chapter 5. "Wreathed in Perpetual Smiles" (1850–1852)

1. E. J. Donnell, *Chronological and Statistical History of Cotton* (New York: James Sutton, 1872), 359, 372–73, 384.

2. "Prospects of East Florida," *Jacksonville Florida News*, May 3, 1851.

3. "Direct Trade with Charleston," *Jacksonville Florida News*, August 16, 1851.

4. *Charleston Mercury* quoted in *Jacksonville Florida News*, September 20, 1851.

5. Alachua County, County Commissioners Minutes, book 1: 30, 34–35. Brown stood for election again in 1851 but lost as he finished fifth out of eleven candidates. Alachua County, County Commissioners Minutes, book 1: 45.

6. Four men, named Massey, Johnson, Thompson, and Mills, were convicted of manslaughter for killing Mobley and fined $1,000 each, except for Mills who was fined $100. See *Tallahassee Floridian and Journal*, August 4, 1849, January 26, 1850.

7. Cabell won reelection in the race. *Jacksonville Republican*, October 17, 1850. See also "Whig Meeting in Newnansville," *Jacksonville Republican*, May 8, 1850; "Maj. Beard," *Jacksonville Republican*, July 25, 1850; "Major John Beard in 1840," *Jacksonville Republican*, August 8, 1850; *Jacksonville Republican*, September 26, 1850.

8. Robert M. Temple, *Florida Flame: A History of the Florida Conference of the United Methodist Church* (Nashville: Parthenon, 1987), 121.

9. Corinna Brown Aldrich to Mannevillette E. D. Brown, March 21, 1850, USMA.

10. See William Shakespeare's *Julius Caesar*, ed. G. Blakemore Evans et al. (New York: Houghton Mifflin Company, 1997), 194–95.

11. Boston & Gunby Cotton Factors and General Commission Merchants of Savannah was a primary consignee of cotton shipments from Palatka and other Florida locations.

12. One of Gen. Stewart's daughters, Martha, married James Stephens Bulloch, and their first daughter—also named Martha, aka "Mittie"—eventually married Theodore Roosevelt Sr. (the president's father) in 1853, one year after George Brown married Matilda. After the marriage, Mittie's mother, Martha Stewart Elliott Bulloch, young Theodore's beloved "Grandmamma Bulloch," resided with the Roosevelt family in New York until her death in 1864. Even though they lived miles apart and there is no evidence they ever met, Matilda and "Mittie" were cousins. See Joseph Gaston Bulloch, *History and Genealogy of the Stewart, Elliott and Dunwoody Families* (Savannah, Ga.: Robinson Printing House, 1895), 1–12; Bulloch, *A History and Genealogy of the Families of Bulloch, Stobo, DeVeaux, Irvine, Douglass, Baillie, Lewis, Adams, Glen, Jones, Davis, Hunter with a Genealogy of Branches of the Habersham King, Stiles, Footman, Newell, Turner, Stewart, Dunwoody, Elliott* (Savannah, Ga.: Braid and Hutton, 1892), 17; David McCullough, *Mornings on Horseback* (New York: Simon and Schuster, 1981), 41–42, 64.

13. Columbia County Census (1850), Columbia County Slave Census (1850), 71–72; Folks Huxford, *Pioneers of Wiregrass Georgia*, 9 vols. (Homerville, Ga: Folks Huxford and Huxford Genealogical Society, 1951–1993), 5: 418–19.

14. Russell D. James, *Too Late for Blood: Florida Volunteers in the Mexican War* (Westminster, Md.: Heritage, 2005), 54, 57, 58; T. Frederick Davis, "Florida's Part in the War with Mexico," *Florida Historical Quarterly* 20 (January 1942): 248–49.

15. *Jacksonville Republican*, June 27, 1850.

16. At the time of Matilda's marriage to George Brown, the Stewart household included Eliza (46), George (22), Matilda (22), Charles (21), Claudius (17), James (15), Alide (10), Thomas (7), Mary (5). Columbia County, Fla., Census, (1850).

17. Executrix's Notice of Eliza M. Stewart, February 8, 1849, in *Jacksonville Republican*, February 8, 1849.

18. Italian for "loveable wife."

19. French for a cradled arm bouquet popular with women during wedding ceremonies.

20. *Jacksonville Republican*, May 8, 1851.

21. Ellen Brown Anderson to Mannevillette E. D. Brown, February 22, 1852, USMA.

Chapter 6. "Picking Steadily Along" (1852–1857)

1. Ward lost to James E. Broome, and Maxwell lost to incumbent Edward C. Cabell.

2. "Discussion at Newnansville," *Jacksonville Republican*, September 24, 1852; Alachua County, Minutes of the County Commission, January 1857, book 1: 68.

3. "Sea Island Cotton," *St. Augustine Ancient City*, November 13, 1852.

4. "Progress of our State," *St. Augustine Ancient City*, July 3, 1852.

5. *Charleston Mercury* quoted in *Jacksonville Florida News*, November 26, 1853.

6. J. W. Bryant to editor, from the *Charleston Courier*, Florida correspondence, in *Jacksonville Republican*, March 23, 1854.

7. *Jacksonville Republican*, February 2, 1854.

8. Edmund L. Drago, *Broke by the War: Letters of a Slave Trader* (Columbia: University of South Carolina Press, 1991), 1–6. For slave trading in Charleston, see Frederic Bancroft, *Slave Trading in the Old South* (New York: Frederick Ungar, 1959), 165–96; Michael Tadman, *Speculators and Slaves: Masters, Traders, and Slaves in the Old South* (Madison: University of Wisconsin Press, 1989), 31–41, 55–57, 113–14, 118–21, 257.

9. George L. Brown to Ziba B. Oakes, November 30, 1854, Ziba B. Oakes Papers, box 52, folio 301, Boston Public Library, Boston, Massachusetts.

10. In 1856, Brown responded to Oakes's inquiry regarding the legal ownership of slaves whom Alachua County Sheriff Charles Wilson had taken to Charleston for sale. He told Oakes that when one of his customers asked about where they could "place negroes for sale in your city, I told him without hesitation to call on you." The purported owner of the slaves was Philip Dell, whom Brown represented as "responsible and as good a man as there is in this county," but since "they left here," Brown wrote, "I have known of other claims against the negroes. I have to advise you that if the negroes are not sold to have nothing more to do with them without advices from Col. P. Dell. His letter will *be good*." And then again on his final trip to Charleston, Brown wrote to Oakes at his office on 7 State Street, "I expect to visit your City next month about the 25th and am desirous to purchase two negro girls—house servants from 15 to 16 years. One for myself and one for a customer. We want *prime* negroes. Let me know by return mail the

probable price and if you expect any at that time. I will be at Savannah for a few days, and without your advices might miss a good purchase." George L. Brown to Ziba B. Oakes, November 28, 1856 and George L. Brown to Ziba B. Oakes, Ziba B. Oakes Papers, box 36, folio 560 and box 35, folio 518, Boston Public Library.

11. "Progress," *Jacksonville Florida News*, January 8, 1853. The *Wm. Gaston, Florida, Welaka* and *Carolina* linked Jacksonville with Charleston and Savannah. The *Sarah Spaulding* and the *Thorn* made weekly trips from Jacksonville to the St. Johns's southernmost landing at Enterprise. "Marine Journal. Port of Jacksonville, Regular Packets," *Jacksonville Florida News*, January 15, 1853.

12. "The Steamers of the St. Johns," *Jacksonville Republican*, January 5, 1854.

13. "Terrible Disaster! The Explosion of the Steamer *Magnolia*," *St. Augustine Ancient City*, January 17, 1852.

14. "Progress," *Jacksonville Florida News*, January 8, 1853.

15. "Jacksonville Florida," *Jacksonville Republican*, June 23, 1853.

16. "Progress," *Jacksonville Florida News*, January 8, 1853.

17. "The Fire in Jacksonville," *Jacksonville Republican*, June 15, 1854; Duval County Grand Jury Presentment, *Jacksonville Republican*, April 5, 1855; "One Year Since," *Jacksonville Republican*, April 12, 1855; "A Glance at Jacksonville," *Jacksonville Florida News*, May 3, 1856; "Disastrous Conflagration—Great Loss of Property!" *Jacksonville Republican*, November 19, 1856.

18. *Jacksonville Republican*, June 17, 1852; "New Hack Line," *Jacksonville Republican*, April 15, 1852; "Central Stage Line," *Jacksonville Florida News*, September 15, 1855.

19. L'Avenie to Friend Blanchard, March 29, 1855, *Jacksonville Republican*, April 5, 1855.

20. "Picolata Ferry," *St. Augustine Ancient City*, July 9, 1853.

21. Richard L. Forstall, ed. and comp., *Population of States and Counties: 1790–1990* (Washington, D.C.: Department of Commerce, U.S. Bureau of the Census, Population Division, 1996), 3–4, 31–32; Edward A. Fernald and Elizabeth D. Purdum, *Atlas of Florida* (Gainesville: University Press of Florida, 1992), 98.

22. *Jacksonville Florida News*, May 21, 1853; *Jacksonville Republican*, May 19, 1853.

23. Lemuel Wilson, "Notice to Government Land Occupants, Land Office, Newnansville," February 11, 1853, *Jacksonville Republican*, March 17, 1853.

24. "Boarding House, Newnansville, Florida," *Jacksonville Republican*, September 21, 1854; Charles Lanman, *Adventures in the Wilds of the United States and British Provinces* (Philadelphia: John W. Moore, 1856), 2: 130–31.

25. Alachua County, Minutes of the County Commission, 1: 45. The Alachua Military Institute (later styled) Alachua Institute was established in 1853. George Brown, J. G. Dell, Philip Dell, William Dell, Stephen Fagen, Benjamin Moody, and T. J. Prevatt were trustees and Jesse T. Bernard was principal. *Jacksonville Republican*, March 3, 1853; *Tallahassee Floridian and Journal*, September 12, 1854.

26. "Hon. Wm. A. Forward," *St. Augustine Ancient City*, January 15, 1853.

27. *Savannah News* quoted in *Jacksonville Republican*, December 23, 1852; "Tribute of Respect," *Jacksonville Republican*, October 7, 1852; *Jacksonville News* quoted in *Tallahassee Floridian and Journal*, October 2, 1852.

28. *Savannah Republican* quoted in *Jacksonville Florida News*, May 14, 1853; *Jacksonville Republican*, May 12, 19, 1853. Alachua County, Minutes of the Alachua and Levy Circuit Court, 1850–1857, 99, 102, 115, 117, 127.

29. Alachua County, Deed Record C: 31.

30. "Medical Notice—Doctors Aldrich and Mott," *San Francisco Daily Placer Times and Transcript*, July 9, 1852.

31. "Mills House," *Jacksonville Republican*, October 4, 1855; Walter J. Fraser, *Charleston! Charleston! The History of a Southern City* (Columbia: University of South Carolina Press, 1989), 231; Iva D. Steen, "Charleston in the 1850s: As Described by British Travelers," *South Carolina Historical and Genealogical Magazine* 71 (January 1970): 36–37.

32. Gregory Allen Greb, "Charleston, South Carolina, Merchants, 1815–1860" (Ph.D. dissertation, University of California, San Diego, 1978), 23–26.

33. Philip N.Racine, ed., *Gentlemen Merchants: A Charleston Family's Odyssey, 1828–1870* (Knoxville: University of Tennessee Press, 2008), xvii.

34. Greb, "Charleston, South Carolina, Merchants, 1815–1860," 62–63; Michael D. Thompson, *Working on the Dock of the Bay: Labor and Enterprise in an Antebellum Southern Port* (Columbia: University of South Carolina Press, 2015), 113–14, 147; Mary C. Oliphant, Alfred Taylor Odell, and T. C. Duncan Eaves, eds., *The Letters of William Gilmore Simms*, 3 vols. (Columbia: University of South Carolina Press, 1952–54), 1: cxxvi–cxxvii.

35. In July 1852, the steamboat *Henry Clay* with more than three hundred passengers on its run on the Hudson River from Albany to New York City caught fire. The *Henry Clay* was racing another steamboat, the *Armenia*, when its hull overheated and ignited the furnace near Yonkers, New York. More than fifty people died in the disaster. The officers were eventually prosecuted for misconduct. "Burning of the Steamboat *Henry Clay*," *Nyack (N.Y.) Rockland County Journal*, July 31, 1852; "Dreadful Calamity on the Hudson River," *New York Times*, July 29, 1852; "Burning of the Steamer Henry Clay," *Haverstraw (N.Y.) Rockland County Messenger*, August 5, 1852.

36. George's sister Adelaide Brown died in 1833.

37. For a brief history of this company, see Walter Barrett, *The Old Merchants of New York City* (New York: Carlton, 1864), 333–39.

38. On November 2, 1852, Sacramento suffered a devastating fire that torched forty blocks and left almost twenty people dead. See "The Fire," *Sacramento Daily Union*, November 6, 1852.

39. Billy Bowlegs (Holata Micco) and his entourage traveled to Washington with General Luther Blake on board the *Gaston* in September 1852. In Washington, Bowlegs met with President Millard Fillmore and signed an agreement in which they promised to leave Florida and persuade the remaining Seminoles to leave also. Bowlegs also visited New York (where his famous picture with his entourage was made), Philadelphia, and Baltimore. By the time the group had returned to Florida, the agreement had broken down. Continued resistance combined with provocative federal policies in lands claimed by Bowlegs triggered the Third Seminole War in 1855, a conflict that led to Billy Bowlegs's and a large number of his tribesmen's removal. "Bowlegs and Suite en route for Washington," *Jacksonville Republican*, September 16, 1852; "Highly Important—Removal

of the Indians," *Jacksonville Republican*, September 30, 1852; James W. Covington, *The Seminoles of Florida* (Gainesville: University Press of Florida, 1993), 123–31; John Missall and Mary Lou Missall, *The Seminole Wars: America's Longest Indian Conflict* (Gainesville: University Press of Florida, 2004), 209–21.

40. On November 23, a special committee of the Masonic Lodge in Newnansville composed of George Brown, T. J. Prevatt, and J. T. Bernard authored a series of resolutions deploring the death of their fellow member Samuel Russell. *Jacksonville Florida News*, December 10, 1853; *Jacksonville Republican*, December 22, 1853.

41. By this time, Corinna had become addicted to morphine. See James M. Denham and Keith L. Huneycutt, *Echoes from a Distant Frontier: The Brown Sisters' Correspondence from Antebellum Florida* (Columbia: University of South Carolina Press, 2004), 283–85.

42. On June 19, 1854, Claudius Stewart fought a duel with fellow Newnansville lawyer Joseph B. Coker near the Georgia line. One account noted that the cause of the duel was a misunderstanding between them over Stewart's courting of a young woman. Both men were armed with double-barreled shotguns. Stewart received three balls in the shoulder and arm, necessitating amputation. Two buckshot passed harmlessly through Coker's loose-fitting garment. The *Savannah News* reported, "Both appear to be well-practiced in the use of their weapons, and by the result of the first fire, we are, perhaps spared the record of one of the bloodiest tragedies that has ever resulted from this mode of adjusting differences between gentlemen." "A Desperate Duel," *Savannah News*, June 27, 1854; *Camden (S.C.) Weekly Journal*, July 4, 1854; *Wilmington (N.C.) Journal*, July 7, 1854; "The Duel in Georgia," *Richmond Daily Dispatch*, July 1, 1854; "A Desperate and Bloody Duel in Georgia," *Washington Sentinel*, July 1, 1854. According to Stewart's own account, "The difficulty between Mr. Coker and myself occurred because he had assailed my reputation on very many occasions, and had spoken in terms of disrespect of a deceased brother, whom he had never known or seen. When I demanded satisfaction, he challenged me to meet him in an affair of life and death beyond the limits of the State. I accepted the challenge, and am now the injured party." Claude Stewart to the editor of the *Savannah News*, July 7, 1854, in *Jacksonville Republican*, July 27, 1854.

43. The losses in Charleston and Savannah were frightful. The death total in Charleston was 627. In Savannah, 1,040 died out of a population of about 6,000. D. J. Cain, *History of the Epidemic of Yellow Fever in Charleston in 1854* (Philadelphia: T. K and P. G. Collins Printer, 1856), 10; William Harden, *A History of Savannah and South Georgia*, 2 vols. (Chicago: Lewis, 1913), 1: 412.

44. Corinna's death certificate lists the cause of death as "inanitio," exhaustion owing to lack of food.

45. Stewart died of the injuries sustained in the duel with Joseph B. Coker on November 23. On the next day, the court session began with the notification of the loss of "our friend and Professional Brother." Judge Forward adjourned the court and a meeting of the Bar was called. A committee reported out a series of resolutions deploring the loss of Stewart. One of the resolutions noted that "as a token of respect to the deceased," Thomas Douglas, associate justice of the Supreme Court, and Judge William Forward be invited

to "join the members of the Bar here present, in procession to accompany the remains of our deceased Brother to the steamer *St. Johns*, and that we do wear the usual badge of mourning for a space of thirty days." "Death of Claude Stewart," *Jacksonville Florida News*, November 25, 1854; *Jacksonville Republican*, November 30, December 7, 1854.

46. In this old ballad of uncertain origin, Giles Scroggins courts Molly Brown, "the fairest wench in all our town"; he dies, and she dreams that his ghost comes back to take her with him. The song was popular in theaters in the United States in the first two decades of the nineteenth century. "Giles Scroggins Ghost; together with Looney Mactwolter, and Sally MacGee," *Isaiah Thomas Broadside Ballads Project*, accessed August 17, 2017, http://www.americanantiquarian.org/thomasballads/items/show/85.

47. The first of May was the day that leases were up at boardinghouses in New York City and people moved from place to place.

48. Here George references the controversial figure in the Crimean War, Lord Raglan, commander-in-chief of British forces and forever associated with the Charge of the Light Brigade. See George Ryan, *Our Heroes of the Crimea: Being Biographical Sketches of Our Military Officers, from the General Commanding-in Chief to the Subalterns* (London: George Routledge, 1855), 1–13.

49. Haviland and Harral & Co Druggists had two locations in Charleston: one at 260 King Street and one at 23 Hayne Street. The City Directory of 1856 listed five persons associated with the firm: J. C. Haviland (res. New York), James Harral (res. New York), H. W. Risley (res. New York) W. K. Kitchen (res. New York), and W. Stevenson (res. Mills House). Stevenson was a merchant and native of Massachusetts. Charleston County, S.C., Census (1850), 376. Stevenson worked at the shop at 23 Hayne Street. R. S. Purse, *Charleston City Directory and Strangers Guide for 1856* (New York: J. F. Trow, 1856), 78; James W. Hagy, *Charleston, South Carolina City Directories of the Years 1849, 1852 and 1855* (Baltimore: Clearfield, 2002), 167; Racine, *Gentleman Merchants*, 57, 834n.

50. Haviland, Risley and Company of Augusta were wholesale dealers in drugs, medicines, paints, oils, window glass, dye stuffs, cement, and plaster of Paris.

51. This is a reference to book four of Laurence Stern's *Tristram Shandy*, where Tristram is misnamed when the nurse taking him to his baptism forgets the correct name to tell the priest (9 vols., 1759–1766).

52. This is probably a reference to the prominent Irish-born playwright and British Whig politician Richard Brinsley Sheridan (1751–1816), though there is no character with this name (or anything similar) in his published plays.

53. "Destructive Conflagration in New York," *Sacramento Daily Union*, December 19, 1856; "Destructive Fire," *Richmond Daily Dispatch*, November 12, 1856.

54. For George Brown's arrivals into Charleston, see *Charleston Mercury*, February 22, October 13, March 9, 1856.

55. John D. Anthon to Mannevillette E. D. Brown, October 13, 1857, USMA.

56. Samuel B. McLin to Ellen Brown Anderson, October 20, 1857, personal collection of Elizabeth Traynor.

57. "Died in Charleston, October 8, 1857, GEORGE L. BROWN, in the 40th year of his age," *Charleston Mercury*, November 9, 1857.

Epilogue

1. J. Egbert Farnum to Ellen Anderson, July 1, 1858, USMA.

2. Alachua County, Administrators Bonds, 1857–1869, book B, 54–6.

3. Schedule of Property Belonging to George L. Brown Taken in Appraisement, December 1, 1857, Alachua County, Administrators Bonds, 1857–1869, book B, 72–78.

4. Alachua County, Inventories and Appraisements, 1858–1880, book 4, 36.

5. Alachua County, Inventory and Order Book, 1841–1858, book 2, 263.

6. Alachua County, Inventories and Appraisements, 1858–1880, book 4, 15–36; Alachua County, Administrators Bonds, 1857–1869, book b, 90, 131, 175.

7. Matilda Brown to Mannevillette E. D. Brown, February 25, 1859, USMA.

8. Ellen Anderson to Mannevillette E. D. Brown, November 10, 1857, USMA.

9. Eliza Stewart to Mannevillette E. D. Brown, October 4, 1859, USMA.

10. Matilda Brown to Mannevillette E. D. Brown, February 25, 1859, USMA.

11. Alachua County Census (1860), 74. The slave census listed Matilda Brown as owning eight slaves (roughly the same number her deceased husband had owned). Her brother James M. Stewart owned fifteen slaves. Mary Eliza Stewart, Matilda's fifty-two-year-old mother, is listed as owning twenty-nine slaves with an approximate value of $24,000. Alachua County Slave Census (1860), 27–28.

12. Thomas O. Stewart married Olivia Quattlebaum in 1864 in Lexington County, South Carolina. Joseph Gaston Bulloch, *History and Genealogy of the Stewart, Eliot and Dunwoody Families* (Savannah, Ga.: Robinson Printing House, 1895), 6.

13. Matilda swore that "her dower had never been set off and assigned to her and that she is justly entitled to the same." Asked that the sheriff summon "five discreet free holders to set off according to law said dower and allowance. [. . .] Petitioner further shows that a very large amount of offsets have been allowed amounting to $18,000 or some other large sum which should have been postponed until said dower and allowances were first taken out of the estate." Alachua County, Administrators Bonds, book B, 1857–1869, 449–50.

14. Mannevillette Brown to Edward Willoughby Anderson, February 2, 1871, USMA.

15. Mannevillette Brown to Edward Willoughby Anderson, March 4, 1875, USMA.

16. Davidson County, Tennessee Census (1880), 188; Huxford, *Pioneers of Wiregrass Georgia*, 5: 19; Matilda Brown to Mannevillette Brown, October 13, 1891, USMA; Marion County Census (1910), 16B; *Ocala Evening Star*, December 8, 1914.

17. Edward Aldrich to Mannevillette Brown, October 13, 1860, USMA; *Savannah Daily Morning News*, October 25, 1861.

18. Shultz, *Nationalism and Sectionalism in South Carolina*, 226.

19. Ellen Anderson to Edward Willoughby Anderson, April 19, 1861, USMA.

20. *Jacksonville Florida Union*, July 22, 1865; *Jacksonville Florida Herald*, September 15, 1865; Edward Aldrich to Mannevillette Brown, July 5, 1867, USMA.

21. Reed, *History of Sacramento County*, 90; *Sacramento Daily Union*, November 2, 1852, September 17, 1855; *San Francisco Daily Alta California*, May 20, 1885.

Appendix A: The Cast of Characters

1. "Alfred Proctor Aldrich," Oliphant, ed., *Simms Papers*, 1: xc–xci; Barnwell County, S.C., Census (1850), 326B; *Representative Men of the South* (Philadelphia: Chas. Robson, 1880), 131.

2. *Jacksonville Florida Union*, July 22, 1865; *Jacksonville Florida Herald*, September 15, 1865; Edward Aldrich to Mannevillette Brown, July 5, 1867, USMA. Columbia County, Fla., Census (1870).

3. John B. Phelps, *The People of Lawmaking in Florida, 1822–1993* (Tallahassee: Florida House of Representatives, 1993), 1; *Tallahassee Floridian and Journal*, June 23, 1849, February 7, 1852; *Jacksonville Florida News*, October 18, 1851; *St. Augustine Ancient City*, January 24, 1852; Reed, *History of Sacramento County*, 90; *Sacramento Daily Union*, November 2, 1852, September 17, 1855; *San Francisco Daily Alta California*, May 20, 1885.

4. Charleston County, S.C., Census, (1850), 84.

5. Florida Militia Muster Rolls, 1: 43–48; Charleston County, S.C., Census, (1850), 84.

6. Camden County, Ga., Census (1840); Camden County, Ga., Census (1850).

7. James M. Denham and Keith L. Hunneycutt, *Echoes from a Distant Frontier: The Brown Sisters' Correspondence from Antebellum Florida* (Columbia: University of South Carolina Press, 2004), 297.

8. Alachua County, Fla., Marriage Records, book 1: 47; Marion County, Fla., Census (1850); Clarence E. Carter, ed. *Territorial Papers of the United States* (Washington: U.S. Government Printing Office,1934–1962) (hereafter TP), 26: 874–76.

9. Alachua County, Fla., Census (1850); Alachua County, Marriage Records, book 1, 109.

10. Alachua County, Fla., Census (1840); TP, 26: 13; Florida Militia Muster Rolls, 4: 31–32, 5: 15–16; Alachua County, Fla., Census (1850).

11. St. Johns County, Fla., Census (1840); Commission of John Beard as United States Marshal (Eastern District), November 1, 1842, TP, 26: 563–64; Jefferson County Marriage Records, 1842–1872: 35; Leon County Florida Census (1840), Leon County, Fla., Census (1850); "Major John Beard," *St. Augustine Ancient City*, June 29, 1850; *Jacksonville Republican*, January 23, 1851.

12. TP, 26: 607–8; Florida Militia Muster Rolls, 4: 9–10, 10: 76–79; Madison County, Fla., Census (1850).

13. Alachua County, Fla., Census (1840); See George W. Cullum, *Biographical Register of the Officers of the United States Military Academy, West Point*, 2 vols. (New York: D. Van Nostrand, 1868), 1: 157; Francis B. Heitman, *Historical Register and Dictionary of the United States Army*, 2 vols, facsimile reprint (Urbana: University of Illinois Press, 1965), 1: 230.

14. TP, 26: 123–24; *Biographical Directory of the United States Congress*, 642; Denham and Huneycutt, *Echoes from a Distant Frontier*, 157–59; Walter W. Manley, Canter Brown, and Eric Rise, *The Supreme Court of Florida and Its Predecessor Courts, 1821–1917* (Gainesville: University Press of Florida, 1997), 85–88; James M. Denham, *A Rogue's Paradise: Crime and Punishment in Antebellum Florida, 1821–1861* (Tuscaloosa: University of Alabama Press, 1997), 28, 30, 34; James M. Denham, "From a Territorial to a Statehood

Judiciary: Florida's Antebellum Courts and Judges," *Florida Historical Quarterly* 73 (April 1995): 451–52.

15. Mannevillette Brown to Edward Willoughby Anderson, March 4, 1875, USMA.

16. *Savannah Daily Republican*, August 23, 1840.

17. Faye M. Kert, *Privateering: Patriots and Profits in the War of 1812* (Baltimore: Johns Hopkins University Press, 2015), 130–33; Denham and Huneycutt, eds., *Echoes from a Distant Frontier*, xvii–xxi, 1–7.

18. *Portsmouth Columbian Sentinel*, October 20, 1832.

19. Folks Huxford, *Pioneers of Wiregrass Georgia*, 9 vols. (Homerville, Ga.: Folks Huxford and Huxford Genealogical Society, 1951–1993), 5: 418; Alachua County (1860); *Ocala Evening Star*, December 8, 1914.

20. Alachua County, Fla., Census (1830); TP, 26: 874–76; Marion County Census (1850), 130B.

21. Charleston County, S.C., Census (1850), 310; Hagy, *Charleston, South Carolina City Directories for the Years 1849, 1852 and 1855* (Baltimore: Clearfield, 2002), 8, 59.

22. Alachua County, Fla., Census (1840); Alachua County, Fla., Census (1850); Alachua County, Minutes of the County Court, np; TP, 26: 608.

23. Putnam County, Fla., Census (1850); Nassau County, Fla., Census (1860); Putnam County, Fla., Census (1870); Madison County, Marriage Book 1: 33; *Territorial Papers*, 26: 604, 637.

24. "A Desperate Duel," *Savannah News*, June 27, 1854; *Camden (S.C.) Weekly Journal*, July 4, 1854; *Wilmington (N.C.) Journal*, July 7, 1854; "The Duel in Georgia," *Richmond Daily Dispatch*, July 1, 1854; "A Desperate and Bloody Duel in Georgia," *Washington Sentinel*, July 1, 1854; "Alachua County Democratic Meeting," *Jacksonville Florida News*, March 29, 1856; *Jacksonville Florida News*, December 2, 1854; *Jacksonville Republican*, February 2, 1854; Rebecca Phillips, "A Diary of Jesse Talbot Bernard: Newnansville and Tallahassee," *Florida Historical Quarterly* 18 (October 1939): 124.

25. Stafford County, VA, Census (1840); Commission of Valentine Y. Conway as Surveyor General, March 17, 1842, TP, 26: 460; Stafford County, VA, Census (1850).

26. Boston Marriages, 1800–1849, 1: 158; Duval County, Fla., Census (1850), 2; Deane R. Briggs, ed. *Florida Stampless Postal History, 1763–1861* (Miami: David G. Phillips Publishing Company for the Florida Postal History Society, 1999), 139.

27. Franklin Hunter Churchill, *Sketch of Bvt. Brig. Gen. Sylvester Churchill, Inspector General U. S. Army* (New York: Willis McDonald and Company, 1888), 44; Heitman, *Historical Register and Dictionary of the United States Army*, 1: 301.

28. Florida Militia Muster Rolls, 3: 40; Benton County, Fla., Census (1850), 24: See E. Ashby Hammond, *The Medical Profession in 19th Century Florida: A Biographical Register* (Gainesville: George Smathers Libraries, University of Florida, 1996), 146.

29. *St. Augustine Florida Herald and Southern Democrat*, November 13, 1843; *Jacksonville Florida News*, April 9, 1847; Alachua County, Bonds and Letters Probate, vol. A, 1828–1857, 198–200; Rockingham County, N.H., Probate Records, vol. 84: 150.

30. Florida Militia Muster Rolls, 1:48–49, 51–52. Alachua County, Fla., Census (1850), 34; Monaco, "Fort Mitchell and the Settlement of Alachua County," *Florida Historical Quarterly* 79 (Summer 2000): 21–22; James Cusick, *The Other War of 1812: The Patriot*

War and the Invasion of Spanish East Florida (Gainesville: University of Florida Press, 2003), 288.

31. Florida Militia Muster Rolls, 3: 73; Alachua County Marriage Records, 1: 10; Alachua County, Fla., Census (1850), 12A; Briggs, ed., *Florida Stampless Postal History*, 127.

32. Florida Militia Muster Rolls, 3: 69, 71; Alachua County, Fla., Census (1850), Alachua County, Marriage Records, book 1: 60; TP, 26: 607–08; Briggs, ed., *Florida Stampless Postal History*, 207; *Jacksonville Florida News*, November 11, 1854; *Tampa Herald* quoted in *Jacksonville Republican*, November 9, 1854; Alachua County, Fla., Census (1850).

33. Duval County, Fla., Census (1840); Pleasant Daniel Gold, *History of Duval County, Including Early History of East Florida* (St. Augustine, Fla.: Record Company, 1929), 104–5; T. Frederick Davis, *History of Jacksonville and Vicinity, 1513 to 1924* (St. Augustine: Florida Historical Society, 1925), 65; Phelps, *The People of Lawmaking in Florida, 1822–1993*, 28; *Jacksonville Courier*, January 1, 1835; TP, 25: 477, 26: 34, 673; St. Augustine *Florida Herald and Southern Democrat*, January 16, 1844.

34. Duval County, Fla., Census (1850), 94; Denham, *A Rogue's Paradise*, 216–17; Manley, Brown, and Rise, *The Supreme Court of Florida and Its Predecessor Courts, 1821–1917*, 123–27; *Jacksonville Florida News*, September 15, 1855.

35. Davidson County, TN, Census (1880), 188; Folks Huxford, *Pioneers of Wiregrass Georgia*, 9 vols. (Homerville, Ga.: Folks Huxford and Huxford Genealogical Society, 1951–1993), 5: 19; Joseph Gaston Baillie Bulloch, *History and Genealogy of the Stewart, Eliot and Dunwoody Families* (Savannah, Ga.: Robinson Printing House, 1895), 6–7; Matilda Brown to Mannevillette Brown, October 13, 1891, USMA; Marion County, Fla., Census (1910), 16B; *Ocala Evening Star*, December 8, 1914.

36. See Hammond, *The Medical Profession in 19th Century Florida*, 180.

37. Arch Fredric Blakey, *Parade of Memories: A History of Clay County, Florida* (Jacksonville: Drummond Press for the Clay County Bicentennial Steering Committee, 1976), 17; TP, 26: 1022; Phelps, *The People of Lawmaking in Florida, 1822–1993*, 34; St. Johns County, Fla. (1850), 207B; Briggs, ed., *Florida Stampless Postal History*, 248; *Jacksonville Florida News*, February 20, 1846; *St. Augustine Ancient City*, September 24, November 19, 1853; St. Johns County, Wills, Letters of Administration, 1840–1862, 1: 285.

38. St. Johns County Marriage Records; St. Johns County, Fla., Census (1850); Manley, Brown, and Rise, *The Supreme County of Florida and Its Predecessor Courts, 1821–1917*, 169–70; Phelps, *The People of Lawmaking in Florida, 1822–1993*, 34; *St. Augustine Ancient City*, November 15, 1851.

39. Florida Militia Muster Rolls, 5: 21–22, 8: 99–100; Alachua County, Will Book A, 17; Alachua County, Bonds and Letters Probate, 1828–1857, vol. A: 178–79.

40. Alachua County, Fla., Census (1840); Alachua County, Fla., Census (1860).

41. Alachua County, Fla., Census (1840); Florida Militia Muster Rolls, 5: 13–14: Alachua County, Marriage Records, book 1: 11; Benton County, Fla., Census (1850), 28B; New River County, Fla., Census (1860), 58.

42. Cullum, *Biographical Register of the Officers of the United States Military Academy, West Point*, 2: 84–85.

43. Canter Brown, *Ossian Bingley Hart: Florida's Loyalist Reconstruction Governor* (Baton Rouge: Louisiana State University Press, 1997), 7–120.

44. Alachua County Marriage Records, book 1: 12; Alachua County, Fla., Census (1840); Levy County, Fla., Census (1850); TP, 26: 721.

45. Cullum, *Biographical Register of the Officers of the United States Military Academy, West Point*, 1: 372–74; Heitman, *Historical Register and Dictionary of the United States Army*, 1: 520.

46. See Hammond, *Medical Profession in 19th Century Florida*, 259; Heitman, *Historical Register and Dictionary of the United States Army*, 1: 521; *New York Evening Post*, June 14, 1842; Washington, D.C., Census (1850), 87; *Virginia Compiled Marriages, 1740–1850*.

47. TP, 26: 986–89; Antonio Rafael de la Cova, *Colonel Henry Theodore Titus: Antebellum Soldier of Fortune and Florida Pioneer* (Columbia: University of South Carolina Press, 2016), 27; Putnam County, Fla., Census, (1850); Phelps, *The People of Lawmaking in Florida, 1822–1993*, 48; Fred L. Robertson, *Soldiers of Florida in the Seminole Indian, Civil, and Spanish-American Wars* (Tallahassee: Board of State Institutions, 1903), 10, 16.

48. See Cullum, *Biographical Register*, 1: 545; Heitman, *Historical Register*, 1: 542.

49. Florida Militia Muster Rolls, 4: 29, 5: 21–22; Alachua County, Fla., Census (1850), 26; Alachua County Marriage book 1: 40.

50. Alachua County Census (1830); TP, 25: 451; Hammond, *The Medical Profession in 19th Century Florida*, 331–32.

51. Alachua County Census (1840); Florida Militia Muster Rolls, 5: 15–16, 19–20, 27–28; Alachua County, Marriage Records, book 1: 46, book 2: 4; Alachua County (1850), 21.

52. Duval County, Fla., Census (1850); Cullum, *Biographical Register of the Officers of the United States Military Academy, West Point*, 1: 233–34.

53. James D. Russell, *Too Late for Blood: Florida Volunteers in the Mexican War* (Westminster, Md.: Heritage, 2005), 53–86; T. Frederick Davis, "Florida's Part in the War with Mexico," *Florida Historical Quarterly* 20 (January 1942): 248.

54. Denham, *A Rogue's Paradise*, 52–53; Phelps, *The People of Lawmaking in Florida, 1822–1993*, 60; Rossiter Johnson, ed., *Twentieth Century Biographical Dictionary of Notable Americans*, vols. 1–10 (Boston, Mass.: Biographical Society, 1904), 7: 26; Raab, W. W. *Loring: Florida's Forgotten General* (Manhattan, Kans.: Sunflower University Press, 1996).

55. TP, 26: 140, 607; Joe Knetsch, *Faces on the Frontier: Florida Surveyors and Developers in the 19th Century* (Cocoa: Florida Historical Society, 2006), 95.

56. TP, 26: 1025; Knetsch, *Faces on the Frontier*, 82.

57. Cullum, *Biographical Register of the Officers of the United States Military Academy, West Point*, 1: 425.

58. Madison County Marriage Book, 149. Alachua County, Fla., Census (1860); *Newnansville Florida Dispatch*, May 11, 1860; Robertson, *Soldiers of Florida*, 174; Orange County, Fla., Census (1880).

59. *Biographical Directory of the U.S. Congress*, 1,406.

60. TP, 25: 510, 629; Duval County, Fla., Census (1850).

61. Briggs, ed., *Florida Stampless Postal History*, 207; Alachua County, Fla., Census (1840), 161; Alachua County, Marriage Records, book 1: 24; TP, 26: 607; Florida Militia Muster Rolls, 4: 13–16; Hartford County, CT, Census (1850); Hartford, CT, Probate Packets, 1641–1880, Olmsted, H-Outerson, James.

62. Florida Militia Muster Rolls, 1: 30–33; TP, 26: 650, 872–73; *Jacksonville Florida*

News, August 7, 1846; *Jacksonville Republican*, May 31, 1849; Alachua County, Fla., Census (1850).

63. TP, 26: 607–8; Alachua County, Fla., Census (1840); Alachua County, Fla., Census (1850).

64. Alachua County, Fla., Census (1850); *Jacksonville Florida News*, August 19, 1854; *Jacksonville Republican*, June 22, 1854; Duval County, Probate Packets, File #1722

65. Columbia County Census (1850).

66. Florida Militia Muster Rolls, 4: 9–10; TP, 26: 607–8.

67. Florida Militia Muster Rolls, 3: 68; Duval County, Fla., Census (1840); Duval County, Fla., Census (1850); Blakey, *Parade of Memories*, 34.

68. Hammond, *Medical Profession in 19th Century Florida*, 508–9.

69. Alachua County, Fla., Census (1830); Alachua County, Fla., Census (1840); Alachua County, Fla., Census (1850), 13B; TP, 26: 60; Alachua County Marriage Records, book 1: 13, 114; Briggs, ed., *Florida Stampless Postal History*, 207.

70. Knetsch, *Faces on the Frontier*, 9–25; James M. Denham and Canter Brown, *Cracker Times and Pioneer Lives: The Florida Reminiscences of George Gillett Keen and Sarah Pamela Williams* (Columbia: University of South Carolina Press, 2000), 160.

71. Alachua County Marriage Records, book 1: 69; Alachua County, Fla., Census (1850); TP, 26: 542, 650, 722, 872–73; *Jacksonville Florida News*, June 19, 26, August 7, 1846, October 18, 1851, July 30, November 12, and December 10, 1853; *Jacksonville Republican*, October 23, 1851.

72. Florida Militia Muster Rolls, 1: 63–66; Monaco, "Fort Mitchell and the Settlement of Alachua County," 14, 22; TP, 25: 279–82, 478; *St. Augustine Florida Herald and Southern Democrat*, July 25, 1839; Alachua County, Marriage Book 1: 28. Alachua County, Fla., Census (1840), 162; Alachua County, Bonds and Letters Probate, vol. A, 1828–1857; Administrators Bonds, Etc., vol. B, 1857–1869, 216–17.

73. Florida Militia Muster Rolls, 3: 76, 4: 58–59, 5: 19–20; TP, 26: 607–08; Alachua County, Fla., Census (1850); Alachua County, Fla., Census (1860); Alachua County, Fla., Census (1870); Gilchrist County, Fla., Census (1900).

74. Florida Militia Muster Rolls, 1: 41–46; Jane Landers, *Colonial Plantations and Economy in Florida* (Gainesville: University Press of Florida, 2000), 92–93; TP, 25: 427–28, 26: 379–40; Denham, *A Rogue's Paradise*, 27, 145, 216; Phelps, *The People of Lawmaking in Florida, 1822–1993*, 86–87; *St. Augustine Ancient City*, September 17, 1853.

75. TP, 26: 607, 737, 876, 988; Marion County, Fla., Census (1850), 120B; Phelps, *The People of Lawmaking in Florida, 1822–1993*, 88.

76. Denham, *Florida Founder*, 45, 47, 58; Phelps, *The People of Florida Lawmaking, 1822–1993*, 88; *United States v. Segui*, 35 U.S. 306 (1836); St. Johns County, Fla., Census (1840), 109; St. Johns County, Fla., Census (1850), 202A; Briggs, ed., *Florida Stampless Postal History*, 248.

77. Florida Militia Muster Rolls, 2: 34–35, 4: 9–10; TP, 26: 60.

78. See Denham, *A Rogue's Paradise*, 28, 30–31; Manley, Brown, and Rise, *Supreme Court of Florida and Its Predecessor Courts, 1821–1917*, 25–30; Denham and Huneycutt, *Echoes from a Distant Frontier*, 158; *Jacksonville Florida News*, May 29, 1846.

79. Alachua County, Fla., Census (1830); Alachua County, Fla., Census (1840); TP,

26: 12; Florida Militia Muster Rolls, 2: 34, 4: 9–10; Herbert Joseph O'Shields, "Women in Antebellum Alachua County" (M.A. thesis, University of North Florida, 2010), 124.

80. Alachua County Census (1830); Jacob Rhett Motte, *Journey into the Wilderness: An Army Surgeon's Account of Life in Camp and Field during the Creek and Seminole Wars, 1836–1838*, ed. James F. Sunderman (Gainesville: University of Florida Press, 1953), 110; O' Shields, "Women in Antebellum Alachua County," 124.

81. Florida Militia Muster Rolls, 4: 9–10, 5: 11–12, 27–28; *St. Augustine Florida Herald and Southern Democrat*, May 16, 1840; *Edgefield (S.C.) Advertiser*, May 21 and June 4, 1840; *Washington, D.C., Madisonian*, May 14, 1840; Alachua County, Fla., Census (1840); Alachua County, Fla., Census (1850), 16B; Alachua County Marriage Records, 1: 15; Phelps, *The People of Lawmaking in Florida, 1822–1993*, 93; TP, 26: 607–8; *Jacksonville Florida News*, October 18, 1851; "Plantation for Sale," *Savannah Daily Georgian*, May 18, 1853; Alachua County, Will Book B: 1–5; Administrators Bonds, Etc, 1857–1869, vol. B: 321.

82. Alachua County, Fla., Census (1830); Alachua County, Fla., Census (1850); O' Shields, "Women in Antebellum Alachua County," 124.

83. Columbia County, Fla., Census (1850); Bulloch, *History and Genealogy of the Stewart, Elliott, and Dunwoody Families*, 4–6.

84. Columbia County, Fla., Census (1850); Bulloch, *History and Genealogy of the Stewart, Elliott, and Dunwoody Families*, 4–6.

85. Columbia County Census (1850); "Death of Claude Stewart," *Jacksonville Florida News*, November 25, 1854; *Jacksonville Republican*, November 30 and December 7, 1854; Bulloch, *History and Genealogy of the Stewart, Elliott, and Dunwoody Families*, 4–6; *Catalog of the Officers, Student and Alumni of Emory College*, 14; *A Catalog of the Students in the Law School of the University at Cambridge*, 81.

86. Columbia County Census (1850), 82A. Columbia County Slave Census (1850), 71–72; Huxford, *Pioneers of Wiregrass Georgia*, 5: 418–19; Bulloch, *History and Genealogy of the Stewart, Elliott, and Dunwoody Families*, 4–6.

87. Bulloch, *History and Genealogy of the Stewart, Elliott, and Dunwoody Families*, 5; James, *Too Late for Blood*, 54, 57, 58; Davis, "Florida's Part in the War with Mexico," 248–49.

88. Huxford, *Pioneers of Wiregrass Georgia*, 5: 418–19; Columbia County Census (1850); Alachua County Census, (1860).

89. Bulloch, *History and Genealogy of the Stewart, Elliott, and Dunwoody Families*, 5; *Savannah News*, quoted in *Jacksonville Republican*, December 23, 1852; "Tribute of Respect," *Jacksonville Republican*, October 7, 1852; *Jacksonville News* quoted in *Tallahassee Floridian and Journal*, October 2, 1852.

90. Columbia County, Fla., Census (1850); Bulloch, *History and Genealogy of the Stewart, Elliott, and Dunwoody Families*, 4–6.

91. Columbia County, Fla., Census (1850); Bulloch, *History and Genealogy of the Stewart, Elliott, Dunwoody Families*, 6–7.

92. Bulloch, *History and Genealogy of the Stewart, Elliott, and Dunwoody Families*, 5; *Jacksonville Republican*, June 27, 1850.

93. Florida Militia Muster Rolls, 7: 33–34, 10: 60–61; Phelps, *The People of Florida Lawmaking, 1822–1993*, 95; Joe Akerman and Mark Akerman, *Jacob Summerlin: King of the Crackers* (Cocoa: Florida Historical Society Press, 2004), 122–23.

94. Florida Militia Muster Rolls, 4: 9–10, 5: 13–14, 8: 37–38; Alachua County, Fla., Census, (1840); TP, 26: 12; Benton County, Fla., Slave Census (1850); O' Shields, "Women in Antebellum Alachua County," 124.

95. TP, 26: 1008; Kings County, N.Y., Census (1860); New York State Census (1875), 42.

96. Florida Militia Muster Rolls: 3: 12, 5: 17–18; Alachua County Marriage Records, 1: 7; TP, 25: 510; Alachua County Census (1840); Benton County, Fla., Census (1850).

97. Alachua County, Fla., Census (1850); See Robert M. Temple, *Florida Flame: A History of the Florida Conference of the United Methodist Church* (Nashville: Parthenon, 1987), 87.

98. Alachua County, Fla., Census (1850), 35; Alachua County Marriage Records, book 2: 42; *Jacksonville Republican*, October 23, 1851; *Jacksonville Florida News*, October 18, 1851; Denham, *A Rogue's Paradise*, 218.

99. Alachua County, Fla., Census (1850), 27; Alachua County Marriage Records, 1: 32; Bowling Green (Mo.) *Democratic Banner*, September 23, 1850; *Washington Daily Union*, March 17, 1854.

100. *Biographical Directory of the American Congress*, 1971; Denham and Huneycutt, *Echoes from a Distant Frontier*, 22–23, 149; Daniel L. Schafer, "U.S. Territory and State," in *The New History of Florida*, ed. Michael Gannon (Gainesville: University Press of Florida, 1996), 215, 221–25.

Appendix B: Two Letters Written before George's Florida Venture

1. George is probably referring to the Boys High School, located at 66 State Street in Portsmouth. It had fifty pupils in 1839. Michael Hugo-Brunt, "A History of the City of Portsmouth in New Hampshire from 1623–1839. Three volumes" (Ph.D. dissertation, Cornell University, 1957), 2: 117.

2. Latin for "love of money."

3. George perhaps is using the noun "cue" as in the OED's third definition: "The tail (of an animal). Humorous use."

BIBLIOGRAPHY

Primary Sources

Archival Sources and Unpublished Sources

Alachua, Columbia, and Hillsborough Counties, Minutes of the Superior Court, 1828–35. University of Florida Library, Gainesville, Fla.

Alachua County, Administrators Bonds, 1857–69, Book B. Alachua County Court, Gainesville, Fla.

Alachua County, Bonds and Letters (Probate), 1840–1857, Book A. Alachua County Court, Gainesville, Fla.

Alachua County, Book of Records (Deeds of Lands), 1826–1846. Alachua County Court, Gainesville, Fla.

Alachua County, County Court Minutes, 1833–1845. University of Florida Library, Gainesville, Fla.

Alachua County, Deed Book, 1846–1852, Book A. Alachua County Court, Gainesville, Fla.

Alachua County, Deed Book, 1852–1854, Book B. Alachua County Court, Gainesville, Fla.

Alachua County, Deed Book, 1857–1859, Book C. Alachua County Court, Gainesville, Fla.

Alachua County, Inventories and Orders, 1841–1861, Book 1. Alachua County Court, Gainesville, Fla.

Alachua County, Inventories and Settlements, 1843–1859, Book 3. Alachua County Court, Gainesville, Fla.

Alachua County, Inventories and Appraisements, 1858–1880, Book 4. Alachua County Court, Gainesville, Fla.

Alachua County, Marriage Records, 1837–1849, Book 1. Alachua County Court, Gainesville, Fla.

Alachua County, Record of Wills, 1840–1859, Book A. Alachua County Court, Gainesville, Fla.

Alachua, Hernando, and Hillsborough Counties, Minutes of the Superior Court, 1838–43. Alachua County Court, Gainesville, Fla.

Alachua, Hillsborough, Benton, and Marion Counties, Superior and Circuit Court Minutes, 1844–50. University of Florida Library, Gainesville, Fla.

Alachua, Hillsborough, Benton, and Marion Counties, Superior and Circuit Court Minutes, 1840–1849. Florida Historical Society Library, Cocoa Beach, Fla.

Alachua and Levy Counties, Circuit Court Minutes, 1850–57. Alachua County Court, Gainesville, Fla.

Book of Record (Governor's Proclamations), RG 156, ser. 13, Book 1. Territorial Auditors Vouchers, RG 352, Ser. 584. Florida State Archives, Tallahassee, Fla.

Brooks, Whitfield. Travel Diary, 1845–1846. College of Charleston Library, Charleston, S.C.

Brown Letters. Ah-Tah-Thi-Ki Seminole Museum Big Cypress Seminole Indian Reservation, Clewiston, Fla.

Cason, William A. Papers. University of Florida Library, Gainesville, Fla.

Charleston Death Records, 1819–1872, Charleston Public Library, Charleston, S.C.

Florida Militia Muster Rolls, Seminole Indian Wars, vols. 1–10. Florida National Guard, Florida Department of Military Affairs, St. Augustine.

Heintzelman, Samuel Peter. Diaries and Papers. Library of Congress, Washington, D.C.

Ledger from U.S. General Land Office Regarding Land Grants under the Armed Occupation Act, 1842–1843. University of Florida Library, Gainesville, Fla.

Miles, William Porcher. Papers. University of North Carolina Library, Chapel Hill, N.C.

Oakes, Ziba B. Papers. Boston Public Library. Boston, Massachusetts.

Sanchez Papers, University of Florida Library. Gainesville, Fla.

U.S. Manuscript Census, Population, 1840, for the following Florida counties: Alachua, Duval, St. Johns, and Columbia.

U.S. Manuscript Census, Population, 1850 for Charleston County South Carolina and the following Florida counties: Alachua, Duval, St. Johns, Columbia, Marion, and Putnam.

U.S. Manuscript Census, Slave, 1850, for the following Florida counties: Alachua, Duval, St. Johns, Columbia, Marion, and Putnam.

U.S. Manuscript Census, Population, 1860, for the following Florida counties: Alachua, Duval, St. Johns, Columbia, Marion, and Putnam.

U.S. Manuscript Census, Slave, 1860, for the following Florida counties: Alachua, Duval, St. Johns, Columbia, Marion, and Putnam.

Newspapers

Athens (Ga.) Southern Whig, 1842
Burlington (Vt.) Free Press, 1836
Charleston Mercury, 1841–1857
Camden (S.C.) Weekly Journal, 1854
Charleston Southern Patriot, 1833, 1843–1846
Edgefield (S.C.) Advertiser, 1839, 1840, 1842
Haverstraw (N.Y.) Rockland County Messenger, 1852
Holly Springs (Miss.) Banner, 1840
Jacksonville Courier, 1835–1837

Jacksonville East Florida Advocate, 1839–1840
Jacksonville Florida Herald, 1865
Jacksonville Florida News, 1846–1858
Jacksonville Florida Republican, 1849–1857
Jacksonville Florida Union, 1865
Macon Southern Post, 1838
New York Times, 1852
Nyack (N.Y.) Rockland County Journal, 1852
Ocala Evening Star, 1914
Ocala Home Companion, 1857–1860
Palatka Whig Banner, 1846–1846
Portsmouth (N.H.) Journal of Literature and Politics-Rockingham Gazette and State Herald, 1833
Richmond Daily Dispatch, 1854, 1856
Richmond Enquirer, 1843
Raleigh North Carolina Standard, 1837, 1839
Sacramento Daily Union, 1852
St. Augustine Ancient City, 1850–1854
St. Augustine Florida Herald, 1834–1838
St. Augustine Florida Herald and Southern Democrat, 1838–1849
St. Augustine News, 1838–1847
San Francisco Daily Alta California, 1885
San Francisco Daily Placer Times and Transcript, 1852
Sacramento Daily Union, 1852, 1855, 1856
Savannah Daily Republican, 1839–1840, 1845, 1849
Savannah Daily Georgian, 1841, 1847
Savannah Daily Morning News, 1861
Savannah News, 1854
Savannah Weekly Georgian, 1839
Tallahassee Floridian, 1836–41
Tallahassee Floridian and Journal, 1849–1850
Washington D.C. Madisonian, 1840, 1842
Washington D.C. Sentinel, 1854
Wilmington (N.C.) Journal, 1854

Published Sources (Contemporary Works, Diaries, Memoirs, Public Documents)

Bagget, J. H. Directory of the City of Charleston for the Year 1852. Charleston: Edward C. Councell, 1852.
The Bankers Journal of the Money Market and Commercial Digest, 1857.
Bleser, Carol, ed. Secret and Sacred: The Diaries of James Henry Hammond, a Southern Slaveholder. New York: Oxford University Press, 1988.
Cain, D. J. History of the Epidemic of Yellow Fever in Charleston in 1854. Philadelphia: T. K and P. G. Collins Printer, 1856.

Carter, Clarence E., ed. *The Territorial Papers of the United States*. 26 vols. Washington, D.C.: U.S. Government Printing Office, 1934–1962.

Charleston City and General Business Directory for 1855. Charleston: David M. Gazlay, 1855.

Churchill, Franklin Hunter. *Sketch of Bvt. Brig. Gen. Sylvester Churchill, Inspector General U. S. Army*. New York: Willis McDonald and Company, 1888.

Clancy, Anne Robinson, ed. *A Yankee in a Confederate Town: The Journal of Calvin L. Robinson*. Sarasota, Fla.: Pineapple, 2002.

Compendium of the Enumeration of the Inhabitants and Statistics of the United States as Obtained at the Department of State, from the Returns of the Sixth Census. Washington, D.C.: Printed by Thomas Allen, 1841.

Cullum, George W. *Biographical Register of the Officers of the United States Military Academy, West Point*. 2 vols. New York: D. Van Nostrand, 1868.

Dawson, J. L., and H. W. DeSaussure. *Census of the City of Charleston for the Year 1848*. Charleston, S.C., 1849.

DeBow, James D. B. *The Seventh Census of the United States: 1850, Embracing a Statistical View of Each of the States and Territories Arranged by Counties*. Washington: Robert Armstrong, Public Printer, 1853.

———. *Statistical View of the United States, Being a Compendium of the Seventh Census*. Washington: Beverly Tucker, Senate Printer, 1854.

Directory of the City of Charleston to which Is Added Business Directory, 1860. Charleston: S.C.W. Eugene Ferslew, 1860.

Drago, Edmund L. *Broke by the War: Letters of a Slave Trader*. Columbia: University of South Carolina Press, 1991.

Fay, T. C. *Charleston Directory and Strangers Guide for 1840–1841, Embracing Names of Heads of Families—firms and Individuals Composing Them*. Charleston: T. C. Fay, 1840.

Forstall, Richard L., ed. and comp. *Population of States and Counties: 1790–1990*. Washington, D.C.: Department of Commerce, U.S. Bureau of the Census, Population Division, 1996.

Gazley, David M. *The Charleston City Directory and General Business Directory for 1855*. Charleston: David M. Gazley, 1855.

Hagy, James W. *Charleston, South Carolina City Directories of the Years 1849, 1852 and 1855*. Baltimore: Clearfield, 2002.

———. *Charleston South Carolina City Directories of the Years 1830–1841*. Baltimore: Clearfield, 2002.

Heitman, Francis B. *Historical Register and Dictionary of the United States Army*. 2 vols. Facsimile reprint, Urbana: University of Illinois Press, 1965.

Honour, John H. *A Directory of the City of Charleston and Neck for 1849: Containing the Names, Residences and Occupations of the Inhabitants Generally*. Charleston: Printed by A. J. Burke, 1849.

Hundley, *Social Relations in Our Southern States*. New York: Henry D. Price, 1860. Reprint, Louisiana State University Press, 1979.

Lanman, Charles. *Adventures in the Wilds of the United States and British Provinces.* Philadelphia: John W. Moore, 1856.

List of Taxpayers of the City of Charleston for 1859. Charleston: Evans & Cogswell, 1860.

Mayors Report on City Affairs. Charleston: A. E. Miller, 1857.

Miles, William Porcher. *Report of the City of Charleston, 1857.* Charleston, 1858.

Minutes of the Annual Conferences of the Methodist Episcopal Church, South for the Year 1858. Nashville: Southern Methodist Publishing House, 1859.

Motte, Jacob Rhett. *Journey into the Wilderness: An Army Surgeon's Account of Life in Camp and Field during the Creek and Seminole Wars, 1836–1838.* Edited by James F. Sunderman. Gainesville: University of Florida Press, 1953.

Oliphant, Mary C., Alfred Taylor Odell, and T. C. Duncan Eaves, eds. *The Letters of William Gilmore Simms.* 3 vols. Columbia: University of South Carolina Press, 1952–1954.

Phillips, Rebecca. "A Diary of Jesse Talbot: Newnansville and Tallahassee." *Florida Historical Quarterly* 18 (October 1939): 115–26.

Purse, R. S. *Charleston City Directory and Strangers Guide for 1856.* New York: J. F. Trow, 1856.

Racine, Philip N., ed. *Gentlemen Merchants: A Charleston Family's Odyssey, 1828–1870.* Knoxville: University of Tennessee Press, 2008.

Register of Deaths in Savannah, Georgia, 1833–1847, vol. 5. Savannah: Georgia Historical Society.

Representative Men and Old Families of Rhode Island—Genealogical Records and Historical Sketches of Prominent and Representative Citizens and of Many of the Old Families. Chicago: J. H. Beers, 1908.

Representative Men of the South. Philadelphia: Chas. Robson, 1880.

Ryan, George. *Our Heroes of the Crimea: Being Biographical Sketches of Our Military Officers, from the General Commanding-in Chief to the Subalterns.* London: George Routledge, 1855.

Sprague, John T. *Origins, Progress, and Conclusion of the Florida War.* 1848. Facsimile reprint. Tampa, Fla.: University of Tampa Press, 2000.

Weston, George M. *The Poor Whites of the South.* Washington, D.C.: Buell and Blanchard, 1856.

Whipple, Henry Benjamin. *Bishop Whipple's Southern Diary, 1843–1844.* Edited by Lester B. Shippee. Minneapolis: University of Minnesota Press, 1937.

Secondary Sources

Akerman, Joe. *Florida Cowman: A History of Cattle Raising.* Kissimmee: Florida Cattleman's Association, 1976.

Akerman, Joe, and Mark Akerman. *Jacob Summerlin: King of the Crackers.* Cocoa: Florida Historical Society Press, 2004.

Andrus, Ann. *Charleston's Old Exchange Building: A Witness to American History.* Charleston: History, 2005.

Atherton, Lewis E. *The Southern Country Store, 1800–1860.* Baton Rouge: Louisiana State University Press, 1949.

———. *The Frontier Merchant in Mid-America*. Columbia: University of Missouri Studies, 1926. Reprint, Columbia: University of Missouri Press, 1971.

Bancroft, Frederic. *Slave Trading in the Old South*. New York: Frederick Ungar, 1959.

Barrett, Walter. *The Old Merchants of New York City*. New York: Carlton, 1864.

Bartlett, Irving. *John C. Calhoun: A Biography*. New York: Norton, 1993.

Bauer, K. Jack. *The Mexican War, 1846–1848*. New York: Macmillan, 1974.

Bellows, Barbara L. *Benevolence among Slaveholders: Assisting the Poor in Charleston, 1670–1860*. Baton Rouge: Louisiana State University Press, 1993.

Blakey, Arch Fredric. *Parade of Memories: A History of Clay County, Florida*. Jacksonville: Drummond Press for the Clay County Bicentennial Steering Committee, 1976.

Brown, Canter. *Florida's Peace River Frontier*. Orlando: University of Central Florida Press, 1991.

———. *Ossian Bingley Hart: Florida's Loyalist Reconstruction Governor*. Baton Rouge: Louisiana State University Press, 1997.

———. *Tampa before the Civil War*. Tampa, Fla: University of Tampa Press, 1999.

Briggs, Deane R., ed. *Florida Stampless Postal History, 1763–1861*. Miami: David G. Phillips Publishing Company for the Florida Postal History Society, 1999.

Buchholz, F. W. *History of Alachua County, Florida: Narrative and Biographical*. St. Augustine: Record Company, 1929.

Bulloch, Joseph Gaston Baillie. *A History and Genealogy of the Families of Bulloch, Stobo, DeVeaux, Irvine, Douglass, Baillie, Lewis, Adams, Glen, Jones, Davis, Hunter with a Genealogy of Branches of the Habersham King, Stiles, Footman, Newell, Turner, Stewart, Dunwoody, Elliott . . .* Savannah, Ga.: Braid and Hutton, 1892.

———. *History and Genealogy of the Stewart, Elliott and Dunwoody Families*. Savannah, Ga.: Robinson Printing House, 1895.

Burrows, Edwin G., and Mike Wallace. *Gotham: A History of New York City to 1898*. New York: Oxford University Press, 1999.

Byrne, Frank L. *Becoming Bourgeois: Merchant Culture in the South, 1820–1865*. Lexington: University Press of Kentucky, 2006.

Caroli, Betty Boyd. *The Roosevelt Women*. New York: Basic, 1998.

Childs, Arney R., ed. *Planters and Business Men: The Guignard Family of South Carolina*. Columbia: University of South Carolina Press, 1957.

Clark, Thomas, ed. *South Carolina: The Grand Tour, 1780–1865*. Columbia: University of South Carolina Press, 1973.

Coker, P. C. *Charleston's Maritime Heritage, 1670–1865: An Illustrated History*. Charleston: CokerCraft, 1987.

Coulter, E. M. *George Walton Williams: The Life of a Southern Merchant and Banker, 1820–1903*. Athens, Ga.: Hibriten, 1976.

Covington, James W. *The Seminoles of Florida*. Gainesville: University Press of Florida, 1993.

Cusick, James. *The Other War of 1812: The Patriot War and the Invasion of Spanish East Florida*. Gainesville: University of Florida Press, 2003.

Davis, Jess G. *History of Gainesville Florida with Biographical Sketches of Families*. Privately published, 1966.

Davis, T. Frederick. *History of Jacksonville and Vicinity, 1513 to 1924*. St. Augustine: Florida Historical Society, 1925.

Day, Thomas G., ed. *The United States Postal Service: An American History, 1775–2006*. Washington, D.C.: United States Postal Service, 2012.

De La Cova, Antonio Rafael. *Colonel Henry Theodore Titus: Antebellum Soldier of Fortune and Florida Pioneer*. Columbia: University of South Carolina Press, 2016.

Denham, James M. *Florida Founder William P. Duval, Frontier Bon Vivant*. Columbia: University of South Carolina Press, 2015.

———. *A Rogue's Paradise: Crime and Punishment in Antebellum Florida, 1821–1861*. Tuscaloosa: University of Alabama Press, 1997.

Denham, James M., and Canter Brown. *Cracker Times and Pioneer Lives: The Florida Reminiscences of George Gillett Keen and Sarah Pamela Williams*. Columbia: University of South Carolina Press, 2000.

Denham, James M., and Keith L. Huneycutt. *Echoes from a Distant Frontier: The Brown Sisters' Correspondence from Antebellum Florida*. Columbia: University of South Carolina Press, 2004.

Donnell, E. J. *Chronological and Statistical History of Cotton*. New York: James Sutton, 1872.

Downey, Tom. *Planting a Capitalist South: Masters, Merchants, and Manufacturers in the Southern Interior, 1790–1860*. Baton Rouge: Louisiana State University Press, 2006.

Eaton, Clement. *The Growth of the Southern Civilization, 1790–1860*. New York: Harper and Row Publishers, 1961.

Edgar, Walter. *South Carolina: A History*. Columbia: University of South Carolina Press, 1998.

Eelman, Bruce W. *Entrepreneurs in Southern Upcountry: Commercial Culture in Spartanburg, South Carolina, 1845–1880*. Athens: University of Georgia Press, 2008.

Eisenhower, John. S.D. *Agent of Destiny: The Life and Times of General Winfield Scott*. New York: Free Press, 1997.

———. *So Far from God: The U.S. War with Mexico, 1848–1848*. New York: Random House, 1989.

Faust, Drew Gilpin, *James Henry Hammond and the Old South: Design for Mastery*. Baton Rouge: Louisiana State University Press, 1982.

Fernald, Edward A., and Elizabeth D. Purdum, eds. *Atlas of Florida*. Gainesville: University Press of Florida, 1992.

Fraser, Walter J. *Charleston! Charleston! The History of a Southern City*. Columbia: University of South Carolina Press, 1989.

———. *Savannah in the Old South*. Athens: University of Georgia Press, 2003.

Gale, Steven H., ed. *Encyclopedia of British Humorists: Geoffrey Chaucer to John Cleese*. New York: Garland, Routledge, 1996.

Gannon, Michael, ed. *The New History of Florida*. Gainesville: University Press of Florida, 1996.

Gold, Pleasant Daniel. *History of Duval County, Including Early History of East Florida.* St. Augustine, Fla.: Record Company, 1929.

Gray, Lewis Cecil. *History of Agriculture in the Southern United States to 1860.* 2 vols. Washington, D.C.: Carnegie Institution, 1933. Reprint, Gloucester, Mass.: Peter Smith, 1958.

Green, Fletcher M. *The Role of the Yankee in the Old South.* Athens: University of Georgia Press, 1972.

Hammond, E. Ashby. *The Medical Profession in 19th Century Florida: A Biographical Register.* Gainesville: George Smathers Libraries, University of Florida, 1996.

Harden, William. *A History of Savannah and South Georgia.* 2 vols. Chicago: Lewis, 1913.

Hartman, David W., and David J. Coles. *Biographical Rosters of Confederate and Union Soldiers, 1861–1865.* 6 vols. Wilmington, N.C.: Broadfoot, 1995.

Henkin, David M. *The Postal Age: The Emergence of Modern Communication in Nine-teenth-Century America.* Chicago: University of Chicago Press, 2007.

Hooper, Kevin S. *The Early History of Clay County: A Wilderness That Could Be Tamed.* Charleston: History, 2006.

Huxford, Folks. *Pioneers of Wiregrass Georgia.* 9 vols. Homerville, Ga.: Folks Huxford and Huxford Genealogical Society, 1951–1993.

Jerrold, Douglas. *A Man Made of Money.* London: Punch Office, 1849.

Johnson, Rossiter, ed. *Twentieth Century Biographical Dictionary of Notable Americans.* Vols. 1–10. Boston, Mass.: Biographical Society, 1904.

Kert, Faye M. *Privateering: Patriots and Profits in the War of 1812.* Baltimore: Johns Hopkins University Press, 2015.

Keuchel, Edward F. *A History of Columbia County, Florida.* Tallahassee: Sentry, 1981.

Knetsch, Joe. *Faces on the Frontier: Florida Surveyors and Developers in the 19th Century.* Cocoa: Florida Historical Society, 2006.

Kohn, August. *Charleston, South Carolina: Business, Trade, Growth, Opportunity.* Charleston: Walker, Evans and Cogwell, 1911.

Lander, Ernest. *Reluctant Imperialists: Calhoun, the South Carolinians, and the Mexican War.* Baton Rouge: Louisiana State University Press, 1980.

Landers, Jane. *Colonial Plantations and Economy in Florida.* Gainesville: University Press of Florida, 2000.

Lesesne, Thomas Petigru. *History of Charleston County, South Carolina.* Charleston: A. J. Cranston, 1931.

Mahon, John K. *History of the Second Seminole War, 1835–1842.* Gainesville: University Press of Florida, 1967; revised edition, 1985.

Manley, Walter W., Canter Brown, and Eric Rise. *The Supreme Court of Florida and Its Predecessor Courts, 1821–1917.* Gainesville: University Press of Florida, 1997.

Martin, Sidney Walter. *Florida during Territorial Days.* Athens: University of Georgia Press, 1944.

McCullough, David. *The Greater Journey: Americans in Paris.* New York: Simon and Schuster, 2011.

———. *Mornings on Horseback.* New York: Simon and Schuster, 1981.

McWhiney, Grady. *Cracker Culture: Celtic Ways in the Old South*. Tuscaloosa: University of Alabama Press, 1986.

Michaels, Brian E. *The River Flows North: A History of Putnam County, Florida*. Putnam County Archives and History Commission, 1986.

Missall, John, and Mary Lou Missall. *The Seminole Wars: America's Longest Indian Conflict*. Gainesville: University Press of Florida, 2004.

Monaco, C. S. *The Second Seminole War and the Limits of American Aggression*. Baltimore: Johns Hopkins University Press, 2018.

Mueller, Edward A. *Steamboating on the St. Johns, 1830–1885*. Melbourne: Kellersberger Fund of the South Brevard Historical Society, 1986.

Neu, Irene. *Erastus Corning: Merchant and Financier, 1794–1872*. Ithaca, N.Y.: Cornell University Press, 1960.

Oxford English Dictionary. 2nd ed. 20 vols. Oxford: Oxford University Press, 1989.

Pease, William H., and Jane H. Pease. *The Web of Progress: Private Values and Public Styles in Boston and Charleston, 1828–1843*. New York: Oxford University Press, 1985.

Peterson, Merrill D. *The Great Triumvirate: Webster, Clay and Calhoun*. New York: Oxford University Press, 1987.

Phelps, John B. *People of Lawmaking in Florida, 1822–1993*. Tallahassee: Florida House of Representatives, 1993.

Pred, Allan R. *Urban Growth and Circulation of Information: The United States System of Cities, 1790–1840*. Cambridge: Harvard University Press, 1973.

Prucha, Francis. *The Sword of the Republic: The United States Army on the Frontier, 1783–1846*. New York: Macmillan, 1969.

Pugh, David S. *Sons of Liberty: The Masculine Mind in Nineteenth Century America*. Westport, Conn.: Greenwood, 1983.

Raab, James W. *W.W. Loring: Florida's Forgotten General*. Manhattan, Kans.: Sunflower University Press, 1996.

Reed, G. Walter. *History of Sacramento County, California*. Los Angeles: Historic Record Company, 1923.

Rivers, Larry Eugene. *Slavery in Florida: Territorial Days to Emancipation*. Gainesville: University Press of Florida, 2000.

Robertson, Fred L. *Soldiers of Florida in the Seminole Indian, Civil, and Spanish-American Wars*. Tallahassee: Board of State Institutions, 1903.

Rogers, George C. *Charleston in the Age of the Pinckneys*. Columbia: University of South Carolina Press, 1980.

Rosengarten, Theodore. *Tombee: Portrait of a Cotton Planter*. New York: William Morrow, 1985.

Rowland, Lawrence S., Alexander Moore, and George C. Rogers Jr. *The History of Beaufort County, South Carolina*, vol. 1514–1861. Columbia: University of South Carolina Press, 1996.

Russell, James D. *Too Late for Blood: Florida Volunteers in the Mexican War*. Westminster, Md.: Heritage, 2005.

Schafer, Daniel L. *Thunder on the River: The Civil War in Northeast Florida*. Gainesville: University Press of Florida, 2010.

Schultz, Harold S. *Nationalism and Sectionalism in South Carolina, 1852–1860: A Study of the Movement for Southern Independence.* Durham, N.C.: Duke University Press, 1950.

Sellers, Charles. *The Market Revolution Jacksonian America, 1815–1846.* New York: Oxford University Press, 1991.

Shakespeare, William. *Julius Caesar.* Edited by G. Blakemore Evans et al. *The Riverside Shakespeare,* 2nd edition. New York: Houghton Mifflin Company, 1997.

———. *The Merchant of Venice.* Edited by G. Blakemore Evans et al. *The Riverside Shakespeare,* 2nd edition. New York: Houghton Mifflin Company, 1997.

Shofner, Jerrell H. *Daniel Ladd: Merchant Prince of Frontier Florida.* Gainesville: University Press of Florida, 1978.

Smith, Julia Floyd. *Slavery and Plantation Growth in Antebellum Florida: 1821–1860.* Gainesville: University of Florida Press, 1973.

Ste. Claire, Dana. *Cracker: The Cracker Culture in Florida History.* Daytona Beach: Museum of Arts and Sciences, 1998.

Tadman, Michael. *Speculators and Slaves: Masters, Traders, and Slaves in the Old South.* Madison: University of Wisconsin Press, 1989.

Taylor, Rosser H. *Antebellum South Carolina: A Social and Cultural History.* Chapel Hill: University of North Carolina Press, 1970.

Temple, Robert M. *Florida Flame: A History of the Florida Conference of the United Methodist Church.* Nashville: Parthenon, 1987.

Thompson, Michael D. *Working on the Dock of the Bay: Labor and Enterprise in an Antebellum Southern Port.* Columbia: University of South Carolina Press, 2015.

Thrift, Charles T. *The Trail of the Florida Circuit Rider.* Lakeland: Florida Southern College Press, 1944.

Wallace, David Duncan. *South Carolina: A Short History, 1520–1948.* Chapel Hill: University of North Carolina Press, 1951.

Wells, Jonathan Daniel, and Jennifer R. Green, eds. *The Southern Middle Class in the Long Nineteenth Century.* Baton Rouge: Louisiana State University Press, 2004.

Wilson, Walter E. *The Bulloch Belles: Three First Ladies, a Spy, a President's Mother and other Women of a 19th Century Georgia Family.* Jefferson, N.C.: McFarland, 2015.

Wiltse, Charles M. *John C. Calhoun, Sectionalist, 1840–1850.* New York: Russell & Russell, 1968.

Woodman, Harold D. *King Cotton and His Retainers: Financing and Manufacturing the Cotton Crop of the South, 1800–1925.* Columbia: University of South Carolina Press, Southern Classic Series, 1990; originally published by the University of Kentucky Press, 1968.

Wright, Gavin. *The Political Economy of the Cotton South: Households, Markets, and Wealth in the Nineteenth Century.* New York: Norton, 1978.

Articles and Book Chapters

Atherton, Lewis E. "Itinerant Merchandising in the Ante-Bellum South." *Bulletin of the Business Historical Society* 19 (April 1945): 35–59.

———. "Mercantile Education in the Ante-Bellum South." *The Mississippi Valley Historical Review* 39 (March 1953): 623–40.

———. "The Problem of Credit Rating in the Antebellum South." *Journal of Southern History* 12 (1946): 534–56.

Caudle, Everett W. "Settlement Patterns in Alachua County, Florida, 1850–1860." *Florida Historical Quarterly* 67 (April 1989): 428–40.

Covington, James W. "The Armed Occupation Act of 1842." *Florida Historical Quarterly* 40 (July 1961): 41–52.

———. "The Indian Scare of 1849." *Tequesta* 21 (1961): 53–64.

Cubberly, Fred. "Fort King." *Florida Historical Quarterly* 5 (January 1927): 139–52.

Davis, Ronald L. F. "The Southern Merchant: A Perennial Source of Discontent." In *The Southern Enigma: Essays in Race, Class, and Folk Culture*, edited by Walter J. Fraser Jr. and Winifred B. Moore Jr., 131–41. Westport, Conn.: Greenwood, 1983.

Davis, T. Frederick. "Florida's Part in the War with Mexico." *Florida Historical Quarterly* 20 (January 1942): 235–59.

Denham, James M. "Cracker Women and Their Families in Nineteenth Century Florida." In *Florida's Heritage of Diversity: Essays in the Honor of Samuel Proctor*, edited by Mark I. Greenberg, William Warren Rogers, and Canter Brown Jr., 15–27. Tallahassee: Sentry, 1997.

———. "From a Territorial to a Statehood Judiciary: Florida's Antebellum Courts and Judges." *Florida Historical Quarterly* 73 (April 1995): 443–55.

———. "The Florida Cracker before the Civil War as Seen Through Travelers' Accounts." *Florida Historical Quarterly* 72 (April 1994): 453–62.

———. "'Some Prefer the Seminoles': Violence and Disorder Among Soldiers and Settlers in the Second Seminole War, 1835–1842." *Florida Historical Quarterly* 70 (July 1991): 38–54.

Denham, James M., and Keith L. Huneycutt. "'Everything Is Hubbub Here': Lt. James Willoughby Anderson's Second Seminole War, 1837–1842." *Florida Historical Quarterly* 82 (Winter 2004): 313–59.

———. "'Our Desired Haven': The Letters of Corinna Brown Aldrich from Antebellum Key West, 1849–50." *Florida Historical Quarterly* 78 (Spring 2001): 517–45.

———. "With Scott in Mexico: Letters of Captain James W. Anderson in the Mexican War, 1846–1847." *Military History of the West* 28 (Spring 1998): 19–48.

Denham, James M., and Randolph Roth. "Why Was Antebellum Florida so Murderous?: A Quantitative Analysis of Homicide in Florida, 1821–1861." *Florida Historical Quarterly* 86 (Fall 2007): 216–39.

Dodd, Dorothy. "Letters from East Florida, 1843." *Florida Historical Quarterly* 15 (July 1936).

Jaher, Frederick C. "Antebellum Charleston: Anatomy of an Economic Failure." In *Class Conflict and Consensus: Antebellum Southern Community Studies*, edited by Orville Vernon Burton and Robert C. McMath Jr., 207–31. Westport, Conn.: Greenwood, 1982.

Lander, Ernest M. "Charleston: Manufacturing Center of the Old South." *Journal of Southern History* 26 (July 1951): 125–31.

Mahon, John K., and Brent R. Weisman. "Florida's Seminole and Miccosukee Peoples." In *The New History of Florida*, edited by Michael Gannon. Gainesville: University Press of Florida, 1996.

McWhiney, Grady, and Forrest McDonald. "Celtic Origins of Southern Herding Practices." *Journal of Southern History* 51 (May 1984): 165–82.

Monaco, C. S. "Alachua Settlers and the Second and the Second Seminole War." *Florida Historical Quarterly* 91 (Summer 2012): 1–32.

———. "Fort Mitchell and the Settlement of Alachua County." *Florida Historical Quarterly* 79 (Summer 2000): 1–25.

Mushal, Amanda Reece. "Bonds of Marriage and Community: Social Networks and the Development of a Commercial Middle Class in Antebellum South Carolina." In *The Southern Middle Class in the Long Nineteenth Century*, edited by Jonathan Daniel Wells and Jennifer R. Green, 62–83. Baton Rouge: Louisiana State University Press, 2011.

Ott, Eloise R. "Fort King: A Brief History." *Florida Historical Quarterly* 46 (July 1967): 29–38.

Otto, John Solomon. "Open Range Cattle-Herding in Southern Florida." *Florida Historical Quarterly* 65 (January 1987): 317–34.

Rotundo, Anthony. "Learning about Manhood: Gender Ideals and the Middle-Class Family in Nineteenth Century America." In *Manliness and Morality: Middle-Class Morality in Britain and America, 1800–1940*, edited by J. A. Mangan and James Walvin, 35–51. New York: St. Martins, 1987.

Schafer, Daniel L. "U.S. Territory and State." In *The New History of Florida*, edited by Michael Gannon. Gainesville: University Press of Florida, 1996.

Schweikart, Larry. "Southern Banks and Economic Growth in the Antebellum Period: A Reassessment." *Journal of Southern History* 53 (February 1987): 19–36.

Shofner, Jerrell H., and William W. Rogers. "Sea Island Cotton in Ante-Bellum Florida." *Florida Historical Quarterly* 40 (January 1962): 373–80.

Smith, Clarence M., Jr. "William Porcher Miles, Progressive Mayor of Charleston, 1855–1857." *South Carolina Historical Association Proceedings* (1942): 30–39.

Smith, Julia F. "Cotton and the Factorage System in Antebellum Florida." *Florida Historical Quarterly* 49 (July 1970): 36–48.

Steen, Iva D. "Charleston in the 1850s: As Described by British Travelers." *South Carolina Historical and Genealogical Magazine* 71 (January 1970): 36–45.

Woodman, Harold D. "Itinerant Cotton Merchants of the Antebellum South." *Agricultural History* 40 (April 1966): 79–90.

Yelton, Susan. "Newnansville: A Lost Florida Settlement." *Florida Historical Quarterly* 53 (January 1975): 319–31.

Theses and Dissertations

Greb, Gregory Allen. "Charleston, South Carolina Merchants, 1815–1860." Ph.D. dissertation, University of California, San Diego, 1978.

Hugo-Brunt, Michael. "A History of the City of Portsmouth in New Hampshire from 1623–1839." Three Volumes. Ph.D. dissertation, Cornell University, 1957.

O'Shields, Herbert Joseph. "Women in Antebellum Alachua County." M.A. thesis, University of North Florida, 2010.

Worth, Stephen G. "Douglas William Jerrold." In *Encyclopedia of British Humorists*, edited by Stephen H. Gale, 1: 581. New York: Garland, 1996.

INDEX

Page numbers in *italics* refer to illustrations and sketches in Cast of Characters.

JAMES M. DENHAM is professor of history and director of the Lawton M. Chiles Center for Florida History at Florida Southern College. He is the author or editor of several books, including *Fifty Years of Justice: A History of the U.S. District Court for the Middle District of Florida* and *"A Rogue's Paradise": Crime and Punishment in Antebellum Florida, 1821–1861.*

KEITH L. HUNEYCUTT is professor of English at Florida Southern College. He is the coeditor (with James Denham) of *Echoes from a Distant Frontier: The Brown Sisters' Correspondence from Antebellum Florida.*

CONTESTED BOUNDARIES

Edited by Gene Allen Smith, Texas Christian University

Printed in the USA
CPSIA information can be obtained
at www.ICGtesting.com
JSHW021950290324
60179JS00004B/20

9 780813 080635